A LAYMAN'S BIBLE DIGEST

A LAYMAN'S BIBLE DIGEST

LESLIE PEYTON

Fleming H. Revell Company
Old Tappan, New Jersey

Unless otherwise identified, Scripture quotations are from the New American Standard Bible, Copyright © THE LOCKMAN FOUNDATION, 1960, 1962, 1963, 1968, 1971, 1972, 1973, 1975 and are used by permission.
Scripture quotations identified KJV are from the King James Version of the Bible.

All rights reserved. No part of this book may be reproduced in any manner whatsoever, stored in a retrieval system, transmitted in any form, or by any means, recorded or photocopied, except in case of brief quotations embodied in critical articles and reviews, without the prior written permission of the copyright owner.

Library of Congress Cataloging in Publication Data

Peyton, Leslie.
   A layman's Bible digest.

   1. Bible—Introductions. I. Title.
BS475.2.P47   220.9'5   78-13295
ISBN 0-8007-0981-1
ISBN 0-8007-0979-9 pbk.

Copyright © 1978 by Leslie Peyton
Published by Fleming H. Revell Company
All rights reserved
Printed in the United States of America

This book is dedicated in humble appreciation to—

Dr. Robert T. McFarlane for his life of service to God as a minister to His people, whose exemplary model was an inspiration for me to write this book.

Rita Mattingley whose spiritual integrity was shared in constant encouragement and sacred enlightenment.

Sheridan Cochran and Mary Tossey who cheerfully typed, corrected, and typed, again and again.

My wife, Helen, who lived with me for four years during the writing and editing of this book.

My Lord and God Almighty who gave me the enhanced strength to write this book with four or five hours of sleep a day.

CONTENTS

Preface	10
What Is the Bible? Why Should I Read It?	11
Introduction to the Old Testament	13
Books of the Old Testament	15
Genesis	16
Map—Abraham's Journey to Canaan	18
Developments in Civilization, 100,000 B.C.–1100 B.C.	24
Chronological Summary	26
Exodus	33
Map—The Route of the Exodus	36
Leviticus	39
Numbers	40
Deuteronomy	42
Joshua	44
Map—The Land of the Twelve Tribes	46
Judges	48
Ruth	51
Developments in Civilization, 1100 B.C.–400 B.C.	52
Chronological Summary	54
First Samuel	62
Second Samuel	66
First Kings	70
Second Kings	74
First Chronicles	81
Second Chronicles	84
Ezra	90
Nehemiah	92
Esther	94
Job	97
Psalms	99
Proverbs	101
Ecclesiastes	102
The Song of Solomon	103
Isaiah	104
Jeremiah	106
Lamentations	109

8 / Contents

Ezekiel	110
Daniel	113
Hosea	116
Joel	118
Amos	119
Obadiah	121
Jonah	122
Micah	124
Nahum	126
Habakkuk	128
Zephaniah	129
Haggai	130
Zechariah	132
Malachi	135
Summary of the Old Testament	137
Developments in Civilization, 400 B.C.–A.D. 1	141
Chronological Summary	143
The Jewish Nation Between Testaments	154
Introduction to the New Testament	159
Jesus Christ as Described by Historians	162
The Books of the New Testament	164
Matthew	166
Mark	172
Luke	178
John	185
Map—Territory Covered in Christ's Ministry	192
Developments in Civilization, A.D. 1–A.D. 100	193
Chronological Summary	194
The Twelve Apostles	196
The Acts	199
The Man Paul	211
Map—Paul's Four Journeys	213
Romans	215
First Corinthians	219
Second Corinthians	223
Galatians	226
Ephesians	228
Philippians	230
Colossians	232
First Thessalonians	234
Second Thessalonians	236
First Timothy	238
Second Timothy	240
Titus	242

Philemon	244
Hebrews	245
James	247
First Peter	249
Second Peter	251
First John	253
Second John	255
Third John	256
Jude	257
Revelation	258
Summary of the New Testament	269
Definitions	270

PREFACE

This book is written primarily for people who have never read the entire Bible. It is a digested version of the complete Bible. As a consequence, many of the happenings are stated briefly and many small details left out. Brevity and condensation are mandatory in giving you the story of the whole Bible quickly.

Further, it is impractical to preface every date and every period of years by stating "In the approximate date of." When we go back 2000–5000 years in history, before the time of the printing press, most archaic writings were made at the direction of a king, dictator, or conqueror. These men generally had all writings made for their own glorification and were not generally known to write anything that told of their own greed, errors, stupidity, or failure. Most archaeologists and historians do not agree on many dates. This book is written to give the reader a general overall summary of the Bible and the parallel history of the rest of the world. It is not intended to be an encyclopedia of documented, detailed dates and facts for the historical technician, theologian or student. There are hundreds of books that have that information for those who want to take the time to find them.

The intention of this book is to give the reader an overall idea of the contents of the Bible in as few words, and with as much clarity as possible. Therefore it should be assumed that practically every date and every year quoted could be classified as "approximately."

This book contains no scholarly dissertations, no sermons, no theological interpretation. The sole objective is to give you an idea of what the Bible is all about, in one complete, short story, with the facts as they are. God's plan for your life as told by His Son Jesus Christ is revealed through the story of the Bible.

The author struggled for years in his first reading of the Bible, trying to figure out the whole story. This book tells you the whole story quickly. You are then better able to read the Bible itself, with great expectation and tremendous satisfaction. This book is like reading the AAA booklets and maps before you make the trip.

After reading this, I hope you will be so hungry for the full Bible knowledge and the abundance of living treasures, understanding, and spiritual and material wealth available to you, that you will undertake the reading of the Bible with a ravenous appetite and find satisfactions you never thought possible.

Success is peace of mind. Peace of mind can be acquired, and the reading of the Bible is the way. God be with you on your journey.

WHAT IS THE BIBLE?
WHY SHOULD I READ IT?

The Bible is a book written by forty writers, accepted by Christians as inspired by God and of divine authority. The Old Testament is a record of one segment of humanity, the Jewish nation, starting with one man, Abraham, and God's covenant with him. The New Testament is the story of Jesus Christ and the Church He founded. The Jewish nation was founded and nurtured by God to bring this man (Jesus Christ) into the world for the salvation of all mankind.

The Bible itself, written over a period of 1,600 years, is a miracle. It is the only single book known all over the world. It has always been the world's best seller. One institution, The American Bible Society, has distributed almost 1,000,000,000 copies by itself. Some 20,000,000 copies of the Bible are printed each year. There are more than 250 complete language translations and about 1,130 partial language translations in existence. In 1976, the United Bible Societies distributed 330,900,744 Bibles! There are billions in existence!

The stories and history of the Bible are narrated in the lives of people and display all of the emotions known to man. There are stories of miracles, achievements, victories, accomplishments, fulfillments, love, success, and faith. There are stories of fraud, deception, strategy, immorality, scheming, conniving, corruption, disobedience, traitorship, and misrepresentation. And there are stories of failure, disappointment, disillusionment, discouragement, defeat, and shame.

All the basic principles for human conduct are exemplified by people in the Bible. Thousands of books are written every year, telling ways that people should deal with other people. This one book has them all. If this one book was the only textbook in existence, and it was read and studied by all, the whole world would be richer in the life, love, and experience of each individual.

This digest of the Bible is intended to give you a quick look at the whole Bible as a complete story, in the hope that it will create sufficient curiosity and desire on your part to read and study the Bible itself and that your life will be enriched by so doing.

The best advice that can be offered to the reader after reading this book is to get a copy of a Bible in modern language, such as Tyndale's *The Living Bible* or *The Good News Bible*, published by the American

Bible Society, and read it. The poorest advice that can be offered is what you generally receive: "Just pick up the Bible and open it up and read any part of it."

There are parts of the Bible in which the genealogies, sometimes referred to as "the begats," which are not very interesting to the average reader, are traced out. Skip them. They are extremely interesting to the experienced scholar, because they prove that Christ is in the direct lineage of the house of David. This was God's promise. There are things in the Bible submitted as evidence for proof of the fulfillment of promises and prophecies. The Bible is a story, and it should be read like any other book. Start with the first page and stop with the last page. Afterward, various parts can and should be read and reread, and understood, with great satisfaction and mental enrichment.

Your rewards will be very real. Your accomplishments will be multiplied, your obstacles can be overcome, you will have peace of mind and confidence, and your friends will ask you why you have that radiantly happy look.

It takes eight hours for most people to read this whole book. Speed readers can read it in two hours. Are the rewards worth your time? Make that decision right now. You can receive these rewarding benefits for the investment of a little time. The sole purpose for the writing of this book was to make that time short and the reading easy.

INTRODUCTION TO THE OLD TESTAMENT

The word *testament* means "covenant" or "agreement." The Old Testament tells of the basic agreement between God and His chosen people—the Hebrews—and how faithfully they each kept this agreement.

Most Protestants and Jews accept the thirty-nine books as the Old Testament. Catholics include fourteen more books, called the Apocrypha.

The Old Testament is the story of all beginnings, the creation of all things, and the history of one group of people, the Hebrews, up to 432 B.C. The story concentrates on the lives of Abraham, Isaac, Jacob, Joseph, Moses, and David. The first five books are often referred to as the Pentateuch or Torah. The word *Torah* means "law."

The beginning of the Hebrew nation was vested in Abraham, who was told by God to leave his home in Ur on the lower Euphrates River and go to Canaan.

He and his descendents were detained in Egypt for more than 400 years, but his descendents eventually left Egypt and entered the Promised Land of Canaan, where they settled. They ruled themselves by judges or priests for many years and talked to God through prophets.

The prophets interpret the history of the Hebrews from the standpoint that man's destiny is decided by his obedience or disobedience to God's laws. The earlier prophets are the books of Joshua, Judges, 1 and 2 Samuel, and 1 and 2 Kings. The later prophets are three major books of Isaiah, Jeremiah, and Ezekiel, plus twelve minor prophets. The subject matter of all the books covers law, religious and moral teachings, ritual practices, health and medical counsel, history, poetry, psalms, and great thinkings.

After entering Canaan, the Hebrews decided they wanted to be ruled by kings, against God's advice. Most of the kings turned out to be tyrants and helped to corrupt the morals of the people. The people would become prosperous and then desert their God and worship idols and other false gods. After they were defeated by their enemies, they would return to pray to God to bail them out of their miseries and poverty, generally through the intercession of one of the prophets. God in His grace and mercy would forgive them, and they would become prosperous again. This process was repeated many times.

14 / Introduction to the Old Testament

The story of the coming of Jesus Christ, referred to as the Messiah, is woven throughout the Old Testament by prophets. All pieced together, they tell of Christ's coming, His lineage of the house of David, His birth, death, resurrection, and establishment of His Church. They prove to be so accurate that it is difficult to believe that these prophecies could have been written hundreds of years before His birth. But this is a fact.

Jerusalem and the temple in Jerusalem were the focal points of the Hebrew religion and their place of worship to their God. They lavished the temple with riches of ornaments and gold, which made it the target and bounty for all enemies and conquerors. The temple was ravished and the Hebrews defeated several times. The temple was destroyed for the last time in A.D. 70, and the Jews were scattered throughout the world.

The Old Testament writings are estimated to cover a period of time from 1500 B.C. to 165 B.C. There does not appear to be any positive evidence of specific dates.

BOOKS OF THE OLD TESTAMENT

Pentateuch—The Laws
Genesis
Exodus
Leviticus
Numbers
Deuteronomy

History
Joshua
Judges
Ruth
1 Samuel
2 Samuel
1 Kings
2 Kings
1 Chronicles
2 Chronicles
Ezra
Nehemiah
Esther

Poetry
Job
Psalms
Proverbs

Poetry (Continued)
Ecclesiastes
Song of Solomon

Major Prophets
Isaiah
Jeremiah
Lamentations
Ezekiel
Daniel

Minor Prophets
Hosea
Joel
Amos
Obadiah
Jonah
Micah
Nahum
Habakkuk
Zephaniah
Haggai
Zechariah
Malachi

GENESIS

Time   Written approximately 1500 B.C. No known date of creation.
Author   Reputedly, Moses. Probably written in the wilderness.
Theme   *Genesis* comes from a Greek word meaning birth, beginnings, or originations.

Genesis is the story of all beginnings. It is a simple, direct statement of the facts of all beginnings—creation, birth, sin, man's downfall, and God's concern for man's redemption. The first ten words are a masterpiece of simplicity: "In the beginning God created the heaven and the earth" (Genesis 1:1 KJV).

God created man and then created woman from one of man's ribs and placed them in the Garden of Eden. They were instructed to do as they pleased, but they should not eat of the tree of knowledge. The serpent tempted Eve to eat an apple of the tree, and then she induced Adam to eat one also. God expelled them from the garden for their violation and sin.

They had two sons, Cain and Abel. Abel's offerings to God pleased God, but Cain's offerings displeased Him. Cain, being very jealous of Abel, slew him.

The descendents of Adam and Eve multiplied and did not obey God's instructions to worship Him, so He decided to destroy all mankind except Noah, his devoted servant, and his family. He instructed Noah to build an ark of gopher wood 300 cubits (450') high, with three decks. It took Noah 120 years to build the ark in the face of ridicule and scorn by his fellow men, while God waited patiently for men to repent of their sins. Noah, together with his sons Shem, Ham, and Japheth and all their wives, were to stock the ark with a male and a female of every living creature on earth. They were to take sufficient food for all of them.

God said He would send rain upon the earth for forty days and nights, which would flood the world and blot out every living thing. This He did, and the flood lasted for 150 days. Almost a year after launching, the ark landed on dry ground, and every creature in the ark left the ark at God's command, to go forth and multiply abundantly. There are estimates that 25,000,000 people died in the flood; the Bible does not say how many. God then said to Noah that the rainbow would be the sign of His covenant with man that He would never again destroy all life with a flood.

The descendents of Noah and his sons Shem, Ham, and Japheth had one language and few words. They decided to build, in the land of

Shivar (Babylon), a tower with its top in the heavens. Seeing this, the Lord observed that if they did that, nothing would be impossible for them. He decided to confuse their language, so they could not communicate, and scattered them over the face of the earth before they finished the tower. The tower was called Babel because the Lord confused their language so they could not talk to one another.

Terah, the father of Abram, Nabor, and Haran, at age seventy went from Ur of the Chaldeans (in lower Babylonia) to Haran (in northern Syria), where he died at the age of two hundred and five. The Lord spoke to Abram and said, "Go forth from your country, And from your relatives And from your father's house, To the land which I will show you; And I will make you a great nation . . . I will bless those who bless you, And the one who curses you I will curse . . ." (Genesis 12:1–3).

Abram, at the age of seventy-five, took Lot, his brother's son, and Sarai, his wife, all their possessions and servants, and set forth to go to the land of Canaan. This was the beginning of the Hebrew nation. They went to Shechem, in Canaan, where the Lord appeared and said, "To your descendents I will give this land . . ." (Genesis 12:7). Shechem was about halfway between the Jordan and the Mediterranean Sea and halfway between the Dead Sea and the Sea of Galilee.

Abram built an altar to the Lord, and they journeyed on to Egypt, because there was a great famine in the land. As they entered Egypt, Abram said to his wife, "See now, I know that you are a beautiful woman; and it will come about when the Egyptians see you, that they will say, 'This is his wife'; then they will kill me, but they will let you live. Please say that you are my sister so that it may go well with me because of you, and that I may live on account of you" (Genesis 12:11–13). When Abram entered Egypt, the Egyptians saw that Sarai was beautiful, and she was taken into the Pharaoh's house. Pharaoh treated Abram well.

The Lord afflicted Pharaoh and his house with great plagues because of Sarai, Abram's wife. So Pharaoh called Abram, reprimanded him for his deceit, gave him his wife back, and ordered him to leave the country and take all his possessions. Abram took Sarai, Lot, and all their herds to Canaan, and there he called on the Lord. There was not enough pasture for all the herds of Lot and Abram, which caused strife among the herdsmen. So Lot took his group to the Jordan Valley, to Sodom, and Abram dwelt in the land of Canaan. The people of Sodom were great sinners against the Lord.

The Lord told Abram that He would give him all the land he could see, and this would be the land of his people forever. (This is present-day Israel.) Abram's people would be so numerous that they could not be counted. Abram moved his home to Hebron (about twenty miles south of Jerusalem), where he built an altar to the Lord.

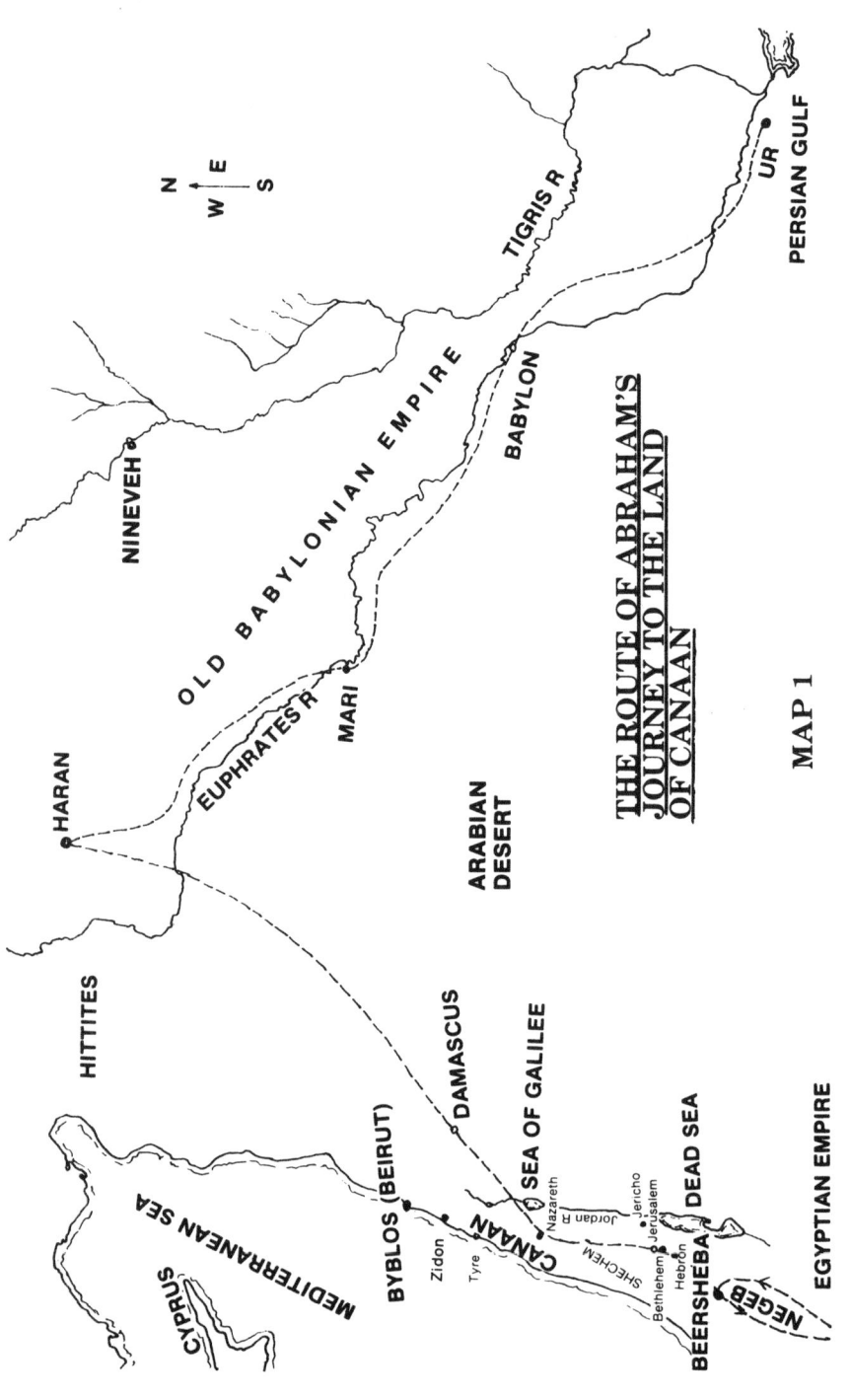

The Word of the Lord came to Abram in a vision, saying that his descendents would be more numerous than the stars; that the Lord would bless him personally with great wealth, and that through Abram's seed (Isaac), all the nations of the world would be blessed. They would live as slaves in a foreign land (Egypt) for 400 years (it was in this manner than an entire nation could come into existence without being polluted through intermarriage with other nations), but they would come out with great possessions and would possess all the land from Egypt to the Euphrates River and the sea to the east of the Jordan.

Abram had no son for an heir. Sarai offered her maid Hagar, an Egyptian, to be his wife; but after she became pregnant, Sarai became jealous and Hagar fled from the camp. The angel of the Lord met her and told her to return to Abram and bear the son, whom she should call Ishmael, and that her descendents would be without number. Abram was eighty-six years of age when Ishmael was born.

When Abram was ninety-nine years old, the Lord appeared to him and said, "I am God Almighty; Walk before Me, and be blameless. And I will establish My covenant between Me and you, And I will multiply you exceedingly" (Genesis 17:1, 2). He changed Abram's name to Abraham and told him that he would be the father of many nations, for He would make him fruitful. Kings would come from Abraham's family, and God would give Abraham all the land of his sojournings. In addition, God would make an everlasting covenant to be their God. God told Abraham that every male should be circumcised, and that every male born thereafter should be circumcised when he was eight days old.

God also told Abraham that Sarai, Abraham's wife, would be called Sarah and that even though she was ninety years old and Abraham was one hundred, she would bear him a son, and his name would be Isaac. God said Ishmael would be a great nation, but His covenant would be with Isaac. When God had finished talking, Abraham had himself and all males circumcised that day, including Ishmael, who was twelve.

The Lord appeared to Abraham in the form of three men, who said they were going to destroy the wicked cities of Sodom and Gomorrah. When they arrived to destroy the cities, they told Lot to take his family and escape to the city of Zoar, but not to look back. Lot's wife looked back at the destruction and was turned to a pillar of salt. Lot and his two daughters later left Zoar and lived in a cave in the hills. The two girls decided there were no husbands available for them, so they got their father drunk on wine and then each of them became pregnant by him. The older girl bore a son, Moab, the father of all the Moabites, and the younger girl bore a son, Ben-Ammi, and he became the father of the Ammonites.

Abraham then went to the Negeb (sixty to seventy miles south of Jerusalem) to live and sojourned in Gerar, ruled by Abimelech, toward the sea. Again in fear, Abraham said his wife Sarah was his sister, and Abimelech took her for his wife. In a dream, God told Abimelech to give her back and make restitution to Abraham, or he would die. God also sealed the wombs of Abimelech's wife and female slaves. Abimelech asked Abraham why he did this, and Abraham explained that he did it in fear of his life. Abimelech gave Sarah back, plus gifts of livestock and money. Abraham prayed to God, and He healed Abimelech's wife and slaves, so they could bear children. The Lord did as He had promised and gave Sarah a son, named Isaac, when Abraham was one hundred years old, and he loved this son very much.

When the son was a young man, God tested Abraham by telling him to go to Mount Moriah and offer the son as a burnt offering. (God made this request at a time when heathen man was engaged in the deplorable act of murdering children by burning them on an altar or burning them alive as an offering to pagan gods. God had made it clear that such acts were despicable. Imagine Abraham's confusion when asked to do this. Abraham obeyed God without question.)

He and Isaac went to Mount Moriah, where they built an altar, placed the firewood, and Abraham bound Isaac and laid him on the wood on the altar. Just as Abraham was taking his knife to slay his son, the angel of the Lord called to Abraham and said, "Do not stretch out your hand against the lad . . . for now I know that you fear God, since you have not withheld your son, your only son, from Me" (Genesis 22:12). Abraham found a ram caught in the brush, which he took and substituted for his son as an offering. The angel of the Lord called to Abraham again and said, ". . . because you have done this thing, and have not withheld your son, . . . indeed I will greatly bless you, and I will greatly multiply your seed as the stars of the heavens, and as the sand which is on the seashore . . ." (Genesis 22:16, 17).

Sarah died at the age of 127 in Hebron. Abraham bought a field with the cave of Machpelah from Ephron, a Hittite, and buried her there.

Abraham arranged for a wife for his son Isaac. He sent his servant to Mesopotamia, where his brother Nahor lived, so that he might select a wife from his own people and not have his son marry a Canaanite of the land where he was living. When the servant arrived at Mesopotamia, he prayed to God to lead him to the right woman and show him a sign that she was the one to be chosen. As the daughters of the city came to the well in the evening to get water, Abraham's servant would say, ". . . 'Please let down your jar so that I may drink,' and who answers, 'Drink, and I will water your camels also';—may she be the one . . ." (Genesis 24:14).

As he finished praying, a beautiful girl named Rebekah, daughter of Nahor, Abraham's brother, came to get water and answered his request. After the exchange of gifts and explanations, the servant took Rebekah back, and she became the wife of Isaac, and he loved her.

Abraham took another wife, Keturah, who bore him six sons. He gave gifts to the sons of his concubines and sent them to the east country, but Abraham gave his estate to Isaac before he died at the age of 175 and was buried with Sarah in the cave of Machpelah, east of Mamre, which he previously purchased from Ephron.

Isaac's wife, Rebekah, had twin boys, Esau and Jacob. Esau was a skillful hunter, while Jacob was a quiet man who dwelt in tents. Isaac loved Esau, but Rebekah loved Jacob. Esau married two Hittite women, who made life miserable for Rebekah. Esau was impetuous, and once when he was hungry, he sold his birthright to his cunning brother Jacob for a bowl of pottage. Jacob's mother, Rebekah, helped him plan a scheme to deceive his father Isaac into giving Jacob his blessing, which made all the brothers servants to Jacob.

Isaac did not want Jacob to marry a Hittite such as Esau's wives, so he sent him north at Haran, to Bethuel, his mother's father, to marry a daughter of her brother Laban. One night on this trip Jacob had a dream and saw a ladder reaching to heaven, with angels ascending and descending. The Lord, standing above it, told Jacob He would give him and his descendents all the land on which he stood, and they would expand in all directions, until their numbers were as the dust of the earth. Jacob arose and erected a monument on that place called Bethel and swore that he would give a tenth of all he received to the Lord.

When Jacob met Laban, he also met his two daughters, Leah and Rachel, and he immediately loved Rachel. He arranged with Laban to serve him for seven years to pay for Rachel as his wife. After the seven years' service, Laban tricked Jacob and gave him Leah, because she was the older daughter. Jacob agreed to work another seven years to get Rachel. He had six sons and one daughter, Dinah, by Leah, and one son, Joseph, by Rachel. After seven more years of service, Jacob took all his possessions and returned to Canaan. Much to Jacob's pleasure and surprise, he received a friendly reception from Esau.

Jacob journeyed to the city of Shechem, where Shechem, the son of Hamor, the Hivite, raped Dinah, Jacob's daughter. After some negotiations between Hamor and Jacob, they agreed to intermarry sons and daughters, provided all the males of Shechem were circumcised. On the third day after the circumcision, when the men were all sore, two of Jacob's sons, Simeon and Levi, murdered all the males of Shechem. Jacob's sons then took all of the herds, wealth, children, and wives of Shechem and continued their journey to Bethel.

All the cities were afraid of Jacob because of the power of his God. Jacob erected an altar to God at Bethel, and God changed Jacob's name to Israel. Rachel died while giving birth to a son, Benjamin, on the way from Bethel to Jerusalem, and Jacob erected a pillar for her grave. Jacob had two sons, Joseph and Benjamin, by Rachel, and ten other sons by Leah.

Jacob (Israel) journeyed on to his father at Hebron, where his father died at the age of 180. There was not sufficient pasture, so Esau took all his possessions and moved to Seir (or Edom), south of the Dead Sea. Jacob remained in Canaan. Joseph, son of Rachel and Jacob, while only seventeen years of age dreamed many dreams that depicted him as superior to his brothers. He was also Jacob's favorite, and Jacob made him a long robe with sleeves, which added to his brothers' hatred of him.

Joseph's brothers conspired, with Reuben dissenting, to sell Joseph to some Midianite traders. On arrival in Egypt, they sold him to Potiphar, the captain of the guard for the Pharaoh. He was an able servant to his master and was put in charge of all of Potiphar's affairs. Potiphar's wife asked Joseph to lie with her, but when he refused, she told her husband that Joseph had tried to rape her, and Potiphar had him imprisoned.

At the prison, Joseph was placed in charge of administration. He interpreted dreams for a servant of the Pharaoh who, when released from prison, told the Pharaoh about Joseph's ability to interpret dreams. The Pharaoh had a dream which no one could interpret, so he sent for Joseph, who explained that God would give the Pharaoh his answer.

Joseph explained the Pharaoh's dream. There would be seven years of prosperity and abundant harvests, followed by seven years of drought and famine. The Pharaoh should appoint someone discreet and wise, over all the land, to take twenty percent of all the crops during the plenteous years and store them in the cities to feed the people during the lean years. The Pharaoh determined that the only person with the spirit of God in him was Joseph. He appointed Joseph second in authority only to the Pharaoh himself, and at age thirty, Joseph was told to prepare for the famine years. Pharaoh also gave Joseph a wife, Asenath, who bore him two sons, Manasseh and Ephraim, before the famine.

At the end of seven years, there was famine in Egypt and in all the earth. When Jacob learned that grain could be purchased in Egypt, he sent his ten sons (but not Benjamin, the brother of Joseph) to Egypt to buy grain. Joseph recognized them, but they did not recognize Joseph. Joseph accused them of being spies. He put one of them, Simeon, in prison as security, and told the others to bring Benjamin to prove they were not lying. He filled their bags with grain and put their money in the tops of the sacks. On the way home the brothers discovered the money, and they were conscience stricken and feared God for their sin in selling Joseph to the traders.

When they had eaten all the grain and needed more, their father Jacob was reluctant to let them take Benjamin with them, but finally consented. Joseph finally revealed himself to them and told them it was

God's will that directed his brothers to sell him into slavery so that they could all eventually be saved from starvation. He forgave them and, with Pharaoh's blessing, sent them home with food and wagons, so they could move all their possessions and people to live in the best land in Egypt. Israel (Jacob) took all his people and possessions and started for Egypt. At Beer-sheba, he offered sacrifices to God. God spoke to Israel and told him not to be afraid to go to Egypt, because God would be with him, and in due time would also deliver him out of Egypt. Israel continued on to Egypt.

Joseph presented his brothers and his father to the Pharaoh, who instructed Joseph to give them the best of the land at Goshen, in the land of Rameses, and also to place them in charge of his cattle.

During the famine, Joseph administered the food for the Pharaoh, until he had all the money in the land. He then traded for all the livestock and finally all the land. When the famine was over, the Pharaoh owned all the land, the Egyptians were his slaves, and they tilled his land and paid him one-fifth of their harvest.

At the age of 147, Israel (Jacob) died. Before he died, he blessed Joseph's two sons, Ephraim the younger and Manasseh the elder, placing Ephraim ahead of Manasseh. He then outlined the characters of his twelve sons and how they would become the twelve Tribes of Israel, and blessed them. He asked that he be buried in the tomb of Abraham and Sarah, with Isaac and Rebekah, in the field of Ephron in Canaan. Joseph received the Pharaoh's permission to embalm Israel and take a great entourage to go to Canaan and bury his father.

After their father died, Joseph's brothers feared that he would do evil to them for their sins, but he assured them he would protect them. Joseph told his brethren that they would some day leave Egypt and possess the land of Canaan, as promised by God to Abraham. He asked them to take his body with them when they left, and he died at the age of 110.

DEVELOPMENTS IN CIVILIZATION 100,000 B.C.–1100 B.C.

Egypt was the predominant civilization during much of this time period. Before 1500 B.C., the Egyptians had developed agriculture, irrigation, dams, shipbuilding, commerce, law, the finest art forms, mathematics, and architecture. The people had mined gold, silver, copper, and tin. They had used contraceptives (3500 years ago).

The Egyptians had been conquered and ruled by the Hyksos kings (c. 1730 B.C.–1580 B.C.) and had regained their freedom again. Amenhotep I (c. 1557 B.C.–1540 B.C.) and Thutmose I (1540 B.C.–1493 B.C.) had been the first kings to be buried in The Valley of the Tombs of the Kings.

Egypt had engaged in commerce with Babylon and had introduced horses. The Upper and Lower Nile Valley had united in Egypt. Cities had developed, and sea trade had become important. The Egyptians had created the first libraries. Egypt reached the height of its power and achievements during this time (1550 B.C.–1085 B.C.), but began declining about 1300 B.C. The Egyptian Empire continued its decline following the Hebrews' escape under Moses' leadership (1250 B.C.). It never rose to as high a level of development again.

The inhabitants of Babylonia used copper, alloys, and gold. They developed cuneiform, a wedge-shaped style of writing, and used wheeled chariots and carts. Various gods and deities were worshipped in the first terraced temples. The people discovered the healing qualities of mineral springs. They used the potter's wheel and oil-burning lamps. They had a numerical system of 6's and 12's, and they produced the first written set of laws (c 1700 B.C.) and studies in mathematics, astrology, and other sciences. In the northern areas, the first iron was manufactured by the Hittites. The bow and arrow was used in warfare. In 2100 B.C., Abraham left Ur in Chaldea.

Before 1500 B.C., the people on the island of Crete, who were called Minoans (named after Minos, king of Crete), developed Europe's first civilization and were skilled sea traders, artists, and builders. They built the famous Palace of Knossos, known as the Palace of Minos, on Crete. They developed a decimal system. This civilization was suddenly destroyed in 1400 B.C. The people of the islands of Keos, Melos, Syros, and others were fishermen, makers of pottery, and traders. They were taken over by the Cretans about 1900 B.C.

Greece was also a dominant force in this period of history (2000 B.C.–1000 B.C.). By 1600 B.C., Greece was rich and powerful. Around 1500 B.C., the people built fortified cities; they also wrote on clay tablets that were not deciphered until A.D. 1953. At this same time, the Troadic culture was flourishing in Asia Minor. Troy was destroyed by fire and rebuilt seven times. The Trojans, who were farmers, wove woolens, built fortified cities and houses, and had treasures of gold, silver, and copper. The famous Greek war with the Trojans, so eloquently sung by Homer, occurred about 1200 B.C. (as Moses was leading the Hebrews out of Egypt).

Between 1500 B.C. and 1100 B.C., a primitive Greek alphabet was being utilized.

In China, silk was discovered in 2700 B.C. At the same time, the people were using marijuana. From 1500 B.C. to 1100 B.C., the first Chinese dictionary emerged. Bronze sculptures were made, and the people worked with advanced mathematical equations. They measured the height of the sun in relation to the incline of the polar axis. Also during this time, prohibition was decreed in China.

From 2000 B.C. to 1500 B.C., the Holy Land established trade routes to Asia Minor and Babylon, and there were sea routes from Egypt to the eastern Mediterranean. In 1200 B.C., Moses received the Ten Commandments on Mount Sinai.

The inhabitants of Turkey, who were known as Hittites, were the first rulers of Asia Minor around 1190 B.C. They used musical instruments such as the guitar, the lyre, the trumpet, and the tambourine. After 1500 B.C., the library in the Hittite capital contained tablets in eight languages. In 1100 B.C., iron was developed from the mines.

The inhabitants of India were using marijuana for pleasure, in ceremonies, and as medicine around 2700 B.C. Around 2500 B.C., the inhabitants of the Indus Valley of Pakistan had systems of counting, measuring, weighing, and writing. They had ditches and canals for irrigation and brick-lined sewer systems for brick houses. These people disappeared about 1700 B.C. Between 1500 B.C. and 1100 B.C., leprosy emerged in India and Egypt.

From 8000 B.C. to 3000 B.C., people from France and Spain, called Celts, settled in Briton; they made flint tools, grew crops, made pottery, and raised cattle and sheep. Around 2000 B.C., people from the Rhine and Danube valleys settled in Briton. These people wove cloth, mined tin, and made bronze tools. The Scandinavians utilized their advanced knowledge of shipbuilding; at the same time, the Bronze Age began in Scandinavia.

There was the first evidence of the Mayan civilization in Central America around 3300 B.C. Between 1500 B.C. and 1100 B.C., the earliest-known settlement in Mexico, Chiapa de Carzo, came into being.

CHRONOLOGICAL SUMMARY

EGYPT
(includes areas of Africa, Ethiopia, Cush)

6000 B.C.	Copper was being used. Silver was known to primitive people.
5000 B.C.	Agriculture was introduced from Asia Minor.
4236 B.C.	The Egyptians had a calendar of 360 days, with twelve months of thirty days each; the calendar was changed to 365 days in 2700 B.C.
4000 B.C.	The Egyptians wove linen and used harps and flutes.
3500–3100 B.C.	Gold was being used. The Upper and Lower Nile were united. King Menes became the first ruler of Upper and Lower Egypt. Agricultural methods included plowing, raking, and fertilizing. The Egyptians used lyres and clarinets.
2940–2400 B.C.	This was the Age of Pyramids. Twenty pyramids were built during this period. Imhotep, who designed the step pyramid of Pharaoh Zoser, was also a physician. Egyptian art and architecture reached their highest development during this time.
2500 B.C.	A mummy cloth made in 2500 B.C. contained 540 warp threads per inch, as compared to present-day fine percale sheeting, which contains 180 threads per square inch. Pharaoh, a god-king type of ruler, was prominent in this time period. The Egyptians discovered the use of papyrus for paper. They also made glass beads and used metal mirrors. The Cheops Pyramid at Gizeh and the great Sphinx of Gizeh were built, conforming to astronomical measurements. A civil service and postal systems were introduced. The Egyptians domesticated dogs. The study of astrology flourished not only in Egypt, but in Babylon, India, and China. A canal was begun from the Nile to the Red Sea. This was built by Amenemhet III, 1849 B.C.–1802 B.C.
1730–1580 B.C.	Egypt was ruled by the Hyksos kings.
1480 B.C.	Egypt extended its rule to the eastern Mediterranean

and to the Euphrates River. "Cleopatra's Needles," two obelisks of red granite, were erected at Heliopolis *c*. 1475 B.C. (In A.D. 1878, one was removed to London, England. In A.D. 1880, the other was sent to the United States, where it now stands in New York's Central Park.)

1300 B.C. Egypt's power began to decline. The Israelites, led by Moses, left Egypt and entered Canaan (*c*. 1200 B.C.). Iron was imported from Asia. Ethiopia became an independent power. Amenhotep IV, assuming the name Ikhnaton, tried to destroy the system of belief in multiple gods and to create the worship of one sun god (*c*. 1375 B.C.). Tutankhamen reinstated the system of belief in multiple gods a short time later (*c*. 1358 B.C.). This time period marked the first mention of the Israelites in an Egyptian song. The Egyptians made tapestries during this time. Tutankhamen's body was embalmed and buried in wood and gold caskets (*c*. 1358 B.C.), one inside the other. Thebes became the capital, replacing Memphis (*c*. 1550 B.C.). A mural in Thebes (Luxor-Karnak) showed female musicians, entertainers. Egypt established regulations concerning the sale of beer. There was widespread robbery of royal tombs.

1250 B.C. The Egyptian Empire continued its decline following the Hebrews' escape under Moses' leadership; it never would rise to the same level of development again.

BABYLONIA

The areas which comprised Babylonia included Mesopotamia, Iran, Syria, Assyria, Arabia, Iraq, Saudi Arabia, Media Chaldea, and Persia. The inhabitants of these areas were referred to as Amorites, Iranians, and Elamites, and later as Persians and Sumerians.

6000 B.C. Copper was known to the people of the Tigris and Euphrates River valleys.

5000–4000 B.C. The Sumerians established the earliest cities in the delta area of the Tigris and Euphrates Rivers.

4000–3000 B.C. The Sumerians moved up the rivers to Babylon. The first Sumerian writings appeared on clay tablets. Copper and alloys were used for the first time between the Stone Age and the Iron Age.

3500 B.C. The Sumerians produced linen and used gold in their

28 / *Chronological Summary*

	jewelry. A wedge-shaped style of writing (cuneiform) was developed. The Sumerians used wheeled chariots and carts.
2500 B.C.	Semitic (Hebrew) tribes moved north in the Tigris and Euphrates valleys. Mis-anni-padda, of Ur, was the first ruler of Mesopotamia. The people worshipped various gods and deities in the first terraced temples. The healing qualities of mineral springs were discovered. The Great Wall of Exech (Uxuk), with 900 towers, was built at this time. There was a numerical system of 6's and 12's. The people used the potter's wheel and oil-burning lamps. During this time, the first iron was manufactured by the Hittites in the northern areas. The people first domesticated chickens. They grew grains, baked bread, and made beer. They produced the first set of laws and studies in mathematics, astrology, and other sciences. The bow and arrow was used in warfare.
2300 B.C.	Sargon established world's first empire in Mesopotamia.
2100 B.C.	Abraham left Ur in Chaldea.
1500–1100 B.C.	Kikkuli of Mitanni (in northern Mesopotamia) wrote the first treatise on horse breeding and training.
1300 B.C.	King Shalmaneser I established Assyrian supremacy and built the fortified city of Nimrud.
1140 B.C.	Nebuchadnezzar I became the king of Babylon.

GREECE

The area of Greece included the isles of the Aegean Sea. The inhabitants of Crete were the first Greeks.

4000–3000 B.C.	The "Cavemen Barbarian" type (Paleolithic-Azilian) began to civilize (into Neolithic) along the shores of the Mediterranean.
3000 B.C.	Bronze was used.
2500 B.C.	This was the period of the earliest Trojan culture. The weaving loom was known at this time. Wrestling was the first highly developed sport.
1700 B.C.	The Greeks made ships that were sturdy enough to reach Egypt for trading purposes. They were skilled traders, artists, and builders. The Greek Hellenic culture on the mainland of Greece was developed by invading Cretans who took over the Hellenic villages of Greece in 1900 B.C.

Chronological Summary / 29

1600 B.C. By this time, Greece had grown rich and powerful.
1500 B.C. The people built fortified cities. They also wrote on clay tablets that were not deciphered until A.D. 1953.
1450 B.C. The Greeks conquered the Minoans.
1400 B.C. By this time, the people had built Cretan-like palaces at Mycenae, Sparta, Aryolis, Peloponnesus. Mycenae became the most powerful Greek city.
1900–1184 B.C. This period marked the flourishing of the Troadic culture. Troy, in Asia Minor, was destroyed by fire and rebuilt seven times. The Trojans were farmers; they wove woolens; built fortified cities and houses, and had treasures of gold, silver, and copper.
1500–1100 B.C. A primitive Greek alphabet was utilized at Knossus. This time marked the beginning of the Cretan-Mycenaean culture, which produced the famous Cretan terra-cotta vases.

CHINA

The area known as China included the countries to the north and peoples such as the Mongolians, Scythians, Huns, and Tartars.

4000 B.C. China was peopled the same way as Asia Minor, Egypt, and the Indus Valley in Pakistan.
3500 B.C. There is some written history of China in this time period.
3000 B.C. At this time, the rule by kings in China began.
2700 B.C. Silk was discovered in China by Si-ling-Shi, the wife of Emperor Huang-Ti, when the worms were damaging his mulberry trees. The secret of silk was kept for 3000 years; traitors who divulged the secret met with disgrace and death. There were silk routes from China to Damascus and the rest of the world through the Persians. In A.D. 550, the Roman or Byzantine emperor, Justinian, sent two monks to China. They brought out silkworm eggs and mulberry seeds in hollow canes. The people used marijuana.
1500–1100 B.C. The Shang Culture was the ruling power. The first Chinese dictionary, which contained 40,000 characters, emerged during this time. Bronze sculptures were made. The people worked with advanced mathematical equations. They measured the height of the sun in relation to the incline of the polar axis. Prohibition was decreed in China. A religion based upon animism and ancestor worship formed.

30 / *Chronological Summary*

1028–256 B.C. Chou dynasty developed ideas about living and thinking which have endured into modern times.
604–531 B.C. Lao-tzu developed his philosophy of Taoism, a liberal religion based upon right conduct.
551–479 B.C. Confucius developed his philosophy of religion.
221 B.C. Chin dynasty, founded by Shih Huang Ti, gave China its name, brought great unity and strength, and built the Great Wall.

THE HOLY LAND

The Holy Land included Israel, Jordan, Lebanon, and parts of Syria, Phoenicia, Palestine, and Canaan.

4000–3000 B.C. The Jewish calendar started with the year 3760 B.C.
3000 B.C. Sidon and Tyre were settled on the Mediterranean coast by the Phoenicians, who probably were from Crete.
2000–1500 B.C. There were trade routes to Asia Minor and Babylon, and sea routes from Egypt to the eastern Mediterranean.
1500–1100 B.C. In 1200 B.C., the Phoenicians became the principal traders in the Mediterranean. Also at this time, Moses received the Ten Commandments on Mount Sinai. This was the Age of the Judges selected from the twelve tribes. Tin was imported to Phoenicia from Briton.
1500 B.C. Book of Genesis.
1425–1250 B.C. Books of Joshua and Ruth.
1290–1140 B.C. Books of Exodus, Leviticus, Numbers, and Deuteronomy.
1200–1000 B.C. Book of Judges.

TURKEY

The area of Turkey included Asia Minor, Armenia, Kurdistan, and Anatolia; many of the inhabitants were referred to as Hittites.

3000–2500 B.C. During this time, iron was first manufactured.
1190 B.C. The Hittites were the first rulers of Asia Minor.
1500–1100 B.C. The Hittites held religious dances and used the guitar, the lyre, the trumpet, and the tambourine. A Hittite princess became a queen for an Egyptian Pharaoh.
1193 B.C. Troy was destroyed during the Trojan War. The library in the Hittite capital contained tablets in eight languages.
1100 B.C. Iron was developed from the mines.

SPAIN

People have lived in Spain for 100,000 years. Since 5000 B.C., the first of recorded history, the Iberians, natives of the Spanish Peninsula, have occupied much of Spain.

10,000 B.C. The Cro-Magnon man occupied and painted their animal paintings on the walls of caves in northern and central Spain. The people farmed and lived in villages. Cartagena and Tarragona have existed since 5000 B.C.

INDIA

India included areas of Pakistan and Afghanistan.

2700 B.C. The people used marijuana for pleasure, in ceremonies, and as medicine.
2500 B.C. In the Indus Valley of Pakistan, the Harappas and the Mohenjo-daros had systems of counting, measuring, weighing, and writing. They had ditches and canals for irrigation and brick-lined sewer systems for brick houses. These people disappeared about 1700 B.C.
1500–1100 B.C. During this time, the Ganges civilization was developing. Leprosy emerged in India and Egypt.

GERMANY

Germany included areas of Denmark, Norway, and Sweden and extended south and east into Hungary, Bohemia, and Romania.

3000 B.C. The settlers in the valley and the plains of the Danube River had developed a culture.
2500 B.C. The people worshipped various gods and deities. Lake dwellers were developing in Middle Europe.
1000 B.C. Tribes came into Germany from the north, and some moved as far south as the Rhine and Danube rivers by 100 B.C. A system of government evolved, based upon devotion to a tribal leader, which during the Middle Ages would develop into the system of feudalism. A communal form of living very similar to modern Communism developed.

BRITON (BRITAIN)

Briton included all of the British Isles of Scotland, Wales, and Ireland.

10,000 B.C. Primitive people lived in caves during the Stone Age.
8000–3000 B.C. People from France and Spain settled and made flint

tools, grew crops, made pottery, and raised cattle and sheep.

2000 B.C. People from the Rhine and Danube valleys settled. They wove cloth, mined tin, and made bronze tools.

2000–1500 B.C. This marked the earliest beginnings of Stonehenge near Salisbury.

FRANCE

2000–1500 B.C. The Bronze Age existed in western Europe.

SCANDINAVIA

100,000 B.C. People lived in Denmark, but the country turned cold and was deserted.

14,000 B.C. The country began to turn warmer, and resettlement began.

6000 B.C. The first settlers in Sweden came from the south.

2500 B.C. People began farming in Denmark. Pictures of skiers were carved on rock in southern Norway.

1500–1100 B.C. The Bronze Age began in the area. The people had advanced knowledge of shipbuilding.

OTHERS

3300 B.C. There was the first evidence of the Mayan civilization in Central America.

3000–2500 B.C. Pepis papyrus was one of the earliest preserved documents.

2500–2000 B.C. There are vague indications that cotton was cultivated in Peru.

1500–1100 B.C. This period of time marked the existence of the earliest known settlement in Mexico, Chiapa de Carzo. The Mexican sun pyramid was built in Teotihuacán. The Olmec culture was beginning in Mexico.

EXODUS

Time   About 1290 B.C. to 1140 B.C., thirty years after Genesis.
Author Reputedly, Moses.
Theme Name means "going out." God's fulfillment of His promises to Abraham, Isaac, and Jacob is shown by His deliverance of Israel from Egypt and His revelation of His faithfulness, power, and wisdom.

Joseph and his brothers died, but their descendents increased until Egypt was populated with the Hebrews. The king, growing fearful of their numbers, told the midwives to kill all male Hebrews at birth, but the midwives, fearful of God, did not obey him. Then the king commanded that every Hebrew son born should be drowned in the Nile. The wife of a Levite bore a son, and when he was three months old, she put him in a basket and put it in the Nile, where the Pharaoh's daughter bathed daily. A sister watched, and when the Pharaoh's daughter found the babe and took pity on it, the sister asked if she should get a Hebrew woman to nurse the child. Pharaoh's daughter said yes, so the girl went and got the child's mother. Pharaoh's daughter paid the mother to raise the child for her. When the child grew, the mother brought him to Pharaoh's daughter, who named him Moses.

When Moses became a man and became powerful in the Pharaoh's rule, he saw an Egyptian beating a Hebrew, so he killed the Egyptian and buried him in the sand. When the Pharaoh heard of this, he planned to kill Moses. After having lived in Egypt for forty years, Moses escaped to Midian, east of Sinai. Here he met Jethro and married his daughter Zipporah. Moses lived in Midian forty years. One day while he was tending his flock, the angel of the Lord appeared to him in a flame of fire out of the midst of a bush. As Moses looked, the bush burned, but was not consumed; and God spoke to Moses, telling him that he was to go to Egypt and lead his people out of Egypt into the Promised Land of Canaan, a land flowing with milk and honey.

Moses pleaded, saying, "Who am I that I should go to Pharaoh and that I bring the sons of Israel out of Egypt?" (Exodus 3:11). God instructed him to go to Egypt and gather the elders of Israel, then go to Pharaoh to secure the release from the Egyptians. Moses would be given power to perform miracles and bring plagues on the Egyptians. The Lord showed

Moses how to turn his staff into a serpent, cause his hand to become leprous and be cured by putting it into his bosom, and cause the water of the Nile to turn to blood when poured on the dry sand. Moses pleaded that he was not an able speaker, so God said He would have Moses' brother Aaron speak whatever words God gave to Moses.

Moses and Aaron went to the Pharaoh to secure release of the Hebrews, but the Pharaoh hardened his heart and made the work of the Hebrews greater by telling them they would have to get their own straw to make bricks and they would have to make the same number of bricks each day. The people were discouraged and bitter with Moses and Aaron.

Moses, at God's instruction, then went to the Pharaoh and said that unless he released the Hebrews, God would turn the River Nile to blood, and all the fish would die. Moses struck the river with his rod and this happened, but still the Pharaoh refused to release them.

After seven days the Lord told Moses to say to the Pharaoh that the land would be covered with frogs, and they would be in the houses and beds and even in the food. The Pharaoh refused, Aaron struck the waters with his rod, and the frogs swarmed the land. The Pharaoh promised to release the Hebrews if God would eliminate the frogs, which He did, but then the Pharaoh refused to keep his word.

The Lord spoke to Moses, telling him to say to the Pharaoh that he would strike the earth with his rod and the dust would turn to gnats. The gnats swarmed the earth, but still the Pharaoh refused to let the Hebrews go.

Subsequently the Lord gave the power to Moses to plague the Pharaoh with five more plagues: flies, death of all the livestock, boils on all the people and cattle, hail and lightning, and locusts. Each time the Pharaoh would lie to Moses about releasing the Hebrews. In each of the plagues, the Hebrews were not afflicted. Only the Egyptians were afflicted. The Egyptian people were becoming aware of the God of the Hebrews and Moses' power, but the Pharaoh remained immovable.

The God of Moses and Aaron said to them that one more plague would be necessary and the Pharaoh would relent. Moses was told to say to the Egyptian people and Pharaoh that, on a given day at midnight, the life of the firstborn of every living person in Egypt, except the Hebrews, and the firstborn of all the cattle, would be taken, including the firstborn of the Pharaoh.

The Pharaoh still refused to listen. The Lord instructed Moses and Aaron that on the tenth day of the month they should have every Hebrew family choose a lamb, kill it on the fourteenth day, take some of the blood, and put it on the side doorposts and on the lintel. They should then roast the lamb and eat all of it before morning. This is the Lord's Passover. The Lord said the angel of death would pass through the land and kill the firstborn of both man and beast, but at the sign of the blood, he would pass over that household and no plague would fall on the Hebrews. This is known as the seven-day feast and celebration of the Passover, celebrated by the Hebrews to this day.

At midnight, when the Lord smote the Egyptians, there was great panic, because there was not a house where there was not one dead. The Pharaoh sent for Moses and Aaron and told them to take all their possessions and leave. The Hebrews asked the Egyptians to give them gold, silver, and clothing, and they gave them all that they asked. The Lord instructed the Hebrews that they were to eat no leavened bread for seven days.

There were six hundred thousand men, plus the women, children, flocks and herds who left Egypt that night. They had lived in Egypt 430 years. They had not gone far when the Pharaoh realized he no longer had the Hebrews for slaves. He ordered six hundred picked chariots and all the other chariots and army to pursue the Hebrews and bring them back.

When the Hebrews saw the Egyptians in pursuit, they cried out to Moses and accused him of leading them into destruction. Moses told them to fear not and stand firm. The Lord told Moses to stretch out his rod and the waters of the sea would part. Then the Hebrews could cross through the sea on dry ground and see the salvation of the Lord their God.

That night Moses did this, and the Hebrews crossed the sea on dry ground, with a wall of water on their left and right. The Egyptians followed, but their chariots became clogged in the mud, and after the Hebrews were safely across the sea, the waters closed in at Moses' command and covered all the Egyptians. Not one remained alive.

Thus the Lord saved Israel and the Egyptians were dead and scattered on the seashore. The people feared the Lord and believed in the Lord and in His servant Moses. There were probably 2,000,000 Hebrews in the exodus from Egypt.

Moses led the people into the wilderness of Shur and on into the Sinai area. The people complained that they had no food and told Moses and Aaron they would be better off as slaves in Egypt. Moses prayed to God, who said He would send them quail in the evenings and manna in the mornings. He did this for the forty years they wandered in the desert. They could gather enough manna to eat each day, but must not save any. On the sixth day, they should gather enough to eat on the Sabbath.

At God's command, Moses went before the people, taking the elders with him as witnesses, and struck a rock with his rod at Horeb. Enough water came from the rock to provide the needs of all the people.

Jethro, the priest of Midian, Moses' father-in-law, came to Moses, bringing Moses' wife and two sons to him. Jethro praised the God of Moses and helped him organize a way to rule and maintain order among so many people.

The people moved into the wilderness of Sinai and camped before the

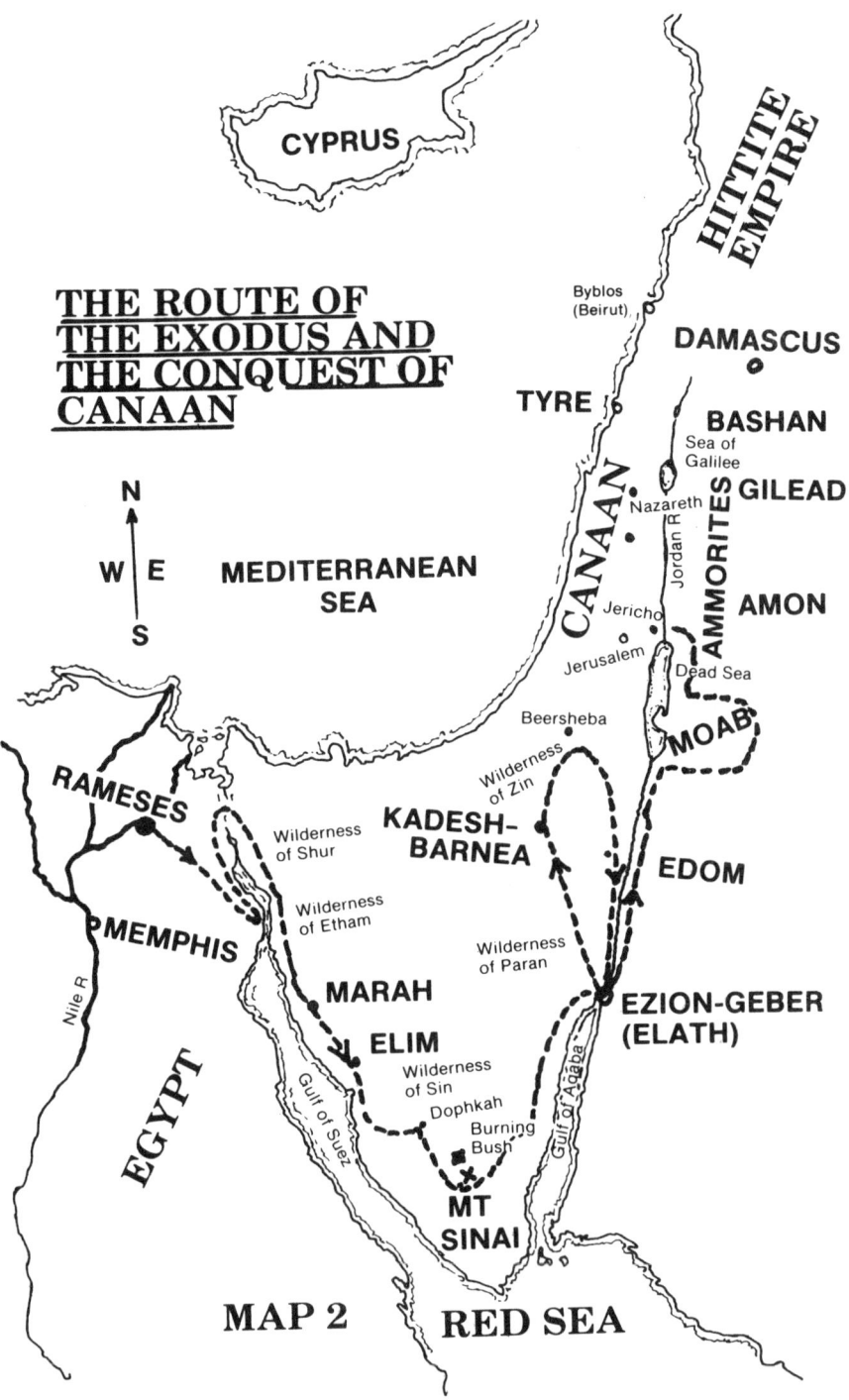

mountain. God instructed Moses to have the people assemble at the front of the mountain to meet God. They were to come no closer, but Moses was to ascend the mountain. There was thunder and lightning and a great cloud on the mountain, plus a great quake and the sound of a loud trumpet blast. God spoke, giving Moses all the laws of the Ten Commandments and many ordinances for the Hebrews' guidance and conduct. Moses wrote them down, and the people agreed to abide by them.

The Lord then told Moses to come to Him on the mountain, to receive the tablets of stone with the law and the commandments. Moses told the people to wait for him. He was on the mountain forty days and forty nights. God spoke to Moses, telling him to gather from the people much gold and silver, precious gems, and other materials to make the Ark of the Covenant, a mercy seat, an altar table, and a lampstand. He also gave him the complete, exact specifications for building a portable, demountable tabernacle. Moses was to appoint his brother Aaron and his sons to tend the temple from morning to evening, wearing robes designed and sewed according to exact specifications.

God told Moses how Aaron and his sons should be consecrated to serve as priests, how and when offerings should be made, and how to build an incense altar and a washing bowl for the priests. He also gave Moses a formula for the sacred anointing oil of oils and spices. God told Moses He would give certain men the craftsmanship to build all these things. He also told Moses that the Sabbath was a day of rest, a holy day, and was to be kept as a covenant between the Lord and the people.

When God had finished speaking, He gave Moses two tablets of stone written with the finger of God. In the meantime, the people, thinking Moses had deserted them, made a golden calf as their god and were worshipping it and feasting and celebrating when Moses returned. Moses was furious and broke the tablets of stone. He had the Levites go among the people and slay 3,000 of them for their sins, and God had a great plague come upon the people.

God was very angry with these stiff-necked people, but Moses begged Him to forgive them. God forgave them and repeated that He would help them defeat all the inhabitants of Canaan and give to the Hebrews this land flowing with milk and honey.

He then instructed Moses to make two new stone tablets and go up into the Mount of Sinai for his instructions, to be written on the stone tablets. Moses was on the mountain forty days and nights, and he neither ate nor drank. When he returned, his face shone brightly, because he had talked to God. He instructed the people to contribute all the things necessary to make the Ark and the Tabernacle and all the furnishings. All whose hearts were moved did this.

The craftsmen, who were endowed with skill by God, completed the Ark and the Tabernacle and all the furnishings with fine woods, gold, silver, elaborate weavings, and precious gems. They also made the elaborate robes for the priests of the Tabernacle. Moses blessed them for their work.

Then Moses had the Tabernacle erected and all the furnishings put in place as God had specified. A cloud covered the Tabernacle, and the glory of the Lord filled it. Throughout all their journeys, when the cloud was taken up from the Tabernacle, the people would move onward. But if the cloud was not taken up, they would not move. The cloud was over the Tabernacle by day and a fire was in it by night, for all to see that the Lord was with Israel.

LEVITICUS

Time At Sinai during the early part of forty years in the wilderness.
Author Reputedly, Moses.
Theme Name means "concerning the Levites and the laws." The members of the tribe of priests and priests' aides in charge of the Tabernacle, the sacred vessels, and later, the Temple.

The third book of the Pentateuch (first five books) gives the instructions of God to Moses as to the conduct of the Hebrew nation. These instructions are intended to strengthen and govern the spiritual life of the Jews and to explain how God should be worshipped. The book includes priestly regulations and laws concerning marriage, sacrifices, and religious festivals.

The Levites, or priests, were also teachers, scribes, musicians, and judiciary officers. They were supported by the offerings and tithes of the other eleven tribes.

Chapters 1–7 outline offerings; 8–9, priests' consecration; 10, Nadab and Abihu, sons of Aaron, burned to death by God for their sin before the Lord; 11–15, purity of life; 16–17, Day of Atonement; 18–22, warnings of sin; 23–25, various feasts; 26–27, obedience to God, vows, and tithes. The command was given ". . . you shall love your neighbor as yourself . . ." (Leviticus 19:18).

God demanded capital punishment for crimes of murder, kidnapping, negligence, cursing a parent, idolatry, and others. God promised rewards for obedience and severe penalties for disobedience. On the annual Day of Atonement, Yom Kippur (chapter 16), the high priest entered the Holy of Holies in the Tabernacle to make atonement for the sins of the people.

God did not consider taking a man's life as excessive punishment for certain crimes. He was more concerned with those who had respect for Him and His laws. Yearly feasts were holidays of joyfulness and thanksgiving.

His edicts included three vacations yearly and a whole year off every seven; slavery was condoned, with humane treatment; the once-in-a-lifetime year of jubilee was a joyous event; and every fifty years, all the land reverted back to the original owners. Chapter 11 outlined basic dietary laws that traditional Jews still observe as Kosher. If God were to give mankind a set of laws today, this book would probably be it.

NUMBERS

Time   1500 B.C. Covers forty years.
Author Reputedly, Moses.
Theme The name is taken from the two censuses, or numberings of the people. Numbers covers a period of thirty-eight years of wandering in the desert rather than being permitted to enter the Promised Land, because the people lacked faith and disobeyed God. It is a book of instruction for obedience, penalties for disobedience, and preparation to enter the Promised Land.

God told Moses to take a census of all males twenty years old or older, who numbered 603,550, excluding the Levites, who were to take care of the Tabernacle. It is estimated that the total population was 2,000,000. Each of the twelve tribes was told where to pitch its tents around the Tabernacle. Duties were assigned to the Levites. Moses, his brother Aaron, and the priests guarded the entrance to the Tabernacle. The total circumference of the camp was twelve miles.

A cloud was over the camp by day and a flame of fire by night. When the cloud moved, the people broke camp and moved with it. When the cloud stopped, the people encamped, whether for a day or a month.

Many new laws were given to the people by God through His servant Moses. Some of the people complained about their misfortunes, and God caused a fire to consume their camps. Others complained that they had no fish to eat, nor the Egyptian cucumbers, melons, leeks, onions, and garlic—nothing except manna. Moses prayed to God to unburden him of the responsibility of these unworthy people and give them meat. The Lord sent enough quail to feed all the tribes for thirty days.

Moses' brother Aaron and sister Miriam were jealous of Moses' power with God, because God spoke face-to-face with Moses, but they had to speak through prophets with others. God smote Miriam with leprosy for punishment, but healed her again after Moses asked God to forgive her. But she was banned from the camp for seven days, and the camp could not move till she came back.

The Lord told Moses to send one man from each tribe to spy out the Promised Land of Canaan. Ten of them reported a land of milk and honey, but said that the people could not be conquered. Caleb and Joshua, however, had great faith in God and said the people could be conquered. God was angered by the lack of faith of the people and was going to destroy the whole nation, but Moses interceded. God compromised by saying the Israelites must wander another thirty-eight years in the desert, until all now over twenty years of age were dead, except Caleb and Joshua, who had faith.

Korah, Dathan, and Abiram and all their families were swallowed alive by the earth as punishment for their criticism of God, and then 14,700 more were killed by the plague for criticizing Moses. Miriam died at Kadesh.

The tribes encamped in an area where there was no water. God told Moses to speak to the rock and it would yield water, but Moses struck the rock in anger with his people, and water gushed forth. God told Moses that as punishment for his disobedience, he would not enter the Promised Land.

The Israelites moved toward the capture of various lands. They conquered the Amorites. Balak, king of Moab, sent word to Baalam the prophet, together with gifts, to persuade Baalam to curse the Israelites, but Baalam was instructed by God to bless them, instead. Moses took another census, and there were 601,730 males—no gain in thirty-eight years.

Midian was captured without the Israelites' losing one warrior of their 12,000. The lands of Moab were divided to the tribes of Reuben and Gad and one half of the tribe of Manasseh. During the thirty-eight years of wanderings in the desert, the shoes and garments of all the people showed no wear, and there was no food or water except as provided by God.

DEUTERONOMY

Time   1500 B.C. Actual time about one month before entering and starting the conquest of Canaan.
Author   Reputedly, Moses. Last book of the Pentateuch. Last chapter probably written by Joshua.
Theme   Title from the Greek word meaning "second giving of the Law" or "repetition of the Law."

The Lord had allowed the Israelites to conquer Shihon, the Amorite, king of Heshbon; and Og, king of Bashon, and all their lands which were east of the Jordan. This land was divided between the tribes of Reuben, Gad and one half of the tribe of Manasseh. The peoples and armies of all the tribes were poised to enter and conquer the Promised Land of Canaan. God had told Moses that he would never enter Canaan, because He was angry with him. Moses was to go to the top of the Mount of Pisgah (opposite Jericho) and see the Promised Land, but he would die before the Israelites entered. God commissioned Joshua, son of Nun, to replace Moses and lead the conquest.

In this setting, Moses spent forty days talking to the people, reviewing their history, their objectives, and the laws as previously given, plus giving additional explanation and some new laws. This was explained in Chapters 1 and 2, with emphasis over and over again on God's love for His chosen people, the Hebrews, and His urgings for them to be loyal and faithful.

Moses set aside three cities: Bezer of the Reubenites; Ramoth of the Gadites; and Golan in Bashan of the Manassites, as refuge cities where men might flee who were guilty of manslaughter without enmity.

Chapters 12 to 29 are a recitation by Moses of all the laws that cover the discipline of the people. Even as Moses was instructing the people, he knew that they were a stiff-necked, obstinate, and easily influenced people. Among the many laws were the ones saying that every three years all tithes were to go to the poor and the Levites; every seven years everyone was to be forgiven for all borrowings; and slaves were to serve for six years and then be granted their freedom. Moses repeated the great warning that obedience to God brings rewards, but disobedience brings disaster, curses, and death. Moses was preparing for his own death.

In Chapter 28:1, God said, "Now it shall be, if you will diligently obey the Lord your God, being careful to do all His commandments which I command you today, the Lord your God will set you high above all the nations of the earth." Then in 28:15, 16, He said, "But it shall come about, if you will not obey the Lord your God, to observe to do all His commandments and His statutes which I charge you today, that all these curses shall come upon you and overtake you. Cursed shall you be in the city, and cursed shall you be in the country." In Chapter 29:4, Moses said, "Yet to this day the Lord has not given you a heart to know, nor eyes to see, nor ears to hear." In Chapter 31:16, "And the Lord said to Moses, 'Behold, you are about to lie down with your fathers; and this people will arise and play the harlot with the strange gods of the land, into the midst of which they are going, and will forsake Me and break My covenant which I have made with them.'" Chapter 32 is the beautiful song of Moses, which stresses the relationship of God's love and loyalty for the children of Israel. Chapter 33 outlines the blessing of Moses and the future destiny of the tribes of Israel. The book ends with the account of the death of Moses.

Throughout this book, Moses told the people of God's love for them and His covenant to deliver to them the Promised Land. He knew of their weaknesses and warned them repeatedly of the penalties if they disobeyed God's laws. In Chapter 31:20, the Lord said, "For when I bring them into the land flowing with milk and honey, which I swore to their fathers, and they have eaten and are satisfied and become prosperous, then they will turn to other gods and serve them, and spurn Me and break My covenant." Moses died when he was 120 years old. He was the only prophet to whom the Lord talked face-to-face. He was truly a man of great power and deeds, and a humble, patient, compassionate servant of God. The reader grieves for the death of this man.

JOSHUA

Time Covers about twenty-five years. Debatable—1425 B.C. to 1250 B.C.

Author Joshua, grandson of Elishama, chief of Ephraim. His family called him Hoshea, meaning *salvation*. (Some scholars say there were several authors.)

Theme This book tells of the conquest of Canaan, the Promised Land, the method of possession, and the allocation of the territories to the tribes of Israel. God's guidance and power are demonstrated, and disobedience is not tolerated.

God instructed Joshua to enter and take the Promised Land and said, ". . . be careful to do according to all the law which Moses My servant commanded you . . ." (Joshua 1:7).

Joshua sent two men from Shittim to spy out Jericho. They stayed with Rahab, a harlot, who saved them from capture, and to reciprocate, they vowed to save her and her family when they took Jericho. The tribes of Hebrew warriors were led by the priests carrying the Ark of the Covenant. When they reached the Jordan, Joshua commanded the waters to stop, so the armies could cross on dry ground. This experience exalted Joshua before all the people. A memorial of twelve stones was built to commemorate the spot. At that time, all the males who had been born during the forty years in the wilderness were circumcised at the place called Gilgal. This was the last day they ate manna.

The story of the conquest of Jericho was to be heard all over the Promised Land. The seven priests with the Ark of the Covenant, followed by the warriors, went around the city once each day for six days, and on the seventh made the trip seven times. Then when all the warriors shouted, the walls of the city fell flat, and every person and beast was slaughtered except Rahab, the harlot, and her family. One warrior kept some booty against God's instruction, and the next battle at Ai was lost because of this sin. Achan was guilty, and he and all his family were stoned to death. The next day Ai was taken and burned. Afterward, Joshua read the law, the blessing, and the curses to all, as commanded by Moses.

All the kings of the lands west of the Jordan heard of these things and, filled with fear, banded together to fight Israel. The people of Gibeon deceived Joshua into making a pact with them, allowing the people of Gibeon to live as Israel's servants. Adonizedek, king of Jerusalem, asked four other kings to join with him to destroy Gibeon for doing this. Gibeon told Joshua and asked him to protect them. Joshua and his warriors attacked and slew many of these five kings' people and chased the rest. As they were retreating down Bethhoron, a great hailstorm killed more of them than did the Israel warriors. As Israel had conquered the Amorites, Joshua asked the Lord to stop the sun and moon, to enable him to make this conquest—and God did so for a whole day. The five kings hid in a cave at Makkedah and were found by Joshua, who had them all hung. Joshua then took Makkedah and hanged its king.

Then Joshua conquered the cities of Libnah, Lachish, Gezer, Eglon, Hebron, Debir, and the Negeb area from Kadesh-barnea to Gaza to Gibeon, which is all a principal area of modern Israel. In every country, every man, woman and child was slain, because the Lord did not want the Israel nation contaminated with foreign sinners. God was fulfilling His promise to Israel.

Jabin, king of Hazor, organized thirteen other kings of territories in the northern half of Canaan, which is modern Israel, and parts of Lebanon and Syria, to meet at the waters of Merom to fight Israel. Joshua's armies, fortified with faith in God, destroyed all of them, "and they did not leave any of them that breathed." Joshua in time destroyed all the people in the Promised Land, except the Hivites and a few in Gaza, Gath and Ashdod along the Mediterranean Sea coastal strip.

Joshua was getting old and was told by the Lord that there were some additional lands to be conquered and that he should allocate all the lands to the other nine and one-half tribes, which he did. He made no allocation of land to the Levites, but the tribes gave them forty-eight cities later. Caleb requested the land he and Joshua had originally spied out. He wanted to follow God's instructions to take this land, so Joshua granted his request. After a survey of the land made by three men from each tribe, all of the territories were divided by lot. The people then gave Joshua his request for the city of Timnath-serah in Ephraim. Joshua then established six cities of refuge.

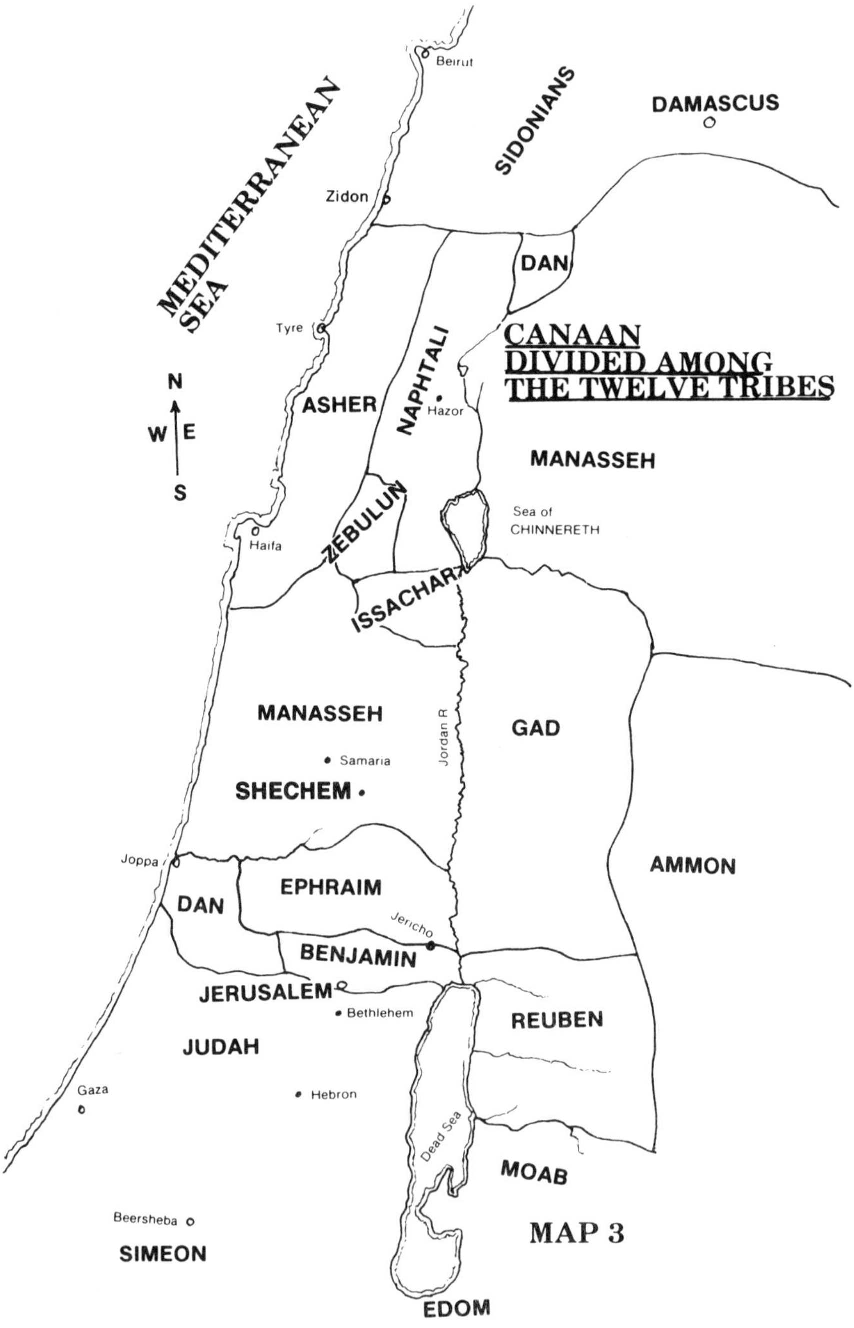
MEDITERRANEAN SEA
Beirut
SIDONIANS
DAMASCUS
Zidon
DAN
Tyre
CANAAN DIVIDED AMONG THE TWELVE TRIBES
N
W
E
S
ASHER
NAPHTALI
Hazor
MANASSEH
Sea of CHINNERETH
Haifa
ZEBULUN
ISSACHAR
MANASSEH
GAD
Jordan R
Samaria
SHECHEM
Joppa
AMMON
DAN
EPHRAIM
Jericho
BENJAMIN
JERUSALEM
Bethlehem
REUBEN
JUDAH
Gaza
Hebron
Dead Sea
MOAB
Beersheba
SIMEON
MAP 3
EDOM

After all the lands were conquered, the warriors of the tribes of Gad and Reuben and half the tribe of Manasseh east of the Jordan were sent home to rest. As they were going home, they built an altar of great size on the west side of the Jordan. This displeased the other nine and one-half tribes on the east side, who appointed Phinehas and ten chiefs to accuse the two and one-half tribes east of the Jordan of rebelling against the Lord, like Achan. The eastern tribes explained that the altar was built so that in later times their children would see the altar on the west side as a symbol that they intended no rebellion against the Lord. This pleased Phinehas, and he took this pleasant message back to the western tribes, who were pleased that all the tribes were in harmony with God. This is the same area where today's Israelites are in dispute with the Palestinians and Jordanians.

Then Joshua, getting old, gathered all the twelve tribes of Israel to Shechem, which is probably near modern Janin or Nabulus in Israel, where he told them that their God had given one of them the power to conquer one thousand; that they should love the Lord; that they should not intermarry with foreigners, as this would create a snare and a trap for them to do evil; that everything God had promised, He had delivered; that if they transgressed the covenant of the Lord, they would surely be punished. They all swore they would gladly follow these instructions. Joshua wrote these covenants in the book of the law and erected a great stone as a witness of their covenant. Joshua died a true servant of God at 110 years of age. Joseph's bones, which had been brought from Egypt, were buried at Shechem in the ground bought by Jacob when he traveled that way.

JUDGES

Time Covers 305 years, from the time of Joshua's death to King Saul. Various opinions run from a 180- to a 410-year time period. Possibly 1200 B.C. to 1000 B.C.
Author Probably the prophet Samuel, but undoubtedly a gathering of all traditional stories and written documents.
Theme A historical account of the activities of the twelve judges who ruled from the time of the death of Joshua to the coronation of King Saul. Tells of the spiritual failures of the Israelites, and the steadfastness of God's love.

The seventh book of the Bible received its name from those who judged Israel. The judges were actually military leaders, rather than judicial judges as known in modern times. The well-known stories of Deborah, Gideon, and Samson are told in this book. There were twelve judges, one of whom was a woman. The activities of six were detailed and the other six were mentioned. The book is a history of Israel's defection from God's rule, oppression by its warring neighbors, and deliverance by the judges, who, when the crises were passed, gave up the judgeship.

Judah conquered some of the Canaanites and Perizzites and then captured Adonibezek. According to his own custom, they cut off his thumbs and great toes. Judah captured many other cities and territories of their allotment but could not defeat the coast people, because they had chariots of iron. None of the tribes completely ridded their territory of the enemy; and after Joshua's death they became disobedient, worshipped the gods of Baal, and permitted intermarriage of their sons and daughters. Because of their disobedience, God permitted the king of Mesopotamia to conquer them; but He then raised up Othniel as judge, to deliver them for forty years.

Then Eglon, king of Moab, defeated and ruled them for eighteen years. God raised Ehud as judge, who by cunning trickery killed the fat King Eglon with his sword. Ehud then defeated ten thousand Moabite warriors, regained their territory, and lived in peace for eighty years.

After Ehud died, the people of Israel sinned again. The judge Shamgar fought and saved Israel again, and then Jabin, king of Canaan, reigned over it. His commander was Sisera. Deborah, a prophetess and judge, summoned Barak to gather ten thousand men, and she asked God to deliver Sisera and his nine hundred chariots to him, which He did. Sisera fled on foot to a woman named Jael, who pretended to protect him but drove a tent spike through his head after he went to sleep. This resulted in the destruction of Jabin, king of Canaan. Israel had peace for forty years. The song of Deborah is one of the great war poems of all literature.

The people sinned against God, and the Midianites on the east then harassed and plundered Israel. God sent His angel to Gideon, a member of a small clan of the tribe of Manasseh, who was a very humble man. The angel told Gideon to save Israel from the Midianites. Gideon could not believe that God had selected him, so he tested God twice with a fleece on the threshing floor, and he was convinced that God had chosen him. Gideon assembled 32,000 men from the tribes, but God said that if they won, they would think it was through their own strength, so through elimination by tests, all but 300 were sent home. Gideon, with these 300 men divided into three groups with trumpets and flares, set the Midian soldiers into revolt against one another and eventually caused the death of 120,000 men and a final 15,000, plus their kings. Midian was subdued, and there was peace for forty years. Gideon died, and the people returned to their sinful ways.

Abimelech, a son of Gideon by a concubine, and one of seventy sons, talked his family into having him become its leader and giving him seventy pieces of silver, which he used to hire murderers to kill all seventy brothers except Jotham, the youngest son. Jotham reviled the city of Shechem for electing Abimelech and prophesied its downfall. Abimelech, in shame, had his armorbearer kill him after a woman wounded him by hitting him on the head with a rock.

Tola, the next judge, judged Israel for twenty-three years, and then Jair judged it for twenty-two years. The Israelites sinned against God, and the Canaanites ruled them for eighteen years. Jephthah, the son of a harlot, was cast out by his brothers, but when the Ammonites threatened war with Israel, his brothers and the townspeople of Gilead asked him to come back to be their judge.

Jephthah made a vow that if God was with him and if he conquered the Ammonites, he would sacrifice the first person to meet him on his return, who turned out to be his only child, his daughter. He kept his vow, but with great sorrow. He ruled for six years. Ibzan ruled Israel for seven years. Elon ruled for ten years. Abdon ruled for eight years.

The Israelites sinned against God, and the Philistines ruled them for forty years. The angel of the Lord appeared to the wife of Manoah, who was barren, and told her that she would bear a son, Samson, and that no razor was to touch his head. Samson married a Philistine girl, who betrayed the answer to a riddle to her countrymen and caused Samson to lose a bet, much to his embarrassment. Samson ruled for twenty years. He feuded with the Philistines on several occasions and went into hiding. His own countrymen came and bound him over to the Philistines. He slew one thousand of them with the jawbone of an ass. The Philistines hired a harlot to find the source of his strength, then had his head shaved. They captured him, gouged out his eyes, and worked him as a slave. He was put on display at a celebration to Dagon, their god, and Samson pressed the two supporting pillars of the stadium, causing it to collapse. Several thousand Philistines, as well as Samson, were killed.

Also included in the Book of Judges are the stories of Micah and the tribe of Benjamin.

The Book of Joshua is one about victories for God. The Book of Judges is one about defeats, caused by failure of the Israelites to obey God.

RUTH

Time The time period is during the rule of the judges, about 1373 B.C., and this book covers a period of about ten years. Many scholars think the story was written about 400 B.C.
Author Unknown, possibly Samuel. The setting suggests this period, but some of the writings suggest the latter date.
Theme An early story of racial tolerance. While the nation of Israel was being punished, God's love was shown through Ruth.

In the days of the judges, a famine caused Elimelech, his wife Naomi, and their two sons, Mahlon and Chilion, to move from Jerusalem to Moab. While living there, the sons took wives named Orpha and Ruth. The father and both sons died within ten years. Naomi started to return to Israel and told her two daughters-in-law to stay in Moab, where they could find husbands. Orpha stayed, but Ruth, who loved Naomi very much, said, "... where you go, I will go .... Your people shall be my people, and your God, my God" (Ruth 1:16). So they returned to Bethlehem.

Naomi knew a rich kinsman of her husband, named Boaz. Ruth asked to glean in the barley fields of Boaz, and was working in his field when he visited and saw her. Boaz told her that he had heard she had left her relatives and country to be with Naomi and comfort her. He told her to stay in his fields and be protected. He allowed her to eat with his workers and told them to leave extra sheaves for her to glean. She took food and the grain home to Naomi and told her about her relative Boaz. Naomi praised God for Boaz's favors and for protecting Ruth from molesters.

Naomi advised Ruth to go to the threshing floor and lie at Boaz's feet where he slept, which she did. When Boaz recognized her, he praised her for her kindness and said he would redeem her through purchase of Elimelech's land, if Naomi's next of kin, who had priority redemption rights according to Jewish custom, did not do so. A hearing was held at the gate of the city and first of kin refused to redeem Naomi's husband's land, so Boaz did so, which gave him the right to take Ruth as his wife.

Ruth bore him a son, Obed, the father of Jesse, who was the father of David, who became king of Israel.

This book establishes the family tree to David, which will later be traced to Jesus. The grace of God is extended to a foreign Moabite and demonstrates His love for all who love Him and respect Him.

DEVELOPMENTS IN CIVILIZATION
1100 B.C.–400 B.C.

The most dominant civilization of this time was that of Greece. In the early stages of the time period, Greek script developed, and the *Iliad* and the *Odyssey* were written. Later on, approximately 590 B.C., Solon's Laws developed in Athens, where public libraries were in use. Greek art and architecture developed their own advanced styles and forms, and important discoveries were made in medicine.

The triumphs over the Persians and the successes in forming the League of Delos brought the Golden Age of Athens, 450 B.C.–400 B.C., also called the Age of Pericles. All free inhabitants of Athens were granted citizenship, and this city was the intellectual and artistic center of Greece. The great dramatists, writers, philosophers, and historians had their beginnings. Philosophers, poets, comedians, authors, historians, and artists flourished. Aspasia, the mistress of Pericles, ruled Athenian society, and the Spartans used chemicals in warfare. Socrates taught, and in 407 B.C., Plato became a pupil of Socrates.

The civilization of Babylon-Assyria also flourished. Arts and crafts were developing, and the earliest recorded music was written. The library at Nineveh contained poetry and educational texts. King Essarhaddon rebuilt Babylon, and construction of the Tower of Babel was begun. There were water aqueducts, bucket wells, and water clocks.

Between 700 B.C. and 600 B.C., the Assyrian king, Assurbanipal, assembled the great library of Nineveh, which contained more than 22,000 clay tablets that covered history, medicine, astrology, and the planets.

During the Babylonian captivity of the Jews, many books of the Old Testament, based on word-of-mouth traditions, were written in Hebrew. In 600 B.C., the first courier (mail) service, which used messengers on horseback, was established. The banking business was practiced in Babylon. In 539 B.C., the Persians under Cyrus captured Babylon. The year 500 B.C. marked the peak of, and the beginning of the decline of, Persian power.

Legend says that Rome was founded in Italy in 753 B.C. The twelve-month calendar was developed. Five hundred B.C. was the high point of Etruscan political power and civilization, and the rule of Rome. Iron mining and trade created wealth. There were developments in the making of laws.

In the Holy Land, David became the king of Judah and Israel; he was succeeded by Solomon. The Hebrews reached the height of their civilization. There was a water-supply system of tunnels in Jerusalem. In 586 B.C., Jerusalem was destroyed by the Chaldeans.

The Phoenicians invented the alphabet, which was adapted by the Greeks. From this, the Romans later developed the alphabet now used by all western civilizations.

The Turkish people used battlefield surgery, and there were several inventions: the soldering iron, the water level, the lock and key, the carpenter's square, and the turning lathe. *The Fables of Aesop* appeared.

The caste system was developing in India, and the Brahminic religion was expanding. The Indian vina was the origin of all hollow-string instruments. Buddhism was founded 500 B.C. by a religious philosopher, Gautama Buddha. The year 450 B.C. marked the beginning of the Indian Empire, which was expanded by Asoka about 240 B.C. to include most of modern India.

In China, there were developments in the study of mathematics and in the study of astrology. Sundials were in use. During this period of time, 551 B.C.–479 B.C., Confucius was teaching.

Marseilles, founded by the Greeks in France, flourished as western Europe's portal to the Etruscan and Greek trading areas of the western Mediterranean.

In what is now California, there were huts built of wood, reeds, and mud, by the Pinto Indians.

The Mayan Indians in Mexico had an advanced civilization.

CHRONOLOGICAL SUMMARY

GREECE

1100 B.C. There were invasions from the north. The Ionians, who were dispossessed in Greece, established the cities of Miletus and Ephesus on the west coast of Asia Minor. Greek script developed, with only capital letters. Fabric dyes were made from purple snails and stained with alum. This time period marked the earliest use of iron. The Greek epics, the *Iliad* and the *Odyssey*, written at this time, were attributed to Homer.

776 B.C. The first recorded Olympic games (which possibly existed since 1350 B.C.) included: horse racing, boxing, wrestling, pentathlon, and running. There were no women spectators. Poetry, literature, and music were developing throughout the Mediterranean, as well as in India and China. The worship of Apollo, the god of manly youth and beauty, knowledge and the sun, and many other entities, gained support.

750 B.C. There were immigrations to the Black Sea, Sicily, southern Italy, France, and Spain. Foreign trade made the rich richer and the poor poorer.

700 B.C. The Acropolis in Athens was begun. The seven-string lyre was introduced, and the people did ornamental weaving.

700 B.C. Hesiod, the first major poet after Homer, told in his *Works and Days* about the cultivation of barley, wheat, legumes, grapes, olives, and figs, and about the raising of horses, cattle, goats, sheep, and pigs. Solon's Laws in 594 B.C. concerning debtors' bondage; land ownership; a class system for citizens; taxes; and the popular vote, developed in Athens as an attempt to ameliorate the harsh law code of Draco (621 B.C.). Public libraries were in use in Athens. The fables of Aesop were written (620 B.C.–560 B.C.). Greek art developed its own advanced style and form. Architecture developed from the more severe Doric into the graceful Ionic. Alemaeon discovered the difference between veins and arteries. There

Chronological Summary / 55

was a decline in women's position in civil rights. This was the time of the first use of papyrus in Greece.

490 B.C. Darius I of Persia, having crossed the Aegean Sea, was defeated by the Athenians at Marathon.

480 B.C. A large Persian army under the leadership of Xerxes, Darius' son, captured Athens and burned the Acropolis; however, the Greeks defeated the Persian navy at Salamis and then the army in 479 B.C. These two battles are among the most decisive in history. Had the Persians prevailed, the seeds of Western civilization would have been destroyed and a Persian culture would have supplanted the Greek culture, so that Western civilization could not have been formed.

469 B.C. This was the year of the birth of Socrates, the Athenian philosopher.

460 B.C. The temple and statue of Zeus, the mythical god, carved by Phidias, was built at Olympia, and is one of the Seven Wonders of the Ancient World. The soldiers and judges of Athens received regular salaries.

461–431 B.C. This was the Golden Age of Athens, also called the Age of Pericles. The Constitution of Cleisthenes gave citizenship to all free inhabitants of Athens. Pericles was the leader of the people. Athens was the intellectual and artistic center of Greece, where the Parthenon, the supreme example of classical architecture, was built. The great dramatists, poets, comedians, writers, philosophers, historians, scientists, and artists flourished, encouraged by the blossoming of intellectual freedoms. The Acropolis was rebuilt. Many new, famous temples were built. A bust of Pericles was done by Cresilas. Aspasia, the mistress of Pericles, ruled Athenian society. Carrier pigeons were used. The population of Greece was composed of 2,000,000 citizens and 1,000,000 slaves. In Athens, 50,000 people were citizens and 100,000 were slaves. The Spartans used chemicals in warfare: charcoal, sulphur, and pitch. This was the time of the birth of the Harbor of Rhodes.

438 B.C. There was a consecration of the completion of the Parthenon, the Temple of Athena on the Acropolis of Athens. It has been cited as the supreme example of Classical architecture.

431 B.C. Corinth, Megara, and Sparta were envious of Athens; Athens fell to the Spartans in 404 B.C. Socrates wrote and taught during this period when Sparta ruled.

56 / *Chronological Summary*

427 B.C. This date marked the birth of Plato and Herodotus, the historian.
421 B.C. The Peace of Nicias was established between Athens and Sparta for fifty years, after there had been constant wars between them for centuries.
411 B.C. There was a coup d'etat in Athens, and the power was transferred to the Peoples' Assembly.
407 B.C. Plato became a pupil of Socrates.

BABYLON-ASSYRIA

1000–600 B.C. The people developed brass (copper plus zinc).
884–859 B.C. Assurnasirpal II of Assyria rebuilt the city of Calah (Nimrud).
859 B.C. Shalmaneser III was the king of Assyria. Leather scrolls with translations of old Babylonian texts into Aramaic and Greek were a link between clay tablets and Greek papyrus.
800 B.C. Arts and crafts flourished, while carpet weaving began. There were five-tone and seven-tone scales in music; the earliest recorded music was written in cuneiform on a tablet in Sumeria. Assyrian clothes were almost identical for men and women.
722–705 B.C. Sargon II of Assyria conquered the Hittites in the north, the Chaldeans in the east, and the Sumerians in the south. He later conquered Judah and Egypt.
707–705 B.C. The royal palace at Nineveh was rebuilt. The favorite sport in Calah was hunting from chariots (nimrods).
705–681 B.C. Sennacherib built a water aqueduct; Nineveh had bucket wells; and there were water clocks in Assyria.
700 B.C. The Assyrians destroyed Babylon and diverted the Euphrates River to cover the site of the city.
681–669 B.C. King Esarhaddon rebuilt Babylon, and the Tower of Babel was begun.
669–626 B.C. The Assyrian king, Assurbanipal, a conqueror and sports hunter of lions, assembled the great library of Nineveh, which contained more than 22,000 clay tablets that covered history, medicine, astrology, and the planets—including the signs of the zodiac. These tablets also revealed information regarding sales, exchanges, rentals, leases, loan interest rates, and mortgages.
612 B.C. The Chaldean general, Nabopolassar, declared Baby-

Chronological Summary / 57

lon's independence from Assyria. The Medeans, Babylonians, and Scythians destroyed Nineveh and divided the Assyrian Empire.

605–562 B.C. Nebuchadnezzar II built a palace with terrace gardens in Babylon (one of the Seven Wonders of the Ancient World). A tunnel under the Euphrates River connected the palace with the Temple of the Sun.

600 B.C. Cyrus established the first courier (mail) service, using messengers on horseback. The banking business was being practiced in Babylon. The first Persian coin illustrated with a picture of the ruler was made.

586 B.C. During the Babylonian captivity of the Jews, many books of the Old Testament, based on word-of-mouth traditions, were written in Hebrew.

539 B.C. The Persians warred with the Greeks. This time marked the peak of, and the beginning of the decline of, Persian power. The Persians, under Cyrus, captured and destroyed Babylon.

ETRURIA

800 B.C. The Etruscans from Asia Minor moved into Italy and took urban civilization with them.

753 B.C. This date marked the founding of the city of Rome. The Greeks and the Spartans settled in southern Italy and founded Syracuse in Italy. Romulus, the legendary first king of Rome, divided the calendar into ten months; Numa Pompilius, the second king (715 B.C.), added January and February.

600 B.C. The Romans adopted arched ceilings from Etruscan architecture. Olive trees were brought to Italy by the Greeks.

500 B.C. This time marked the high point of Etruscan political power and civilization, and the rule of Rome. Sardinia was captured by the Greeks, Phoenicians, and Carthaginians.

451 B.C. Three Roman senators were sent to Athens to study the laws of Solon. Wooden barrels were used in the wine culture.

450 B.C. The Etruscans had settled most of northern Italy; the Gauls broke their control. Iron mining and trade created wealth. The Assembly of Roman Plebeians was given the right to share in making laws.

449 B.C. The Decemvirs codified Roman laws into a form known as Twelve Tables.

HOLY LAND

1100–930 B.C.   The Phoenicians established colonies in Morocco. During this time, David ascended the throne as King of Judah and Israel, and was succeeded by Solomon. The Hebrews reached the height of their civilization. Professional musicians sang and played in religious ceremonies, much the same as they do today. There was a water-supply system of tunnels in Jerusalem. The Phoenicians settled in Cyprus. The earliest Jewish prophets lived at this time. The prophet Elijah opposed the worship of Baal and had Queen Athalia killed for supporting it.

1100–950 B.C.   Time of the Book of First Samuel.
1000–961 B.C.   Time of the Book of Second Samuel.
961–843 B.C.   Time of the Book of 1 Kings.
925–586 B.C.   Time of the Book of 2 Kings.
1500–587 B.C.   Time of the Books of 1 and 2 Chronicles.
961–200 B.C.   Time of the Book of Job.
1500–100 B.C.   Time of the Book of Psalms.
975–950 B.C.   Time of the Book of Ecclesiastes.
1000–950 B.C.   Time of the Book of Song of Solomon.
900 B.C.   The invention by the Phoenicians of their alphabet, the root of the alphabet now used by all Western civilizations.
800 B.C.   The Syrian language changed from Phoenician to Aramaic.
742–701 B.C.   Time of the Book of Isaiah.
790–697 B.C.   Time of the Book of Hosea.
850–838 B.C.   Time of the Book of Joel.
810–750 B.C.   Time of the Book of Amos.
820–746 B.C.   Time of the Book of Jonah.
749–693 B.C.   Time of the Book of Micah.
700–400 B.C.   Time of the Book of Proverbs.
663–607 B.C.   Time of the Book of Nahum.
625–598 B.C.   Time of the Book of Habakkuk.
639–608 B.C.   Time of the Book of Zephaniah.
626–580 B.C.   Time of the Book of Jeremiah.
589–587 B.C.   Time of the Book of Lamentations.
586 B.C.   Nebuchadnezzar II burned Jerusalem, sending the Hebrews into exile for fifty years.
597–567 B.C.   Time of the Book of Ezekiel.
586–583 B.C.   Time of the Book of Obàdiah.
606–534 B.C.   Time of the Book of Daniel.

539 B.C. Cyrus destroys Babylon, restores the Hebrews to their land, and permits them to rebuild Jerusalem and its Temple.
520–516 B.C. Time of the Book of Haggai.
520–518 B.C. Time of the Book of Zechariah.
536–432 B.C. Time of the Book of Ezra.
536–432 B.C. Time of the Book of Esther.
536–432 B.C. Time of the Book of Nehemiah.
470–397 B.C. Time of the Book of Malachi.

TURKEY

800 B.C. Battlefield surgery was used. Sledges with rollers were used to carry heavy loads.
700 B.C. Glaucus of the Isle of Chios invented the soldering iron. Coins of gold and silver alloys were made in Lydia.
600 B.C. The Temple of Artemis, one of the Seven Wonders of the Ancient World, was built at Ephesus. (The temple was destroyed in 356 B.C. and later rebuilt.) On the island of Somos, a water system built by Eupalinus used a three-quarter-mile long tunnel; construction was started simultaneously at both ends. Theodorus of Somos was credited with the invention of the water level, the lock and key, the carpenter's square, and the turning lathe.

INDIA

1100 B.C. The caste system was developing. Iron and steel were produced in the Indo-Caucasian culture.
800 B.C. Medicine was separated from the priesthood.
700 B.C. The Brahminic religion was expanding. Mohaviro Jina was the first known rebel against the caste system.
600 B.C. The Indian vina, two hollow gourds connected by strings and bamboo reed, was considered the origin of all hollow-string instruments.
563–483 B.C. Buddhism was founded by Siddhartha (Gautama Buddha, called Sakyamuni), a son of a royal and powerful prince, who was born in Nepal.
500 B.C. The Persians were conquered in India, but Afghanistan became part of the Persian Empire. The Indian surgeon, Susruta, performed cataract operations. Dams were being constructed for irrigation purposes.
450 B.C. This time marked the beginning of the Indian Empire. Magadha was the cradle of Buddhism.

CHINA

1100 B.C. Peking came into existence. Chinese script was fully developed. Brush and ink paintings developed (lacquers had been used previously). There was rapid advancement in the study of mathematics, and a mathematics textbook was created.

900 B.C. The people were studying astrology.

775 B.C. September 6, the date of the solar eclipse, was the first authenticated date in Chinese written history.

551–479 B.C. This period of time marked the teachings of Confucius (Kung Fu-Tze), the Chinese philosopher. Sundials were in use in China and Greece.

500 B.C. The Chinese feudal state under the Chou dynasty was declining.

SPAIN

900 B.C. The Celts and Anglo Saxons moved in from the north and settled in the northern areas of Spain.

800 B.C. The Greeks settled on the coast of Spain.

600 B.C. The Greeks established trading posts.

EGYPT

930 B.C. Sheshonk I conquered and pillaged Jerusalem. Carthage was founded by Phoenicians as a trading center with Tyre.

800 B.C. A woman reigned as the high priest in Thebes. Ivory carving was practiced in Egypt, Phoenicia, and Sumeria.

700 B.C. The Assyrians destroyed Memphis and Thebes. Nebuchadnezzar II defeated Egypt. Pharaoh Necho of Egypt started a canal from the Nile to the Red Sea. According to Herodotus, the Greek historian, he also ordered the Phoenicians to circumnavigate Africa from the Red Sea to the Mediterranean; this took three years.

600 B.C. The use of iron spread from Egypt into Spain.

500 B.C. The kingdom of Cush was established in Sudan.

FRANCE

600 B.C. This date marked the founding of Massilia (Marseilles) by the Greeks.

450 B.C. Marseilles flourished as western Europe's portal to the Etruscan and Greek trading areas.

RUSSIA

1000 B.C.   People called Cimmerians were living north of the Black Sea.
700 B.C.   The Russians were invaded from the west by the Scythians, nomadic barbarians, and settled around the north side of the Caspian Sea. (The people probably were originally Iranian.)

GERMANY

1100 B.C.   Gold vessels and jewelry were in use in northern Europe. There was a mass migration of the Germanic people.
800 B.C.   Spokes in wheels and horseshoes were in use in Europe.

BRITON (BRITAIN)

800 B.C.   The Celts invaded again, this time the Gauls in western and northern areas. The Britons used iron and tin; wove woolen cloth; and dyed cloth bright colors.
450–400 B.C.   More Celtic settlements were established in the British Isles.

OTHERS

1100 B.C.   There was evidence of huts built in California, made of wood, reeds, and mud, by the Pinto Indians. The Mayan Indians in Mexico had an advanced civilization.

FIRST SAMUEL

Time   Various estimates, between 1100 B.C. and 950 B.C. Time covered 100 to 120 years.

Author   Samuel, the seer; Nathan, the prophet; and Gad, the prophet-seer.

Theme   The historical account of the transition of the Israel nations from the rule by judges to kings. Hebrew history is different from other histories in that it bares the good and the bad of the rulers as they actually were, regardless of their royal robes.

    The Books of 1 and 2 Samuel were originally one book. The two books basically cover the lives of Samuel, Saul, and David. This book begins the line of writing prophets, ends the judges, and starts the reign of kings. Samuel is also a priest and a kingmaker.

    Samuel, a Zophite, was born in Ramah, about twenty miles northwest of Jerusalem. His father, Elkanah, had two wives, Hannah and Peninnah. Peninnah was arrogant toward Hannah because Hannah was childless, causing Hannah to pray fervently with Eli the priest for a son, whose name should be Samuel. Her prayer was answered, and when Samuel was weaned, she gave him to Eli, the priest at Shiloh, for dedication of his life to God. Eli's sons, Hophni and Phinehas, were sinners and a disgrace to their father and God. Eli was warned of their conduct but could do nothing with them. In the middle of the night, God called to Samuel and told him He was going to destroy the house of Eli and his sinful sons, and Samuel told Eli.

    The Philistines went to battle with Israel and slew 4,000 of its warriors. They followed with another battle, where they slew 30,000 soldiers and killed Eli's sons, Hophni and Phinehas, who were escorting the Ark of the Covenant, and captured the Ark. Eli received this news and dropped dead, followed by Phinehas' wife, who died while giving birth to a son. The presence of the Ark brought a great panic of sickness and a plague of mice to the Philistines, and caused their god Dagon to fall on his face.

    The Ark was moved from Ashdod to Gath to Ekron, causing great suffering and death in each city for a period of seven months. The lords of the Philistines decided to return the Ark, plus five golden emerods and five golden mice, to Israel as a guilt offering. They made a new cart,

First Samuel / 63

attached two milk cows to it, and placed the Ark and the offerings on it, deciding that if the cows headed toward Bethshemesh, it was Israel's God's will that the Ark be returned—which was what happened. The return of the Ark caused the Israelites to lament and turn back to God. Samuel called all the people to Mizpah (located about eight miles north of Jerusalem) and prayed for them. They defeated the Philistines in several cities previously captured.

Samuel became old; he made his sons Joel and Abijah judges; but they were evil, like Eli's sons, and the people demanded a king.

A rich man of Benjamin, named Kish, had a son named Saul, who was tall and handsome. One day Saul's father sent him to find a lost herd of asses. Saul and his companions came near Zuph, where Samuel lived, and they accidentally met Samuel, who, after inviting them to stay with him, anointed Saul to be prince over the Israelites, told him his herd of asses had been found, and gave him instructions as to how he was to be chosen king. Saul's strength was tested by the Ammonites, and he recruited 330,000 warriors to destroy them, which exalted him with all the people of Israel.

Then Samuel called all the people to assemble at Gilgal, to officially make Saul king. Samuel reviewed the history of the Hebrews and warned them to obey the Lord's commandments, or they would be swept away, together with their king.

Saul and his son Jonathan had several encounters with the Philistines. When they were in favor with God, they won. When they sinned, they lost, but they eventually ridded Israel of most of its enemies. Samuel, by instructions from God, sent Saul to destroy the Amalekites, including every man, woman, child, and all their livestock, but Saul kept some of the best of the livestock. This disobedience of God's commands displeased God, who told Samuel that He would instruct him to find a successor king in the family of Jesse. Jesse presented each of six sons, but Samuel said the Lord had not chosen any of them. Samuel asked Jesse if he had other sons, and he said only the one, David, who tended the sheep. They sent for him, and God told Samuel to anoint him as future king of Israel. Saul became depressed and remorseful, so his servants asked David to play the lyre for him, which pleased Saul. He appointed David as his armorbearer.

The well-known story of David and Goliath occurred when the Philistines assembled their armies against the Israelites between Azekah and Shochoh. Goliath, a nine and one-half foot tall Philistine, shouted to the Israelites twice each day for forty days, saying that he would do battle with any one Israelite to the death, and the losers' side would be servants of the other. David heard this, told Saul that he had killed lions and bears that had molested his sheep, and that with the help of the living God of Israel, he could kill Goliath. Saul reluctantly consented. David and Goliath met on the battlefield; David killed him with one rock from his slingshot, cut off his head, and delivered it to Saul. The people acclaimed David as a hero, which made Saul very jealous and angry; he attempted to kill David while he was playing the lyre for him.

Saul's son Jonathan respected and loved David. Saul tried to ensnare David by giving his daughter Michal for his wife. The people loved David, which made Saul hate him and plan his murder. Jonathan tried to convince his father that David was a loyal and innocent man, but Saul tried again to murder him. He sent his servants to murder David in his home, but his wife helped him escape. David went to Samuel, and they hid him at Naioth in Ramah. Jonathan wanted to help David, but Saul became very angry with Jonathan; nevertheless, Jonathan helped David escape again. Ahimelech, the priest of Nob, gave David food and Goliath's sword, but Doeg, the Edomite and chief of Saul's herdsmen, saw him and told Saul. Saul ordered all the priests of Nob murdered, together with all the people of Nob and their livestock.

Abiathar escaped and told David, who had assembled about four hundred dissidents. David and his men fought the Philistines to save Keilah for Saul, but Saul still tried to have David killed. David hid in the wilderness, but Saul pursued him relentlessly. At one time, Saul stopped in a cave in which David was hiding, and David cut off a part of Saul's robe. After Saul left, David stopped him, showed him the piece of garment, and told Saul that he could have killed him if he had wanted to. Saul wept and went home in remorse.

David requested food of Nabal, a rich but evil man, who turned him down and insulted David. David and his men were enroute to kill Nabal and all his people when Nabal's wife, Abigail, met them with much food and drink and begged David's forgiveness. The Lord smote Nabal and he died ten days later. David took Abigail, Nabal's widow, as his wife.

Saul pursued David again in the wilderness of Ziph. During the night, David crept through Saul's warriors and stood at his side while he slept. David took Saul's spear and water jug, and after passing all his sleeping warriors, called from the hilltop to tell Saul that he could have killed him if he had wanted to. Saul said he would seek David's life no more.

David decided to live with the Philistines so Saul would not seek him. King Achish gave him a home in Ziklag to live in, and he lived there one year and four months. David raided other Philistines but said he was raiding Israelites. The Philistines prepared for another war with the Israelites. Achish asked David to fight with them and to be his personal bodyguard. Saul was pleading to God, but received no answer because he had not obeyed God nor kept His commandments. Saul then sought out a woman medium to put him in contact with Samuel, who was dead. Samuel told Saul that he had disobeyed God and would surely die.

Achish's commanders would not let David and his men go with them into battle against the Israelites, so they went back to their home, Ziklag. During their absence, the Amalekites had raided and burned Ziklag and had carried off all the people as slaves. David asked God what he should do. God said that he should pursue and recapture all his people and possessions, which he did. The Philistines battled Saul and his men and killed Saul's sons—Jonathan, Abinadab, and Melchishua. Saul was wounded and asked his armorbearer to kill him with his sword. The armorbearer wouldn't, so Saul fell on his own sword, and the armorbearer did likewise. All of Saul's armies were defeated, and Israel fled in defeat. Saul, an evil king, disobeyed God and died in contempt.

God had warned that the rule by kings was bad. He had love and compassion for the Hebrews, but He knew they would disobey Him and sin against Him time and time again.

SECOND SAMUEL

Time Approximately 1000 B.C.–961 B.C. Time covered, forty years. After Saul's death, David was made King of Judah at age thirty. Seven years later, he was made King of all Israel, which he ruled for thirty-three years, making him king for forty years. He died at the age of seventy.

Author Nathan, the prophet, and Gad, the prophet-seer. There were probably other unknown contributors.

Theme The historical recording of the life and rule of King David. David was many men in one—a shepherd, musician, soldier, true friend, hunted outcast, general, king, loving father, poet, and sinner. Above all, he loved God, and God called him a man after His own heart, yet he sinned against God.

David was in Ziklag after the death of Saul when an Amalekite came and told David that he had killed the wounded Saul at his own command. David had the man killed and grieved greatly for the death of Saul and Jonathan, his true friend. God instructed David to go to Hebron, where he was anointed King of Judah at the age of thirty. Abner, son of Ner, who was commander of Saul's armies, made Ishbosheth, the son of Saul, king of all Israel, except Judah, at the age of forty.

The story is told of the event at the pool of Gibeon, where twelve of Abner's men and twelve of David's men met and killed each other. Abner was criticized by Ishbosheth for taking Saul's concubine, Rizpah, which angered Abner. He went to David to turn over all Israel to him, and returned David's wife, Michal. Unbeknownst to David, his commander, Joab, killed Abner, because Abner had killed his brother Asahel. David mourned Abner's death. Two brothers, Rechab and Baanah, killed Ishbosheth, cut off his head, and delivered it to David, who in turn had them killed.

Then all the elders of Israel came to David at Hebron, and they anointed him king over all Israel at thirty-seven years of age. He ruled all Israel for thirty-three years, until he died at the age of seventy.

David became greater and greater because he loved and obeyed God, and God was with him. He conquered Jerusalem and arranged with Hiram, King of Tyre, to furnish cedars, carpenters, and masons to build him a great house. David had six wives and six sons. He now took more wives at Jerusalem and had more sons, among whom was Solomon.

The Philistines battled two times with David, but David, guided by God, defeated them and enlarged his territory. David then brought the Ark of the Covenant from the house of Abinadab to Jerusalem, the city of David, and placed it in a tent. David's wife, Michal, criticized him for dancing in the streets in celebration of the arrival of the Ark, and she became barren for life. David talked to Nathan, the prophet, saying ". . . I dwell in a house of cedar, but the ark of God dwells within tent curtains" (2 Samuel 7:2). David wanted to build a great house for the Ark, but Nathan received word from God that he should not do so. David was a very righteous man and praised God and did as he was told by God.

David was successful in all encounters with enemies on all sides. He enlarged his kingdom in all directions, until he was probably the greatest power in the world at that time.

David inquired of Ziba, a former servant of Saul, if there were any relatives of Saul that he might befriend. Ziba told him there was one son of Jonathan, named Mephibosheth, who was crippled in both feet. David restored all of Saul's properties to Mephibosheth, and said that Ziba and his family and servants should serve him. Mephibosheth was to eat at the king's table as one of the family.

The Ammonites hired the Syrians to help them gain their freedom from the Israelites, but David's armies prevailed in all encounters and slew thousands of them, so Hadarezer, king of the Ammonites, became subject to Israel.

At one time in the spring, David sent his armies out to do battle while he remained in Jerusalem. Late one afternoon while walking on his roof, he saw a beautiful woman bathing. He was covetous of her and found that she was Bathsheba, wife of Uriah, one of his best and most loyal warriors. David sent for her and lay with her. Later she sent word to him that she was pregnant. David made plans to have Uriah killed in battle, and he then took Bathsheba as his wife. This was a grievous sin for David and displeased God. David confessed his sin to Nathan; Nathan said that God would not take his life but that "the sword shall never depart from your house . . . ," and because he had sinned secretly, the Lord "will raise evil against you from your own household . . . ," and ". . . the child also that is born to you shall surely die" (2 Samuel 12:10, 11, 14). This was the turning point in David's life. He loved God, but he used his power to sin and disobeyed God's commands. Then Bathsheba bore David another son, Solomon.

David's son Absalom had a sister named Tamar. Amnon, another of David's sons, probably by another wife, loved Tamar, or at least coveted her, and by pretending that he was ill, had her attend him at his bedside and raped her. Then his love turned to hatred. Two years later, Absalom planned Amnon's death, and Absalom fled to Geshur. David grieved for his son Absalom, and Joab, with the aid of a very wise woman, persuaded the king to repent and to permit Absalom to return. But he was not permitted to live in David's house, or to see him. After two years, Absalom persuaded Joab to let him see David, who then granted him royal privileges of servants and horses and a chariot.

Absalom then sat at the gate and talked to all the dissidents who came with grievances and could not see the king. By this device, he gained the allegiance of people all over Israel. At the end of four years, he went to Hebron, conspired against his father, and had himself declared king. David, who had sinned and did not know if God would help him or not, fled Jerusalem, but left behind ten concubines and the Ark of the Covenant. Ahithophel, one of the king's counselors, had joined Absalom, so David left Hushai, another loyal counselor, to keep David advised. David and his entourage fled east of the Jordan. Ahithophel advised Absalom to attack and kill David alone, but Hushai advised him to gather greater forces of men and then attack. Ahithophel committed suicide.

The armies of Absalom and David met, and Absalom's troops were defeated, with 20,000 dead. As Absalom was fleeing, he caught his head in a tree, and his mule kept running. When Joab saw him, he had Absalom killed and buried. When all the warriors returned victorious, they found David grieving for Absalom, which made them feel guilty instead of joyous in their victory. Joab told David that all of his people would desert him if he did not change his attitude, which he did.

All of Israel and Judah sent messages for David to return, and all his former loyal friends came to meet him and escort him back. The people of Israel and Judah argued over their loyalties, and a man named Sheba convinced the ten tribes of Israel not to be loyal to David. After David returned to Jerusalem, Joab pursued Sheba to the city of Abel of Bethmaachah, where a very wise woman told Joab that men should settle their affairs peacefully. She threw Sheba's head to Joab, and Joab ceased his attack and returned to Jerusalem.

There was a three-year famine, and David asked God why. God said it was because Saul had put many of the Gibeonites to death after agreeing not to do so. David asked the Gibeonites what he should do to make retribution, and they answered that he should take the lives of the seven sons of Saul, whom David delivered to them. But he spared Mephibosheth, son of Jonathan.

The Philistines warred with Israel four more times. The relatives of Goliath tried to avenge his death by trying to kill David, and David's men insisted that he must not go with the warriors again. David wrote the song of chapters 22 and 23.

David sinned again by ordering Joab to take a census of all Israel and Judah, which numbered 800,000 warriors in Israel, plus 500,000 in

Judah, making a total of probably 6 to 8 million people. God, speaking through Gad, David's seer, gave him three choices as a penalty for his sins: three years of famine; three months of fleeing in defeat from his foes; or three days of pestilence. David chose three days of pestilence, and 70,000 people died, from Dan to Beer-Sheba.

David purchased from Araunah his threshing floor, on which to build an altar and offer a sacrifice. God heeded his supplication and stopped the plague. This is the same spot on which the Temple was later built and on which the Mosque of Omar, which is owned by the Moslems, stands today.

David was truly a man after God's own heart. But he was human and sinned and wholeheartedly repented, knowing that he had to have God's forgiveness. David was a great leader, totally devoid of vindictiveness and kind to Saul and his kin, in spite of Saul's attempts to kill him. He wrote many of the Psalms of the Bible. The promise of an eternal King to arise from David's family was repeated over and over again to David and Solomon, in the Psalms, and by the prophets Amos, Isaiah, Micah, Jeremiah, Zechariah, over a period of 500 years. Mary, Christ's mother, was of the family of David. These things will all be revealed in later books.

FIRST KINGS

Time Approximately 120 years from the death of David— 961 B.C. to 843 B.C.

Author Tradition says Jeremiah. The writer had access to data, the court, temples, and literary records. Official scribes are mentioned in the books of Samuel and Kings. Probably written during the Babylonian exile, 400 years later.

Theme First Kings and the following book, 2 Kings, were one book originally. They tell the historical story of the Kings of the Hebrews, from the death of David in about 961 B.C. until the Judean Hebrews were captured by the Babylonians in 586 B.C. In order to enable the reader to know which kings are rulers of Judah and Israel the letters (J) and (I) follow the names of all rulers. This will be done throughout the books of 1 and 2 Kings and 1 and 2 Chronicles. All of the nineteen kings of Israel were bad. Eight of the twenty kings of Judah were bad.

This book tells of the division of Israel into the two tribes of Judah and the ten tribes of Israel after Solomon's death. It gives the lines of the rulers of both kingdoms, as well as the stories about the prophets Elijah and Elisha, who emphasized obedience to God at a time when there appeared to be nothing but idolatry, immorality and bloodshed.

When David was old, his son Adonijah, by his wife Haggith, unbeknown to David, professed to assume to be king. But another wife, Bathsheba, reminded David that he had promised her that he would make her son, Solomon, king. David instructed Zadok the priest, Nathan the prophet, and Benaiah to take Solomon to Gihon, anoint him king, put him on the throne, and announce to all Israel that he was king, which they did. Just before David died, he instructed Solomon to respect God and to keep His commandments. Solomon stabilized his command by having Adonijah, Joab, and Shimei killed.

Solomon married the daughter of Pharaoh, king of Egypt. When he went to Gibeon to sacrifice, God said to him in a dream, "Ask what you wish me to give you" (1 Kings 3:5). Solomon's famous prayer was "So give Thy servant an understanding heart to judge Thy people to discern between good and evil . . ." (1 Kings 3:9). God answered that He would make him the wisest man in the world, and in addition, would give him great riches and honor.

Two harlots who lived together had sons at the same time. One child died, and both claimed the living child. They asked Solomon to decide. The king said, "Get me a sword . . . . Divide the living child in two, and give half to the one and half to the other" (1 Kings 3:24, 25). But when the rightful mother pleaded to give the living child to the other woman, Solomon gave it to the rightful one. His wisdom spread throughout Israel.

Solomon organized his kingdom with high officials, to provide for his economic support and supply. He established ocean shipping lines from Asia to Africa, controlled all the caravan trade between Asia and Egypt, established copper mining, chariot construction and sale, built cities, levied heavy taxes, wrote 3000 proverbs, 1005 songs, was an authority on botany and zoology, and was considered the wisest man in the world. Peace prevailed on all sides.

Solomon made a treaty with Hiram, King of Tyre, to furnish cedar and cypress and craftsmen to build the Temple to the Lord. Solomon furnished 30,000 laborers, 70,000 burden bearers and 80,000 stone cutters. All cutting was done offsite, so that in the seven years of the building of the Temple, ". . . neither hammer nor axe nor any iron tool [was] heard in the house while it was being built" (1 Kings 6:7). He then spent thirteen years building his own house, and he had stables for 40,000 horses. His wife, Pharaoh's daughter, lived in his house. When the Temple was finished, Solomon assembled the Elders of Israel and the tribal heads and had the Ark brought from Zion and placed in the Temple. He offered praise to God for all His blessings and received God's promise of more blessings if the people kept His commandments, but He warned them that if they forsook the Lord, they would be cast from His sight.

Solomon became very rich with gold, ivory, and precious stones and was known for his wisdom. The Queen of Sheba did not believe this, but after visiting him, she said, "Nevertheless I did not believe the reports, until I came and my eyes had seen it. And behold, the half was not told me" (1 Kings 10:7).

Against God's instructions, Solomon married many foreigners and had 700 wives and 300 concubines, and his wives turned his heart to their other gods. This angered the Lord, who told Solomon that at Solomon's death, He would take all of his kingdom except Judah, for the sake of David, the Lord's faithful servant.

Solomon's adversaries, Hadad, the Edomite; Rezon, ruler of Syria; and Jeroboam, who had charge of all of Solomon's forced labor, plotted against him. Jeroboam (I), advised by Ahijah, the prophet, seized all Israel except Judah. After Solomon's death, Rehoboam (J), Solomon's son, asked the old men how he should rule, and they said he should be kind to the people. He asked the younger men, his friends, and they said to make the burden of taxes higher, and this is what he did. He sent

Adoram, his head taskmaster, and the Israelites stoned him to death. Rehoboam (J) gathered 180,000 warriors to fight with his own people, the Israelites. God told him not to fight, but to stay and rule Judah alone.

Jeroboam (I) set up golden calves at Bethel and Dan for the people to worship, so they would not have to go to Jerusalem, and this displeased God. Jeroboam (I) built Shechem and lived there. Jeroboam's (I) son became ill, and he sent his wife, disguised, to ask the prophet Ahijah what to do. The prophet recognized her and said her son would die. He said that eventually all the men with Jeroboam (I) would die, because they had not kept God's commandments. Jeroboam (I) ruled twenty-two years, and his son Nadab (I) became king. The balance of this Book of Kings is a brief history of nineteen kings, including nine dynasties of Israel and twenty kings, including one dynasty of Judah. The kings of Israel were all bad, and about half of the kings of Judah were as bad. Some were good, but this part of Hebrew history is very degenerate.

Rehoboam (J), king of Judah, was vile and sinful. Shishak, king of Egypt, raided all the treasures of his Temple. Rehoboam (J) died after seventeen years. Abijam (J) became king and ruled for three years and died. Asa (J), his son, became king. Asa (J), who ruled forty-one years, was a good king and found favor in God's sight. His son, Jehoshaphat (J) became king and ruled for twenty-five years. After a reign of two years, Nadab (I), Jeroboam's son, was murdered by Baasha (I), who became king and murdered all the house of Jeroboam (I). Baasha (I) was a bad king and ruled for twenty-four years. Baasha's (I) son Elah (I) became king and reigned for two years. While he was drunk, his commander, Zimri, killed him. Zimri (I) ruled for seven days, and during that time, he murdered all the house of Baasha (I). Omri (I), the commander of the army, became king after half of Israel had tried to follow Tibni, who failed and died. Omri (I) succeeded him and sinned more than his predecessors. He ruled for twelve years and was followed by his son Ahab (I).

Ahab (I) married Jezebel, daughter of Ethbaal, king of the Zidonians, and worshipped Baal with her. He did more to anger God than any other previous king. Jezebel was an unscrupulous, devilish woman, who brought many prophets of Baal from Zidon and ordered Jehovah's prophets killed. She later died as she lived—she was eaten by the dogs in the street. Six chapters are devoted to Ahab (I), to tell the story of Elijah, the prophet, who tried to turn the people back to God.

Elijah told Ahab (I) that there would be no rainfall again, except by his word. He then hid and was fed by the ravens until the brook of Cherith dried up, after which he went, by God's instruction, to Zarephath, where he blessed a widow with a continuous supply of meal in a jar and oil in a cruse. Her son died, and Elijah asked God to restore his life, which He did.

After three years, the Lord told Elijah to go to Ahab (I), and he would meet Obadiah, who revered God and who had hidden one hundred prophets to keep Jezebel from having them killed. Obadiah arranged for Ahab (I) to meet Elijah, who told him to bring his prophets and all the people of Israel to Mount Carmel. Elijah challenged the prophets of Baal to ask their god to put fire to the sacrifice, and he in turn would ask his God. The prophets of Baal failed, but Elijah's Lord not only set fire to the sacrifice, but burned it, the altar, the rocks, and the water completely. The people were amazed and seized all the prophets of Baal and killed them. God caused a great rain, and Ahab (I) told Jezebel. She threatened to kill Elijah, and he escaped and hid. God sent him to Mount Horeb to hide.

God instructed Elijah in "a still small voice" to go to Damascus and anoint Hazael as king of Syria; Jehu as king of Israel; and Elisha to be a prophet to succeed Elijah. They were to slay many sinners. Ahab (I) fought the Syrians and killed 127,000 of them, but saved King Benhadad.

Ahab (I) wanted Naboth's vineyard, which was close to the palace, but Naboth would not sell. Jezebel caused Naboth to be killed. Ahab (I) went into the vineyard, where he was met by Elijah, who told him he had sinned against God and would die and the dogs would eat his flesh. Ahab (I) deeply repented, and the Lord said he would spare him but bring evil upon his sons' houses.

Jehoshaphat (J), king of Judah, asked Ahab (I), king of Israel, to help him take back Ramoth, in Gilead, from Syria. Ahab's (I) prophets said to go to war, but Micaiah, God's prophet, said Ahab (I) would be killed, which turned out to be true. Ahaziah (I), his son, became king of Israel and ruled for two years. He was a bad king and provoked the anger of the Lord. Jehoshaphat (J) was a good king like his father Asa (J) and ruled twenty-five years. Jehoram, his son, became king of Judah and ruled for eight years, but he was a bad king also.

Rehoboam's decision split Israel into the two nations of Judah and Israel, each with separate kings. All the kings of Israel served the golden calf; the worst ones served Baal. Most of the kings of Judah served idols; a few served Jehovah. Some bad kings were partially good and some good kings were partially bad. One wonders sometimes how God had the patience to tolerate the Hebrews and to continue to love them, but this same history of mankind has been repeated over and over, to this very day.

SECOND KINGS

Time   961 B.C. to 586 B.C. 1 and 2 Kings cover from the time of the last days of David to the King of Babylon's release of Jehoiachin.
Author   Some sources suggest Jeremiah, but the author is actually unknown. Whoever authored these two books had access to many written records, but he was not just a compiler; he had a religious aim attuned to his own time.
Theme   Both books of Kings are written with lessons to be learned from history. Did the kings, priests, prophets, and people keep the covenant of God at Sinai? Each king was more or less compared to David, who "Did that which was right in the sight of the Lord" (*see* Deuteronomy 12:25), and Jeroboam, ". . . which made Israel to sin" (2 Kings 10:31 KJV).

This book is a continuation of 1 Kings and covers the last 130 years of Israel, the northern part of the Hebrew kingdom, captured by Assyria; and the last 250 years of Judah, the southern part, captured by Babylon. The stories of the kings of Judah and Israel are interspersed with the stories of the prophets Elijah and Elisha, and are difficult to follow at times. The reader should bear in mind that Judah is the kingdom of the tribes of Benjamin and Judah, and Israel is the ten tribes to the north, on both sides of Jordan.

Ahaziah fell through the lattice in his upper chamber and was sick in bed. He sent his messengers to Baalzebub, god of Ekron, to inquire if he would recover, but Elijah intercepted them with the answer no. The king sent three different groups of men to bring Elijah to him, but Elijah said, "If I am a man of God, let fire come down from heaven and consume you . . ." (2 Kings 1:10). Two groups were destroyed. The third group pleaded with Elijah, so he came down and told the king he would die, and he did. He ruled two years. Jehoram (I) became king of Israel. (His name was the same as the king of Judah, and both ruled at the same time.)

Elijah took Elisha with him to Bethel, Jericho, and to the Jordan, where Elijah struck the waters with his mantle (or cloak) and they parted. Elijah and Elisha crossed on dry ground. Elijah told Elisha he was going to be taken to heaven. Elisha, as his successor, asked for a "double portion of your spirit" (*see* 2 Kings 2:9). Elijah advised him he would receive this if he saw him being taken to heaven by a chariot and horses of fire, which he did.

Jehoram (I), son of Ahab (I), succeeded Ahaziah (I) as king of Israel for twelve years. For the most part, he was a bad king. Mesha, king of Moab and a sheep breeder, had been paying King Ahab (I) 100,000 lambs and the wool of 100,000 rams, but he now refused to pay Jehoram (I). Jehoram (I) enlisted the aid of all Israel and Jehoshaphat (J), king of Judah, and the king of Edom, to subdue Moab. After marching for seven days, they could find no water. They sent for Elisha, who said he would not beseech the favor of the Lord for them, except for his regard for King Jehoshaphat (J). Elisha said "thus says the Lord" and caused the stream bed to be filled with water. They conquered the Moabites and were destroying the countryside when King Mesha gave his eldest son, successor to his throne, as a burnt offering, and Israel withdrew.

Elisha performed several miracles in the name of God. An impoverished widow had only a jar of oil, and he caused it to fill several vessels for her to sell, pay her debts, and yet have enough to live on. In Shunam, a wealthy old woman befriended him, and he decreed that she would have a son. A year later she did, but a few years later, the son died. Elisha came from the Mount of Carmel and, in the name of God, restored the boy to life. During a famine, the sons of the prophets were fixing a meal of wild gourds, which would have killed them. Elisha tossed a handful of meal in it, and there was no harm.

A man of Baalshalisha brought some first fruits for food, but there was not enough for a hundred men. Elisha said to feed the men, and they all ate and still had some left.

Naaman, the commander of the army of the king of Syria, was a leper. An Israelite slave, handmaiden to his wife, told her that a man of God in Samaria could cure him. Naaman told his king, and the king sent him with presents to the king of Israel. The king of Israel didn't know what to do, for he thought it was a trick to provoke a quarrel. Elisha heard of the incident and told Naaman to go and wash himself seven times in the Jordan, and he would be cured. He returned to thank Elisha and to pay him, but Elisha would take no pay. His servant, Gehazi, thought he would profit from the favor and took pay from Naaman; Elisha transferred Naaman's leprosy to Gehazi and his descendents forever.

Elisha caused an axhead that had fallen into the Jordan to float. The king of Syria would try to plan war with Israel; Elisha would advise the king of Israel where he was going to attack, and he would avoid the place. The Syrian king discovered that Elisha was the cause of his failures, so he plotted to kill Elisha by sending a great army of men, chariots, and horses to surround the city where Elisha lived. At Elisha's prayer, God showed the Syrian king that the mountain was covered with horses and chariots of fire, and the Syrian army was struck blind, enabling

Elisha to lead them to Samaria, where the king, at Elisha's bidding, could have killed all of them. Instead, he fed them a great feast and sent them home.

Later, Benhadad, king of Syria, besieged Samaria until the people were so impoverished that they ate their own children. The king was going to kill Elisha, but Elisha prophesied that the next day ". . . a measure of fine flour shall be sold for a shekel . . ." (2 Kings 7:1). At twilight the Syrian army was caused by God to hear the sounds of a great army, and it fled, leaving all its food and treasures, so that Elisha's prophecy was fulfilled. The widow whose son was restored to life testified before the king that Elisha's God had done this.

Elisha visited Damascus while King Benhadad was sick and prophesied to Hazael that the king would live, but that Hazael would succeed him and make terrible wars against Israel.

At the age of thirty-two, Jehoram (J) succeeded Jehoshaphat (J) as king of Judah and reigned for eight years. He was bad, but God would not destroy Judah yet, because of David. Jehoram's (J) son Ahaziah (J) succeeded him at the age of twenty-two, and he ruled for one year, as badly as his father. He went to Joram (I), king of Israel, to join forces against the Syrians at Ramoth-gilead, where Joram (I) became wounded. Elisha sent a messenger to anoint Jehu to become king of Israel. Joram (I) ruled twelve years.

Jehu (I) went to Jezreel and killed Joram and Ahaziah (J), kings of Judah. Jehu then went to Jezreel to have Jezebel, the worshipper of Baal and widow of Ahab (I), put to death. Her eunuchs threw her out of the window and the dogs ate her flesh before they could bury her, as Elijah had foretold. Jehu (I) then plotted by devious ways to have all of Ahab's sons and their families killed. He also had all the prophets, priests, and worshippers of Baal assembled and killed, and converted the house of Baal into a public latrine. Thus he wiped out Baalism in Israel. But he did many other things which were sin against God. He also lost much territory to Syria during his reign of twenty-eight years. He died and was succeeded by his son Jehoahaz (I).

Athaliah (J), the mother of Ahaziah (J), declared herself king and had all members of the royal family murdered. Jehosheba, Ahaziah's sister, hid his one-year-old son, Joash, and had him raised in hiding. Six years later, she connived with the priest Jehoiada, to have Joash made king at the age of seven. Athaliah (J) was killed, the house of Baal was torn down, and the Baal priest was killed. Jehoiada the priest made a covenant between the Lord, the people, and the king that they would be the Lord's people. Then the people tore down the temple of Baal and the altars.

Jehoash (J) (Joash) was seven years old when he began to reign; having the benefit of instruction from Jehoiada the priest, he did what was right in the eyes of the Lord and was mostly good. He maintained the house of the Lord but gave all the gold and treasures of the house of the Lord to Hazael, king of Syria, to save Jerusalem. He had ruled for forty years when two of his servants killed him, and his son Amaziah (J) became king.

Jehoahaz (I), king of Israel, reigned for seventeen years, as badly as his predecessors. He was harassed constantly by Hazael, king of Syria, and his son, Benhadad, but the Lord spared the Israelites from being captive, even though they had few warriors and lived constantly in sin. Joash (I) (same name as the king of Judah) succeeded his father, Jehoahaz (I). He reigned for sixteen years, sinned like his forefathers, fought with Judah, his brethren, and died a bad king. Elisha, the prophet, died during his reign. A man was being buried when the mourners sighted a marauding band of Moabites coming, so they threw him into Elisha's grave. As soon as the body touched Elisha's bones, the man revived and stood up.

Hazael, king of Syria, died. His son, Benhadad, tried to continue the oppression of Israel, but under Joash's (I) leadership, Israel recaptured many cities previously lost.

Amaziah (J), son of Joash of Judah, became king of Judah and ruled for twenty-nine years. He was a fairly good king but was not very smart. He did what was right in the eyes of the Lord in some respects, but permitted the people to burn incense and to sacrifice in high places. He killed all the servants who had killed his father, was successful in a war against the Edomites, and challenged Johoash (I), king of Israel, to war. He was defeated; Jerusalem was sacked of its treasures, and the wall was destroyed from the Ephraim gate to the corner gate. Amaziah (J) fled to Lachish, but his own people slew him and made his son Azariah (J), (Uzziah) sixteen, king of Judah for fifty-two years.

Jeroboam II (I), son of Joash (I), became king of Israel and ruled for forty-one years. He was bad, like all the successors of Jeroboam I (I), and caused Israel to sin. Even so, the Lord permitted him to recapture much territory, in spite of the fact that most of Israel's warriors had already been killed. He was succeeded by Zachariah (I), his son.

Azariah (J), king of Judah, was a good king and did much that was good in the eyes of the Lord, but he did not abolish the sacrifices and burning of incense in high places. The Lord smote him with leprosy, and his son Jotham (J) ruled for him to his death and then was made king. Jotham (J) ruled for sixteen years.

Zachariah (I), king of Israel, was a bad king and was killed by his successor, Shallum, after ruling for only six months. Shallum (I) ruled for one month and was killed by Menahem, who became king. Menahem (I) sacked Tiphsah and its territory and ripped up all the women who were with child. He exacted fifty shekels (224.5 grains) of silver from every rich man in Israel and paid a thousand talents ($1,940,000) of silver to

Pul, king of Assyria, to gain freedom from assault. He ruled for ten years, died, and was succeeded by his son, Pekahiah (I).

Pekahiah (I) did what was evil in the sight of the Lord, just as all other rulers of Israel had done, and after two years, his captain and fifty other officers conspired and killed him. The captain's son, Pekah (I), was made king of Israel, and he ruled for twenty years. The king of Assyria captured much of his territory. Hoshea conspired against Pekah (I), killed him, and ruled Israel in his stead for nine years. Israel collapsed.

Jotham (J), king of Judah at the age of twenty-five, ruled for sixteen years and was a good king. He was harassed by Israel and Syria and never abolished the sins of sacrifices and burning of incense on the high places. He was succeeded by his son, Ahaz (J), age twenty years, who ruled for sixteen years.

Ahaz (J), king of Judah, conspired with Tiglath-pileser, king of Assyria, to help him defend himself from Syria and Israel. They killed Rezin, king of Syria, and took Damascus. Ahaz (J) was intrigued by the Assyrians' altar at Damascus and had one made like it, to replace the bronze altar in the house of the Lord. Ahaz (J) was a wicked king who sinned against God, died, and was succeeded by his son Hezekiah (J), twenty-five, who ruled Judah for twenty-nine years.

This was an epochal period in the history of the Hebrew people. This was the end of Israel, the northern ten tribes. Under Pekah (I), Assyria captured all of northern and eastern Israel and carried away the inhabitants to Assyria. This was the Galilee captivity. Hoshea (I), the Samarian king, had paid tribute annually to Assyria, but he also made an alliance with Egypt. This angered the Assyrians, who captured Samaria, the last part of Israel, exported the people to Assyria, and replaced them with people from other conquered lands. The northern territory lasted about 200 years. The prophets Hosea, Isaiah, and Micah had preached in vain. Jeroboam (I) and all his nineteen successor kings sinned and worshipped idols in spite of God's warnings. Hoshea's (I) reign ended in 721 B.C., and Judah was to fall in 586 B.C., ending the Hebrew nation. The Lord had warned Israel through many prophets and seers, "turn from your evil ways and keep my commandments and my statutes," but they would not listen. Therefore, the Lord was very angry with them and removed them from His sight.

Hezekiah (J), king of Judah, was one of the best, God-fearing kings of Judah.

In the fourteenth year of King Hezekiah, the Assyrian king Sennacherib took all the fortified cities of Judah, and King Hezekiah (J) paid much silver and all the gold in the Temple. The Assyrians again besieged Jerusalem and declared that the Hebrews were doomed ". . . to eat their own dung and drink their own urine . . ." (2 Kings 18:27). Hezekiah (J) consulted Isaiah, who said that God would cause them to retreat, which they did. They returned again, however, and Hezekiah (J) prayed fervently to God. Isaiah the prophet said that God said He would defend the city for His own sake and for the sake of His good servant, David.

That night the angel of the Lord went forth and slew the 185,000 soldiers in the Assyrian army, and in the morning there was an army of dead bodies. Sennacherib fled back to his home, Nineveh, where his two sons killed him. Hezekiah (J) became ill and prayed to God, who healed him and, through Isaiah, said God would let him live another fifteen years.

After Hezekiah's (J) death, his son Manasseh (J) became king, at twelve years of age, and ruled for fifty-five years. He was one of the worst kings of Judah. He did everything he could think of that was abominable to God. He rebuilt the high places where incense was burned, erected altars to Baal, made an Asherah (a wooden, false god image), built altars other than those in the Temple, burned his son as an offering, dealt with mediums and wizards, shed much innocent blood, and did everything evil—even more so than the Israelites and Moabites. This angered God, and He said He would wipe the Judeans out of their homeland. Manasseh (J) died and his son, Amon (J), became king at twenty-two, ruled for only two years, and was worse than his father. Amon's (J) servants killed him and named Josiah (J), his son, king at the age of eight. He reigned for thirty-one years. When he was twenty-six years of age, he ordered the Temple repaired and maintained.

In the repair work, the men discovered the book of the law of God. The high priest sent it to Josiah (J), who had it read to him, and he was greatly grieved because the people had disobeyed God's laws. He read the law to everyone and caused the people to obey the law. He destroyed all the idols and false temples, deposed all the priests of Baal, and reinstituted the Passover. He did everything possible to abolish the sins against God and live up to His laws. He pleased God, who promised him He would not destroy Judah in Josiah's (J) presence. Josiah (J) was killed by Neco, king of Egypt, when Josiah (J) went peaceably to meet him, and his son Jehoahaz (J) was made king at the age of twenty-three. He ruled for only three months; Neco had him imprisoned in Egypt and appointed Jehoiakim (J), another son of Josiah (J), as king. The Judeans were taxed very heavily to pay tribute to Neco. Jehoiakim (J) was twenty-five when he was made king. He was wicked and ruled for eleven years.

According to God's will to wipe the Hebrew nation out of existence because of their sins against God, Nebuchadnezzar took Judah away from the Egyptians in the closing days of Judah. The Lord would not pardon the sins of Manasseh (J), especially all the innocent blood he had shed. Jehoiakim (J) died and Jehoiachin (J), his son, reigned at the age of eighteen for three months. At that time Nebuchadnezzar, king of Babylon, came to Jerusalem and besieged it. Jehoiachin (J), king of Judah, gave himself up to the king of Babylon, together with all his relatives, servants, and officials. The king of Babylon took all the treasures of the Temple, all the princes, 10,000 captives, 1,000 craftsmen and smiths, and then made Jehoiachin's (J) uncle, Zedekiah (J), king of what was left of Judah.

Zedekiah (J) was twenty-one and ruled for eleven years, until the end of Judah. Zedekiah (J) tried to rebel against Nebuchadnezzar, but he was overpowered, and his sons were killed in front of him. The Babylonians put out his eyes and took him to Babylon. About ten years later, the king of Babylon sent his men to burn the Temple and all the buildings in Jerusalem. They broke down the walls and took all but a few of the poorest citizens to Babylon as captives. What few priests and officials were left, were killed. A few remaining escaped to Egypt. Thus ended the Hebrew nation of the ten tribes of Israel and the two tribes of Judah, who were God's chosen people, but most of whom preferred to sin against God rather than to obey His commandments, until they angered Him to the point where He decided to remove them from His sight. They were cast into exile in Babylon for seventy years.

FIRST CHRONICLES

Time — Covers recapitulation of the first twelve books of the Bible, from the beginning of time to the Assyrian captivity of Israel and the Babylonian captivity of Judah, 587 B.C.

Author — Tradition alone indicates that the prophet-priest Ezra chronicled the books of 1 and 2 Chronicles, Ezra, Nehemiah, Esther—which at one time were one book—from many other records previously written, about 350 B.C.–250 B.C.

Theme — Special emphasis is on the history of David and his family lineage. The history, confined mostly to Judah, the southern part of the kingdom, covers the same time as 2 Samuel. The author is concerned with the ritual, music, and hierarchy of the Levites in the Temple.

The first nine chapters record the names of the Jewish families, from Adam to their return from captivity. Saul, king of Israel, and his three sons were killed by the Philistines, and David was made king at Hebron. He captured Jerusalem from the Jebusites, who had resisted the Hebrews for 400 years since Joshua, and made it the City of David, the capital of all Judah and Israel. Warriors of all the tribes, numbering 337,982, came to join David, and he counselled with them. The people of all the tribes decided to bring the Ark of the Covenant to Jerusalem. While enroute, one of the oxen drawing the cart carrying the Ark stumbled. Uzza put out his hand to hold the Ark, and God smote him dead, because he was not a Levite and was not supposed to touch it. The Ark was left with the house of Obededom.

Hiram, king of Tyre, built a house for David in Jerusalem, and David took more wives. David prepared a place and pitched a tent for the Ark. He then gathered 862 Levites to be the priests to care for the Ark and the Temple. He told them to properly sanctify themselves and to bring the Ark to the tent in Jerusalem. David also organized the priests to be in charge of all music, including the singers and players of the cymbals, harps, lyre, and trumpets. They brought the Ark to Jerusalem with a great celebration, and services of thanksgiving and burnt offerings were given to praise God.

David felt that because he lived in a house of cedar, it was not right that God should dwell in a tent. He conferred with Nathan the prophet, who told him to go ahead and build a temple. That night, God spoke to Nathan and told him to tell David not to build a house for the Lord, and in the following words foretold the birth of Christ and His Church: ". . . when your days are fulfilled to go to be with your fathers, I will raise up your offspring after you, one of your own sons [Christ], and I will establish His kingdom. He shall build a house [church] for me, and I will establish His throne forever. I will be His father, and He shall be my son; I will not take my steadfast love from Him, as I took it from him [Saul] who was before you, but I will confirm Him [Christ] in My house and in My kingdom forever and His throne shall be established forever" (*see* 1 Chronicles 17:11–14).

After receiving God's blessing, David expanded the territory of Israel by conquering the lands of Syria, Zobah, Edom, Moab, Ammon, Philistia, Amalek and Hamath—from the Euphrates River on the north, the desert on the east, the Gulf of Aqoba of the Red Sea on the south, and the Great Sea on the west, except a small strip of Philistia and Phoenicia. He killed thousands of warriors, destroyed thousands of horses and chariots, and took much gold, silver, and precious stones, which he dedicated to the Lord. These were later used in the ornamentation of the Temple.

David's ego caused him to order a census of all Israel, against the advice of his commanders and to God's displeasure. There were 1,100,000 warriors in Israel. In Judah there were 470,000, not counting the Levites and the Benjaminites. Women and children were not counted.

This act so displeased God that He gave David his choice of three punishments, three years of famine, three months of defeats from his enemies, or three days of the sword of the Lord. David chose the latter, trusting the mercy of the Lord. God sent a pestilence that killed 70,000 men in all Israel, and the angel of the Lord was ready to destroy Jerusalem when God repented and stopped him. David asked God to punish him, and not his people. The angel of the Lord ordered David to erect an altar to the Lord on the threshing floor of Ornan the Jebusite. (This spot is located in today's Dome of the Rock, now controlled by the Moslems.) David purchased the site from Ornan for 600 shekels of gold ($5,760) and planned the construction of the house of the Lord and the altar for burnt offerings.

God instructed David that he had shed so much blood that he should not be the one to build the Temple, but He would give David a son, Solomon, who would build it. David assembled many materials for the actual construction, including many cut stones, iron for nails, doors and clamps, bronze beyond weighing, many cedar timbers, 100,000 talents of gold ($964,000) and 1,000,000 talents of silver ($640,000). He then instructed all the leaders of Israel to participate and help observe the statutes and ordinances that the Lord commanded for Israel through

Moses. David then organized the 38,000 Levites over 30 years of age: 24,000 to serve in the temple, 6,000 as officers and judges, 4,000 as gatekeepers, and 4,000 as musicians. In addition, he designated an army to serve alternatively each month of the year. David reigned for seven years in Hebron and thirty-three years in Jerusalem, then appointed his son Solomon as king and died in his old age. David was a good king and constantly implored his people to follow God's commandments.

SECOND CHRONICLES

Time   See notes on 1 Chronicles.
Author See notes on 1 Chronicles.
Theme Retells 1 and 2 Kings, as pertaining to Judah, and not the ten tribes of Israel, from the reign of Solomon to the decree of Cyrus releasing the Hebrews from captivity. God's greatness is emphasized by miracles.

Solomon became king of all Israel (Judah and Israel). When asked by God what He should give him, Solomon answered, "Give me now wisdom and knowledge . . ." (2 Chronicles 1:10), and God answered that because Solomon had asked for nothing for himself, He would grant his wish, plus give him ". . . riches and wealth and honor, such as none of the kings who were before you has possessed, nor those who will come after you" (2 Chronicles 1:12).

Solomon's first desire was to build a temple for the Lord, to house the Ark. Four years after becoming king, he arranged with Huram, king of Tyre, to build it. Huram used 153,600 aliens in Israel as workers, and the work took seven years for completion. Estimates of the cost run as high as $5,000,000,000. It was built according to exact measurements specified by God. Solomon had a great dedication and prayer to God, and God showed His presence and acceptance of the Temple by sending a fire from heaven that consumed the burnt offerings and sacrifices. He said that He would bless the Israelites if they were faithful, but would punish them if they weren't. God had said this same thing many times before.

The Queen of Sheba visited Solomon to verify tales of his grandeur and wisdom. They probably negotiated some trade alliances, "And King Solomon gave to the queen of Sheba all her desire which she requested . . ." (2 Chronicles 9:12). Tradition maintains that this included a son by Solomon, named Menelek.

Solomon collected heavy taxes, much wealth from trade in commerce, and presents from kings and governors, until his wealth and wisdom exceeded those of any king on the earth. He ruled a kingdom from the Euphrates to Egypt and from the Philistines to the desert for forty years; then he died. His treasures were to be the principal incentive and bounty for the conquest of Israel and Judah by other kings.

Solomon's son, Rehoboam (J), became king, and contrary to the advice of his father's advisors, told the people ". . . My father made your yoke heavy, but I will add to it; my father disciplined you with whips, but I will discipline you with scorpions" (2 Chronicles 10:14). The ten northern tribes of Israel revolted under Jeroboam, who had returned by way of Egypt. Rehoboam (J) forsook the law of the Lord, and Shishak, king of Egypt, captured all the fortified cities of Judah and all the treasures of the house of the Lord and the king's house. The people repented and God forgave them, but said they would be subservient to Shishak. Rehoboam (J) was king for seventeen years, during which time there was constant war between Israel and Judah; and he died, leaving the throne to Abijah (J), his son.

Abijah (J), king of Judah, was not a good king, but was better than Jeroboam (I), king of Israel. They drew battle lines to fight against each other.

Abijah (J) had 400,000 warriors and Jeroboam (I) had 800,000. Abijah (J) was outnumbered, so he called on the Lord to help him. He warned Israel that it had not obeyed God and he, Abijah (J), did keep God's commandments, so the Lord would help him to win. Abijah (J) did win and killed most of the Israelites, so they did not fight with him again. He was king for three years and died. Asa (J), his son, became king of Judah.

Asa (J) was a good king, doing mostly what was right with God, so he had peace and Judah prospered. He called upon the people to worship and obey God. He tore down the idols and high places which maintained chambers for *kedeshim* (male prostitutes) and *kedeshoth* (sacred harlots) and where firstborn infants were sometimes sacrificed.

Asa (J) built an army of 300,000 men from Judah and 280,000 men from Benjamin. Zerah, the Ethiopian, came to conquer him with 1,000,000 men and 300 chariots, but Asa (J) prayed to God for help. With God's help, Asa's (J) army slew all of the Ethiopians. The prophet Azariah warned Asa (J) to continue to obey God and he would prosper, but to disobey Him would cause suffering. Asa (J) continued to purge the land of idols, had great meetings to worship God, and even went so far as to put to death all who would not worship Him. He even had his mother removed as queen because she had made an image of Asherah, an idol of fertility.

In Asa's (J) thirty-sixth year, he made an agreement with Benhadad, king of Syria, to help him defend himself from Baasha (I), king of Israel. This angered the Lord and he sent Hanani the seer to tell Asa (J) that he had sought help from man instead of from the Lord, so he would be punished with wars for the rest of his life. Asa had a disease of his feet in his thirty-ninth year of reign and sought advice of physicians, instead of from God. He was king for forty-one years and died. His son, Jehoshaphat (J), became king.

Jehoshaphat (J) was a good king. One of his first acts was to set up a program of teaching and reading the book of the law to all the people, so they would love and honor God. God blessed him with great riches, an army of 1,160,000 men, and respect and peace from all the surrounding nations. Ahab (I), king of Israel, came to him to make an alliance to fight the Syrians, but Micaiah the prophet advised against war with the Syrians. Ahab (I) insisted they fight, and he was killed, so Jehoshaphat (J) returned home. He was rebuked by Jehu, the son of Hanani the seer, for joining forces with the ungodly Ahab (I). Jehoshaphat (J) set up a system of judges from among the Levites to help the people settle their disputes.

After this, the Moabites, Ammonites, and Meunites in a great multitude came to war against Judah. Jehoshaphat (J) assembled his advisors and new court in the house of the Lord, to pray to God and to ask guidance. God spoke through Jahaziel, who said that the battle was God's and that they would win. He told the king to send his men to meet the enemy, but they would not need to fight. This proved to be true. When Jehoshaphat's (J) men came upon the enemy, they had engaged in battle among themselves and were all dead, so Jehoshaphat's (J) men picked up a great amount of booty. They gave thanks to the Lord, and all the surrounding countries had great fear of Judah. Then Jehoshaphat (J) joined with the evil King Ahaziah (I) of Israel, to build ships at Eziongeber to go to Tarshish. The prophet Eliezar had said this was evil, and that the ships would be destroyed by God—and they were. Thus, Jehoshaphat (J) reigned for twenty-five years and died at the age of sixty. Jehoram, his son, was king.

Jehoram (J) was a bad king. The first thing he did was to murder all his brothers. His wife was the daughter of Ahab (I), the evil king of Israel. He violated God's wishes, set up worship of false idols in high places, and was unfaithful, leading Judah astray from God. Elijah the prophet wrote to him and told him that because of his evil ways, his family would be struck with a great plague. He would have all his riches plundered by the Philistines and Arabs, and he himself would have an incurable disease of the bowels. He would be in great agony and would die. All this happened. He was thirty-two when he became king, but he only ruled for eight years and died in disgrace. Ahaziah (J), his youngest son, became king.

Ahaziah (J) was twenty-two when he was made king and only ruled for one year. His mother, Athaliah, granddaughter of Omri, a wicked woman, was his counsel. He did everything that was evil. He was murdered while visiting Joram. Athaliah then destroyed all the royal family of Judah, except one son, Joash, son of Ahaziah. He was hidden by Jehoshabeath, Jehoram's daughter and wife of Jehoiada the priest, who kept him for six years. After six years, Jehoiada made an agreement with all of the commanders to restore the house of the Lord, make the young boy king, and kill the evil Athaliah, which they did with a great celebration.

Joash (J) was seven years old when he became king, and he ruled for forty years. While Jehoiada lived and counselled him, he did all that was good in the eyes of the Lord. But when Jehoiada died at 130, the king would not listen to Zechariah, the son of Jehoiada. He did evil things, causing God to permit the Syrians to defeat him, take all the treasures, and kill all the princes. Joash's (J) own servants then killed him for his sins, and Amaziah (J), his son, became king at twenty-five.

Amaziah (J) first killed all the servants who had killed his father. He ruled for twenty-nine years—mostly good ones. He assembled an army of 300,000 men and hired another 100,000 Israelites, but one of his prophets told him not to associate with the men of Israel, so he dismissed them. Then he fought the men of Seir in Edom, killing 10,000 and taking another 10,000 captive, whom he killed by shoving them over a cliff. He then sinned against God by worshipping the captured gods of the Edomites, which angered the Lord. A prophet told Amaziah (J) he would be destroyed for his sin, but he boastfully challenged Joash (I), king of Israel, to war. Joash (I) defeated Amaziah (J), plundered Jerusalem, and seized all the king's treasures. Amaziah (J) fled to Lachish, where his own people eventually slew him. His son, Uzziah (J), succeeded him at the age of sixteen and ruled for fifty-two years.

Uzziah (J) had been tutored by the priest Zechariah, son of Jehoiada, to obey God. He had a strong army of 307,500 men and was successful in battle with the Philistines, Arabs, Meunites, and the Ammonites, even to Egypt. He helped rebuild farms and grazing lands but became very arrogant and boastful in his successes and defied the Lord by entering the Temple to burn incense, a ritual which was reserved only for priests. God struck him instantly with leprosy on his forehead, and he lived alone for the rest of his life. His son Jotham (J) had to rule for him and succeeded him at death.

Jotham (J) was king at twenty-five, ruled for sixteen years, and was considered a good king. He did what was right in the eyes of the Lord and was successful in war and peace. He was succeeded by Ahaz (J), his son.

Ahaz (J) was king at age twenty and ruled for sixteen years, but he was a very wicked king. He made idols and worshipped Baal, made human sacrifices of his own sons, burned incense on the high places, and closed the Temple, all in disobedience to God. God caused him to be defeated by Syria, Israel, Assyria, and Edom. He lost 120,000 men in one day, and the Israelites took captive 200,000 women and children, who were later returned. Ahaz was evil and faithless to God and unsuccessful in everything he did. He was succeeded by Hezekiah (J), his son, twenty-five, who ruled for twenty-nine years. He was to be Judah's best king.

Upon becoming king, Hezekiah (J) immediately started preparations to obey God as faithfully as David had. He reorganized the Levites and priests, and had them open and restore the Temple. He then invited all the people of Judah and Israel to assemble and be consecrated to God. He was ridiculed by many of the Israelites, but some came. He had a great assembly to celebrate the Passover, which lasted for seven days and was extended another seven days. Hezekiah (J) talked to the people and told them they must return to obedience to God in order to obtain God's pardon for their sins and the sins of their fathers. This was the greatest celebration since the days of Solomon, son of David. Then the people were blessed and returned to their homes. They prospered and tithed freely and willingly to the priests, and all Judah praised God and received His blessings.

King Sennacherib of Assyria invaded Judah, trying to take the whole land, but Hezekiah (J) prayed to God for help. The Assyrian king ridiculed God before the people of Judah, but God sent an angel to cause the Assyrians to retreat to their own land, where their king was killed in shame by his own sons in his own house of worship. Hezekiah (J) was exalted in the sight of all nations, prospered, and acquired great wealth and riches; all the nation prospered. He was the king who diverted the waters of the spring of Gihon to the west side of the City of David. He was a good king and was honored at his death. He was succeeded by his son Manasseh (J), twelve, who ruled for fifty-five years, but unfortunately was the opposite of his father and was one of the worst of Judah's kings.

Manasseh (J) did everything evil, the opposite of his father. He rebuilt the high places, erected altars to the Baals, made Asherahs, desecrated the Temple with idols and altars, burned his own sons as offerings, practiced soothsaying, augury, sorcery, and much more that was evil—even worse than the evil nations Manasseh (J) destroyed when he conquered Canaan. God caused the Assyrians to conquer Judah and take Manasseh (J) captive to Babylon. He finally humbled himself and beseeched the true God, who heard him and caused him to be released to Jerusalem, where he cleaned the Temple and righted many wrongs he had previously done. He died and was succeeded by his son Amon (J), twenty-two, who ruled for two evil years.

Amon (J) did all the evil things that his father Manasseh (J) had done, causing his servants to kill him, who in turn were killed by the people. His son, Josiah (J), was made king in his stead at eight years of age and ruled for thirty-one years.

Josiah (J), who was probably nurtured by priests or the prophets, was equally as good a king as Hezekiah (J). He sought God fervently at the age of sixteen, and at the age of twenty, he purged all of Judah of the high places, the Asherim, idols, altars of the Baals, and all other forms of worship displeasing to the Lord. At twenty-six, he ordered the Temple repaired and rebuilt, and while this was being done, the workmen found the book of the law of God, given through Moses. After Josiah (J) had the book read to him, he rent his clothes and repented for the sins of his people, caused by his forefathers. He inquired of Huldah, the prophetess, for guidance from God. She answered that God was angered with the people of Judah for their sins and for their forsaking Him, the Lord, and that the wrath of God would be poured upon the people, but Josiah would live in peace during his reign and would not have to witness the penalty of his people. Josiah (J) gathered all the priests and the people, and the book of laws was read to them; they made a covenant to keep the laws. He then kept the Passover celebration to the Lord, which was the greatest since the days of Samuel, the prophet. Josiah (J) was twenty-six years of age. All Judah mourned his death after he was killed while doing battle with Neco, king of Egypt, who did not want to fight Josiah, but was on his way to fight at the Euphrates. His son, Joahaz (J), became king and ruled for three months at the age of twenty-three.

Joahaz (J) was deposed by Neco, king of Egypt, who put his brother Eliakim on the throne and changed his name to Jehoiakim. At age twenty-five, he began ruling wickedly, for eleven years.

Jehoiakim (J) was evil in the sight of God; and Nebuchadnezzar, king of Babylon, defeated him, took part of the treasures of the Temple, and took Jehoiakim (J) in fetters to Babylon. At age eight, his son Jehoiachin (J) was made king for three months and then shipped to Babylon, along with more of the Temple's treasures. Zedekiah (J), Jehoiachin's brother, was made king at twenty-one, and he reigned for eleven bad years.

Zedekiah (J) was evil. He would not humble himself before God or listen to the good prophet, Jeremiah, or to anyone else who talked for God. He opposed King Nebuchadnezzar, so finally God decided there was no remedy for these evil people and caused the king of the Chaldeans to conquer and kill most of them. What few people were left, the king took captive to Babylon as servants, together with all of the treasures of the Temple and the princes' houses. What he didn't take, he burned and utterly destroyed.

Judah was destroyed by a God who wanted to love its people, but these people could not handle prosperity and the blessings of God. They consistently reverted to evil ways and disobedience to God's laws. Judah lay desolate, and its few survivors were in slavery in Babylon for seventy years. Cyrus, king of Persia, was then urged by God to rebuild the Temple. He released the Hebrew people to return to Jerusalem and rebuild it, all according to the prophecy of Jeremiah the prophet.

EZRA

Time The three books of Ezra, Nehemiah, and Esther cover about 100 years—536 B.C. to 432 B.C.

Author Presumed to be Ezra, but there are differing opinions, varying from 450 B.C. to 330 B.C., as to the time of writing.

Theme An historical account of the end of the Old Testament history, covering approximately 100 years. The return of the Jews from captivity in Babylon; the rebuilding of the Temple and walls; and the revitalizing of the Jewish life, faith, and law.

One of the first acts of Cyrus, king of Persia, was to issue an order permitting the Jews who had been in captivity in Babylon to return to Jerusalem to rebuild the Temple. This was foretold 200 years previously in Isaiah. In the year 536 B.C., 42,360 Hebrew men, plus their families, servants, and livestock returned to Jerusalem. Cyrus also gave to Sheshbazzar, prince of Judah, 5,469 vessels of gold and silver to return to the Temple. Seven months after their arrival, they erected an altar for burnt offerings. In the second year, they started construction of the Temple.

The Persian people who had been imported to Judah and Israel when the Jews were exported protested the building of the Temple to King Artaxerxes (Cambyses), and he issued an order to have construction stopped for fifteen years. The prophets Haggai and Zechariah prophesied, and construction was started again and approved, as well as blessed, by King Darius, who also ordered that costs be paid by the royal treasury. The Temple was finished four years later, with a great celebration and the keeping of the Passover.

In the year 457 B.C., Ezra, scribe-priest, went to Jerusalem from exile in Babylon with the blessing of the king of Persia, Artaxerxes I, taking four months for the perilous journey. The king sent gifts and treasures and told Ezra he could draw on the treasurers of any of the provinces for additional funds if needed. Ezra had a group of about 1,700 men plus their families and servants.

Ezra's mission was to appoint magistrates and judges, to judge the people according to God's laws and to teach those who did not know the laws. The first thing that was called to his attention was the fact that his predecessors in exile, who had returned to Judah, had intermarried their sons and daughters with the foreigners who had inhabited the land while the Jews were in exile. This was contrary to the law of God, and Ezra was greatly distressed.

Ezra prayed to God to forgive his people for their trespasses against God's laws after God had been generous enough to permit them to return to their homeland and rebuild the Temple. After much soul-searching, all the people were assembled; they agreed that they must make a covenant with their God and put aside all the foreign wives and their children. This they did.

NEHEMIAH

Time 444 B.C.
Author Tradition says Ezra; some scholars think Nehemiah wrote at least part of it.
Theme The Jews had been back in Jerusalem for one hundred years and had made little progress, spiritually or materially, in rebuilding. Ezra had been there for thirteen years, trying to rebuild them spiritually. Nehemiah was a civil governor and had secured the king of Persia's blessing to rebuild Jerusalem's walls, making Jerusalem a fortified city not easily harassed by its powerful neighbors.

Nehemiah, cupbearer to King Artaxerxes, heard that the ruined walls and burned gates of Jerusalem had not been rebuilt; after fervent prayer to God and many days of fasting, he secured favorable approval from the king to go to Jerusalem to rebuild the walls and the gates. He was opposed by the non-Jews, but enlisted the help and cooperation of all the priests and people of Judah. The various parts of the walls and gates were assigned to different groups for rebuilding, so that work progressed on all parts at the same time. Half the people stood guard to protect the workers from the surrounding foreigners, while half worked at the rebuilding.

The workers complained that they worked so hard and so many hours that they were neglecting their own crops and were borrowing money at high rates. Jeremiah exacted a promise from the lenders that they would charge no interest and would return the fields and vineyards held as security for loans.

The walls were rebuilt in fifty-two days, one hundred forty-two years after their destruction. Sanballat, governor of Samaria; Tobiah; Geshem the Arab; and other Ammonites and Ashdodites who had opposed the Jews now began to recognize that the God of these Jews was real. Nehemiah then organized the guards for the city and took a census of all the families who had moved there from capitivity in Babylon. There were 42,360 persons, plus servants and much livestock.

Then for seven days, every day from early morning until noon, all the people gathered to hear Ezra, the priest, read and explain the book of the law of Moses. The people wept in repentance, praised God, confessed their sins, and made new vows to abide by God's laws and commandments.

Before all the assembled people, Ezra reviewed the history of the earth, from God's creation, the choosing of Abraham, the history of the Jewish people, their failures to obey God's commandments, and His everlasting love and forgiveness over and over again. The leaders made a written covenant, joined by the voice of all the people, to observe God's laws to Moses and to keep God's commandments. They then drew lots for 10 percent of the people to live in Jerusalem to administer the affairs of Jerusalem and the Temple. They banned the foreign Ammonites and Moabites for their past sins.

While Nehemiah was on a visit to Artaxerxes, king of Babylon, the priests used a part of the storehouse for the offerings as a place for Tobiah to live. When Nehemiah returned, he was angered and had this restored.

He also noted that the people were working on the Sabbath and bringing in food and merchandise to sell on the Sabbath, and he had this stopped.

He prayed to God to forgive his people. He also chastised those Jews who had intermarried with foreigners and were not raising their children to speak the Jewish language. He asked God's forgiveness for the sins of the people. Nehemiah, with Ezra's aid, was a steadfast and righteous Godfearing man.

ESTHER

Time 536 B.C.–432 B.C.
Author Presumed to be Mordecai, but not definitely known. Some scholars say this book is fiction.
Theme Ahasuerus (King Xerxes) of Persia was one of the greatest kings in all history, who ruled all the lands from India to Ethiopia. God showed His power and love for the Jewish people through the life of one Jewish girl and her willingness to sacrifice her life, if necessary, obeying God's will.

Ahasuerus, king of Persia, and up to this time all-powerful in his world conquests, had a great feast and celebration of several days in anticipation of his conquest of Greece. While he was drunk, he ordered his beautiful wife, Queen Vashti, to appear before his guests with her crown, so that they might see her beauty. She refused to obey him.

This angered the king, and in consultation with his advisors, he issued a proclamation to all his kingdom, saying that he had cast her aside as an example to all wives to be subservient to their husbands. He selected a new queen by having all the provinces send their most beautiful virgins to him; he spent one night with each.

Esther, an orphan, was raised by Mordecai because she was the daughter of his uncle. She was a beautiful girl, and, as a candidate, was selected by the king to be his queen. He did not know that she was a Jewess. He loved her deeply.

Two of the king's eunuchs plotted to kill the king, but Mordecai learned of it and told Esther, who told the king in the name of Mordecai. The king confirmed the information and had the eunuchs hanged.

The king made Haman, an egotist, his head prince and decreed that all should bow to him, but Mordecai, being a Jew, refused to bow. This angered Haman, and he secured the king's approval to issue an order to all the kingdom that on the thirteenth day of the twelfth month every Jew, young and old, male and female, was to be destroyed in one day, and all their possessions plundered.

The name of God is not mentioned in this book, but there was great weeping, wailing, and fasting among the Jews, and undoubtedly much prayer; this is not mentioned. Queen Esther learned of this and sent word to Mordecai, asking what had happened. Mordecai sent a message to Esther that she must appear before the king and petition a pardon for the Jews, even if it cost her her life. There was a rule of the court that no one could appear before the king except at his request. Only those to whom the king holds out the golden scepter may live. Esther and Mordecai knew this.

Esther told Mordecai to have all the Jews fast for three days and nights, neither eating nor drinking, and then she appeared before the king, who loved her and held out the golden scepter, that she might live. She invited the king and Haman to dinner that day, and the king told her to ask what she desired, and he would grant it. She asked that he and Haman come to dinner again the next day, when she would make her request.

Haman's ego was exalted greater than ever, and while bragging to his wife and friends, he counselled with them as to what he should do with Mordecai. They decided to build a gallows fifty cubits (seventy-five feet) high, and the next day, before Haman went to dinner, he would get the king's permission to have Mordecai hanged on this gallows. During the night the king could not sleep; he had the book of memorable deeds read to him, and in reviewing the deed of Mordecai, who saved the king's life from the plot of the two eunuchs, he asked what had been done to reward Mordecai. The reply was that nothing had been done.

The king called Haman and asked him what should be done to reward a person whom the king wants to honor. Haman, thinking that the honor was for himself, said he should be given some of the king's robes and placed on the king's horse and paraded through the streets with proclamations of the king's honor. The king said for Haman to have this done for Mordecai. This was devastating to Haman and his exalted ego.

At Esther's dinner that night for the king and Haman, the king asked her to make her request and said he would grant it, even if it was for half of his kingdom, because he loved her devotedly. She asked that he spare her life and the lives of the Jewish people from the decree of death. The king asked who was responsible for this order, and she pointed her finger at Haman and said it was this foe and enemy. The king was furious and walked into the garden for a few minutes. When he returned, Haman had fallen on the queen's couch. The king exclaimed, "Will he even assault the queen with me in the house?" (Esther 7:8). One of the king's eunuchs told the king that Haman had built the gallows to hang Mordecai. The king ordered Haman hanged instead.

The king gave to the queen all of Haman's house and gave to Mordecai the signet ring of authority taken from Haman. The queen again petitioned the king to revoke the order to kill all the Jews, but the law of the land was that a king's order can never be revoked, so he told Mordecai to prepare and issue another order, of Mordecai's own writing. The new order, issued to all the provinces, gave the Jews the right to defend themselves, protect their property, and kill anyone who was their enemy.

On the assigned thirteenth day of the twelfth month, there was great fear of the Jews, because they killed 75,000 enemies and 500 in Susa, the king's city. On the fourteenth day, they hanged all ten of Haman's sons, but they took no plunder.

Mordecai ordered that the thirteenth day should be a festival day in the provinces and the fourteenth day a festival day in Susa. They called these days Purim. Esther and Mordecai decreed that these festival days should be forever celebrated and commemorated among the Jews. Mordecai grew in rank next only to the king and was popular among the people.

This is a great story of love, devotion, and sacrifice, wherein the central character, Esther, is responsible for the salvation of the Jewish nation.

JOB

Time Estimates run from 961 B.C.–200 B.C. Actually unknown.

Author Some scholars say Moses. Could be a Jew, but probably an Edomite; a person of great intellect, a scholar of vast knowledge, a thinker, and an observer. In talent sometimes compared to Shakespeare.

Theme There are conflicting thoughts: The righteous and the wicked receive their just deserts on earth; the inequalities and injustices of life, where a good God permits so much suffering to fall on those who least deserve it. Satan accuses God of being partial in His dealings with man. God proves His point by letting Satan test Job, a very rich, prosperous, and righteous man.

Job lived in the land of Uz (location unknown, but possibly present-day Jordan, east of the Sea of Galilee). He was a minor king, patriarchal chieftain, or desert prince—of great wealth and prestige—who had seven sons and three daughters. God was proud of Job, but Satan said that God had given Job everything a man could want, so why wouldn't he be a good man? Satan said that if Job was denied all these things, he would deny God also. God gave Satan permission to test Job to any degree, except death.

In one day, Job's herds of camels were stolen and his herders killed by the Chaldeans. His herds of oxen were stolen and his herders killed by Sabeans. Seven thousand sheep and their herders were killed by a thunderstorm. His ten children were all killed at once by a cyclone. Later, Job was tortured with horribly painful diseases (probably leprosy and elephantiasis, erythema or smallpox). He wished he had never been born and longed for death.

The rest of the book consists of a dialogue or debate between Job and his three influential friends: Eliphaz the Temanite, a descendent of Esau, an Edomite; Bildad the Shuhite, a descendent of Abraham and Keturah; Zophar the Naamathite. Elihu the Buzite, a descendent of Abraham's brother Nahor, entered into the discussion later. Job spoke nine times, Eliphaz three times, Bildad three times, Zophar two times, Elihu once and God once. The discussions are not easy to follow.

The rhetoric is the finest, but sometimes we wonder if they know exactly what they are trying to say or prove. Sometimes they are in harmony, and at other times there is wide disagreement. Job was reduced to total loss of dignity and prestige from his former position of great prestige and respect. Job's friends take the position that suffering is sent upon man as punishment for his sins and is proof that he has sinned, and if done secretly, is also proof of his hypocrisy.

Elihu's speech was mostly about how smart he was and how dumb everyone else was, but in essence it is possible to determine that he thought suffering was intended by God to be corrective or preventive, rather than punishment, for sin. In the last chapters, God spoke out in eloquence to silence Job and to bring him to his knees in reverence. God vindicated Job as a truly righteous man.

God restored Job to his prestigious position in the community, with twice the possessions he had before. He had 14,000 sheep, 6,000 camels, 1,000 yoke of oxen, and 1,000 she asses. He also had seven sons and three daughters and lived 140 years, to see four generations of his children. The reading of this book clarifies the saying, "the patience of Job."

PSALMS

Time From 1500 B.C.–100 B.C. Mostly 400 B.C.–100 B.C. Many were probably handed down from generation to generation verbally before being written.

Author David, seventy-three; Asaph, twelve; Sons of Korah, twelve; Solomon, two; Heman, one; Ethan, one; Moses, one; anonymous, forty-eight.

Theme The Psalms are probably man's most noble and honest expressions to God of his respect, love, yearnings, pleadings for forgiveness, confessions, adoration, and faith. They are an accumulation of thoughts and ideals of many people, such as the Canaanites, Egyptians, and Babylonians, as well as the Hebrews.

The Psalms are divided into five groups: David's songs; devotionals; church rites; anonymous group; those written late. The collection of the Psalms called the psalter has been the vocal expression of both Jew and Gentile through song and many types of musical instruments. They are poems (not doctrinal treatises or sermons) intended to be sung by man to reflect the ideals of his religious piety, communion with God, sorrow for sin, search for perfection, walking in darkness fortified by faith, obedience to God, joy in the worship of God, fellowship with fellow believers, reverence for the Word of God, humility under chastisement, trust in God when evil triumphs and wickedness prospers, and serenity in the midst of storm. They are an outpouring of the innermost feelings of a man's soul, and belong to all believers.

To understand Hebrew poetry, one must understand that it has no rhyme or meter dependent upon the number of syllables or accents in each line, but rather a parallelism of thoughts from one line to the next.

This parallelism is reflected in four different ways. *Synonymous*—the statement in the first line is repeated exactly, but in different words, in the second line. *Contrasted*—the statement in the first line is affirmed by its opposite in the second line. *Constructive*—the statement in the first line serves as the basis upon which the second line rests; in other words, cause and effect. *Ascending*—the first line is incomplete, but the second line completes it.

The Ras Shamra tablets, found in the ruins of Ugarit, fifty-nine miles southwest of Antioch (present-day Antakya, Turkey), show that at the time Israel invaded Canaan, the type of poetry in the Psalms was already a long-established tradition among the inhabitants of Ugarit, a city probably founded before 2000 B.C. and destroyed at the height of its golden age, about 1200 B.C., at the hands of the Sea Peoples.

The Psalms are often referred to as the Psalms of David, with the belief that he was the principal writer. The generally accepted opinion, however, is that there were Psalms in existence before David's time, which he used as a nucleus for a hymnal of worship. This was enlarged by David and others from generation to generation, and many scholars think it was brought to its present form by Ezra.

W. E. Gladstone said, "All the wonders of Greek civilization heaped together are less wonderful than in this simple book of the psalms. The 23rd psalm is probably the most frequently quoted and should be read as an example—'The Lord is my Shepherd . . . .'"

PROVERBS

Time Covers a period of 700 B.C. to 400 B.C. One of the oldest parts of chapter 22 is a reflection of the ancient Egyptian book *Wisdom of Amenemope*, written before 1000 B.C.

Author Solomon is credited with writing chapters 1–9 and 10–24; the men of Hezekiah copied Solomon in chapters 25–29, Words of Augur in 30, and Words of Lemuel in 31. The "wisdom teachers" had probably taught the principles of some of these sayings verbally before.

Theme Similar to Carnegie's book *How to Win Friends and Influence People*, the Book of Proverbs is Solomon's book, *Best Guide Books to Success That a Young Man Can Follow*. Psalms was a book of devotion, while Proverbs is a book of practical ethics. It is concentrated common sense. The fear of the Lord or respect for the Lord is the beginning of all real wisdom.

A proverb is a short, pithy, instructive saying or a more lengthy moral essay. Solomon had a consuming passion for wisdom and knowledge. His intellectual attainments were the wonder of his age, and kings came from the ends of the earth to hear him. The wisdom philosophy oversimplifies human character by dividing all men into three groups: the *wise*, or *righteous*, who know and do what is right and are successful; the *simple*, who are capable of becoming wise, although they are not yet; and the *fools*, who are utterly corrupt, incapable of moral growth, and doomed to destruction. The fear of God is stressed. One of the greatest proverbs is 3:5, 6.

The Proverbs deal with the results of seeking wisdom as compared to living a life of folly. They are not prophetic or legalistic Judaism, but rather stress the wisdom distilled from life itself, taught primarily to the young as a guide to success.

The subjects covered run the gamut of human behavior, including: wisdom, righteousness, fear of God, knowledge, morality, chastity, diligence, self-control, trust in God, tithes, proper use of riches, consideration for the poor, control of the tongue, kindness to enemies, choice of companions, training of children, industry, honesty, laziness, idleness, justice, helpfulness, cheerfulness, and just plain common sense.

ECCLESIASTES

Time   If written by Solomon, about 975 B.C.–950 B.C.
Author   Solomon, although there are some scholars who say it was not written until about 200 B.C., which would be after his time.
Theme   *Ecclesiastes* is Greek for "the Preacher" or "the Orator" or "the Speaker." The book is a collection of essays and thoughts on life, mostly gloomy. David taught happiness. Solomon's refrain was "all is vanity," and the result was unhappiness.

Solomon was the wisest man in the world. He was also the richest and most powerful. In today's world, we would probably say he had the best public-relations department, because he was the best known. He had 1,000 wives; therefore, he couldn't have had any of the common marital and sexual problems.

In spite of all of this, or because of it, he was unhappy. The question, Is life worth living? was asked. He answered, ". . . Vanity of vanities! All is vanity" (Ecclesiastes 1:2). In his lifetime, he tried pleasure and had 1,000 wives; he tried music, dance, wine, laughter, and gaiety in the court; he became practical and created great works of aqueducts, pools, palaces, public buildings; he tried vineyards, gardens, orchards, and flowers; and Jerusalem bloomed like the Garden of Eden; he tried cattle breeding, art collecting, and even tried to be an amateur musician.

He urged the young man to eat, drink, and find enjoyment, and yet he said, "Although a sinner does evil a hundred times and may lengthen his life, still I know that it will be well for those who fear God, who fear Him openly. But it will not be well for the evil man and he will not lengthen his days like a shadow, because he does not fear God" (Ecclesiastes 8:12, 13). He also said, ". . . I have found one man among a thousand, but I have not found a woman among all these" (Ecclesiastes 7:28). His great question is, "Is life worth living?" His life, research, and mental reasoning end up with, "Vanity of vanities . . . all is vanity!" (Ecclesiastes 12:8.)

The book ends: "The conclusion, when all has been heard, is: fear God and keep His commandments, because this applies to every person. Because God will bring every act to judgment, everything which is hidden, whether it is good or evil" (Ecclesiastes 12:13, 14). The reader should remember that Solomon had not learned about Jesus Christ and the redemption of man's sins, which will be revealed in the reading of the New Testament.

THE SONG OF SOLOMON

Time 1000 B.C. to 950 B.C. Could have been written during the Greek period (300 B.C.) if not written by Solomon.
Author Solomon. Some scholars think it is a collection of poems of anonymous authors.
Theme An intimate poem of love, difficult to understand and to hold to a chain of thought. There are as many interpretations of the meaning as there are scholars.

The characters are a bride, the Shulammite, the king, and a chorus of daughters of Jerusalem. The name of God does not appear in this book. There are many interpretations of the story.

Briefly, the story could be interpreted this way. It includes: the bride's love for the king; her delight in his love; her dream of his disappearance and joy in his return; the bridal procession and greetings; the king's adoration of his bride; another bride's dream of his disappearance and her love; the Shulammite, the loveliest in the palace by the king's acceptance; and their all-consummate love for each other and undissoluble union.

Some present-day scholars parallel the story to the love of God for the Hebrews and Christ's love for the Church, but at the time of its writing, Christ was not known.

ISAIAH

Time Approximately 742 B.C.–701 B.C.

Author Isaiah. There are many opinions, but most scholars say Isaiah wrote chapters 1–39, which are often termed First Isaiah. The poems of chapters 40–55 are considered Second Isaiah, written after 580 B.C. by several writers. Chapters 56–66, Third Isaiah, were written before Nehemiah (444 B.C.), by several prophets. Some scholars think these writings could extend to 200 B.C.

Theme Isaiah was married and had two sons. He was of royal-blood lineage and was considered the greatest of the writing prophets. He warned Judah of its sins and downfall if it did not repent. He foretold the coming of Christ, the captivity by the Babylonians, and the ultimate deliverance by Cyrus, king of Persia. He counselled with kings, denounced evil, and threatened judgment, but still held out hope for the love of God for His people.

In the time of Isaiah, northern Israel was greater than southern Judah, but both were prizes desired by the Assyrians on the north and east and by the Egyptians on the south. Assyria was the stronger aggressor, with its ultimate goal of the conquest of Egypt. Egypt knew this and used Israel and Judah as a buffer zone. This has been Israel's problem for 5,000 years, and remains so to this very day. Israel succumbed to Assyria 135 years before Judah, in about 722 B.C., under the Syrian king Tiglath-pileser III. Judah was next. This was the time in history pertaining to the Book of Isaiah.

Isaiah was a friend and advisor to three kings: Jotham, 742 B.C.–735 B.C.; Ahaz, 735 B.C.–715 B.C.; and Hezekiah, 715 B.C.–687 B.C. Isaiah was a prophet and critic of political policies and a spiritual teacher, but mostly a prophet concerned with the ethical, social, and spiritual conduct of the leaders and their people. Nothing certain is known of his death, but tradition insists that Isaiah resisted Manasseh's idolatrous decrees and was fastened between two planks and "sawn asunder and buried beneath an oak tree."

The book is more or less divided in thought into three areas of message: first, chapters 1–39; second, 40–55; and third, 56–66. In the first, Isaiah says that God is in universal history and extends to all peoples.

Israel is His people, but God uses other nations as instruments for good or bad in reaching His overall objectives. Assyria, for example, is a tool of God to punish Israel for its idolatrous misbehavior. Judah must trust in God and not in material alliances with idolatrous people.

The prophets Amos and Hosea in the northern kingdom of Israel were denouncing the same evils that existed in Judah: the amassing of riches by the rich at the expense of the poor, luxury, complacency, pride, heathen worship, and the corruption of the legal processes by the priests, who were supposed to be the protectors. Isaiah prophesied Christ's birth, His living in Nazareth, and His work to come. He predicted, and lived to see: Judah saved from Israel and Syria; Syria and Israel destroyed by Assyria; Assyria's attempt to take Judah, and Jerusalem's delivery from this attempt; the conquest of the Philistines, Moab, Egypt, Ethiopia, Arabia, and Tyre.

When Sennacherib, king of Assyria, besieged Jerusalem, Hezekiah sent Isaiah to intervene, and he prayed to God to forgive the sins of his people and save the city. God answered his prayers and sent an angel of the Lord, who slew 185,000 of Sennacherib's warriors in one night. Sennacherib left and returned to Nineveh, where his own two sons killed him while he worshipped his false god, Nisroch.

In the second part, Isaiah predicted John the Baptist's foretelling of the coming of Christ. His chief theme is constant trust in God and joy amid sorrow, defeat, and disaster. God's love for His people is tender, but their continued sins hurt deeply His love for them. This prophet is the most evangelical of the prophets. He continually passes on to a sinful humanity the element of hope, the outlook of a coming golden age, and the doctrine of the Kingdom of God on earth, to which all men, without distinction of race, are called. Part of the purpose of these teachings is to rebuild the faith of the Jewish exiles in Babylon for their return to their homeland.

In the third portion of Isaiah, the predictions are made of Christ's program, His entry into Jerusalem, and His ultimate death. This area reflects the period just before or during Jeremiah's return to Jerusalem and is a composite of many moods and teachings. During the exile in Babylon, the Jews had learned to break their isolationism; instead of living in dread of surrounding peoples, they now had a tendency to include them in their missionary zeal. Christ later quoted from Isaiah in this area.

Isaiah lived to see many of his predictions fulfilled, but many were fulfilled after his death. He prophesied about Christ's birth, ministry, area of work, sufferings, might, gentleness, righteousness, justice and kindness, His death, His vast influence, death of the earth, a new heaven and new earth, and the final separation of the righteous and the wicked. Isaiah was a great and powerful servant of God.

JEREMIAH

Time   626 B.C.–586 B.C., possibly twenty-six years more, to 560 B.C. After Isaiah's death by 70–100 years.

Author   Jeremiah is credited, but it is possible that his secretary, Baruch, actually wrote the book. Jeremiah, son of a priestly family that had a landed estate in the northern kingdom of Benjamin, was born in Anatoth, three miles north of Jerusalem. He was called by God to be a prophet when very young (actually before his birth). He died a captive in Egypt. Tradition says he was stoned to death.

Theme   Chapters 1–24 are prophesies; chapters 25–44, experiences; and chapters 45–52, prophesies against other nations. Isaiah had saved Jerusalem from Assyria and Jeremiah tried, but failed, to save it from Babylon. Under God's guidance and direction, he devoted his whole life to trying to get the leaders and the people who had forsaken God to give up their immoral, indifferent, idolatrous, and corrupt lives and follow the teachings of Moses and God's commandments. He failed.

World supremacy for 300 years was being decided among three nations: Assyria, which had ruled the world from Nineveh for 200 years; Babylon, which was growing stronger; and Egypt, which 1,000 years before was a great power, then decayed and was now getting stronger. Hordes of Scythians from south Russia were moving into Assyria in the north; Babylon was pushing from the east; Egypt was collecting tribute from Judah and was a threat from the south. Religion was closely tied to political leadership. Jeremiah lived through the reign of the last five kings of Judah: Josiah, Jehoahaz, Jehoiakim, Jehoiachin, and Zedekiah.

Babylon won Assyria in 607 B.C., partly destroyed Jerusalem in 606 B.C., and defeated Egypt at Carchemish in 605 B.C. Palestine became a Babylonian province. Babylon further devastated Jerusalem in 597 B.C., finally burned and desolated it in 586 B.C. and took 4,600 Jews as captives to Babylon for seventy years.

Jeremiah was born into this period of external historical turmoil and threat, internal moral rottenness and spiritual decay (which was caused primarily by bad kings, apathy of the people and corruption of the priests and false prophets). He was a prophet appointed by God to convey God's messages to the rulers and the people. This was against his wishes, because he was so young and felt inadequate, but God commanded and he obeyed. God ordered him to remain unmarried. He was very unpopular with the people, and he suffered much persecution, threat, and abuse because he advised against the sinfulness of the people, but he remained loyal and devoted to the will of God.

Jeremiah condemned the nation and its leaders for forsaking their Almighty God and serving other gods and idols. He repeatedly told them that their nation would be ravaged and destroyed, and he prophesied as to their doom and ultimate captivity if they did not desist from their evil ways. He assured them of God's blessings, if they would only obey and abide by His commandments.

He told them the story of the linen waistband (chapter 13), the potter and his clay (chapter 18), and the broken potter's flask (chapter 19). He was beaten by the priest, Pashur, and put in stocks. When released, he prophesied to Pashur that he would die in captivity in Babylon. He warned the people to submit to Nebuchadnezzar (chapter 21) or die and have their city ravaged, but he was ignored. He told the story of the good and bad baskets of figs (chapter 24), forecast that Judah would be in captivity for seventy years, and was sentenced to death but was saved by Ahikam. Hananiah, a false prophet, rebuked Jeremiah, and Jeremiah foretold his death within the year (chapter 28). He promised the restoration of Judah after the captivity of seventy years (chapters 30 and 31) and told the story of the purchase of Hanamel's land.

He rebuked the people for setting their slaves free and then taking them back, in violation of God's will (chapter 34). He told of God's blessing of the Rechabites because of their obedience to God (chapter 35). Jeremiah dictated to his secretary, Baruch, God's instructions to the people, so they could be read over and over again, but King Jehoiakim cut up the scrolls and burned them. Jeremiah had them rewritten and was later imprisoned, but released (chapters 36 and 37). He was later cast into an empty, muddy cistern, but was saved by Ebedmelech the Ethiopian (chapter 38).

In the eleventh year of King Zedekiah, all of Jeremiah's prophesies came true (chapter 39). Nebuchadnezzar, king of Babylon, captured Jerusalem, killed most of the people, captured King Zedekiah and gouged out his eyes, took all the treasures, burned the city, and took the king and 4,600 captives to Babylon. Nebuchadnezzar recognized Jeremiah as a servant of God and offered him his choice of going to Babylon in honor or staying in Judah. He decided to stay.

A remnant of the poorest of the Jews remained in Judah under Gedaliah, who was appointed governor by Nebuchadnezzar. Ishmael and others killed Gedaliah, but were then chased from the country. The small Jewish remnant then asked Jeremiah if they should stay in

108 / Jeremiah

Jerusalem or flee to Egypt. He said that God instructed him to tell them to stay, but as usual, they ignored his advice and fled to Egypt. Jeremiah had foretold they would die there and never return, because Babylon would also conquer Egypt, which it did.

Jeremiah then (chapters 46, 47, 48, and 49) prophesied as to the judgment on Egypt, the Philistines, Moab, Ammon, Edom, Damascus, Kedar, and Elam (Persia), the ultimate fall and destruction of Babylon forever, and the ultimate redemption and return of the Jews to Judah.

Jeremiah was a true servant of God, totally dedicated to his mission in life as specified by his God. His was not an easy life, but his ultimate reward will surely be among the greatest.

LAMENTATIONS

Time 589 B.C.–587 B.C., probably the three-month period between the destruction of Jerusalem and the trip to Egypt.
Author Jeremiah.
Theme Jeremiah, who was known as the weeping prophet. He wept over the desolation and ruin of Jerusalem, even though he knew well in advance that this was going to happen. The poetry of this book is in the form of a dirge or funeral hymn.

Jeremiah writes with all the emotions humanly possible to express sorrow, penitence, grief, and suffering of the human conscience for the destruction of Jerusalem by the Babylonians, the exile of its people to Babylon, the death of many, and the exile of a small remainder to Egypt. He laments the sins of his people and the corruption of the leaders who despoiled them.

He still trusts God with all his heart and admits that the judgment and punishment of the people are justified, but he pleads for God's forgiveness of an unrighteous people and asks His mercy. Jeremiah cannot seem to erase from his mind the horrors of the siege of the city, the cries of the starving children, and the agony of the women who boiled their own babies for food. The grief is also God's grief for punishing His own children; the same as any parent would feel. God's sorrow is as deep as the people's grief, because He has to chasten them. Jeremiah appeals to God for mercy and forgiveness.

This book is read in Jewish synagogues at the morning and evening services at the Fast of Ninth of Ab in July each year, which is when Jerusalem was destroyed in 587 B.C. It was later rebuilt and destroyed again by the Romans in A.D. 70. The seat of the government was moved to Mizpah after Jerusalem's destruction.

EZEKIEL

Time   597 B.C.–567 B.C.

Author   Ezekiel, son of Buzi, a priest-prophet taken captive to Babylon with King Jehoiachin in 597 B.C. at about the age of twenty-five. He started his prophetic ministry at about the age of thirty, for the period 593 B.C.–567 B.C.—twenty-six years.

Theme   Ezekiel was taken captive to Babylon ten to twelve years before the final destruction of Jerusalem. He grew up in Jerusalem, probably heard Jeremiah preach, and may possibly have been his student. He lived with other exiles at Tel-abib, about forty miles east of Babylon on the Chebar, a large canal in the Euphrates' irrigation system. Daniel, the subject of the next book, had been in Babylon eight to nine years when Ezekiel arrived. Daniel was in the palace, Ezekiel in the country. They probably met and talked often. Ezekiel's prophesies were based on very vivid visions, which he tabulated exactly as to dates. Chapters 33–48 cover the future restoration of Judah and the coming glory of Jerusalem.

    While Jeremiah was still in Jerusalem and Ezekiel was in Babylon, both were talking about the same things: the love of God for His people, His hopes for them, their punishment for their sins, and the destruction of Jerusalem, but the ultimate salvation and restoration of Judah.

    Ezekiel's first vision was a likeness of the glory of God, who commissioned him to speak to His rebellious people. He was handed a scroll to eat, to fill him with knowledge, and was warned that if he was charged with teachings to the people and did not deliver them, the blood of their sins would be on his hands.

    He was ordered to lie on his left side for 390 days, symbolic of 390 years of punishment for Israel, and on his right side for forty days, symbolic of forty years of punishment for Judah. He was ordered to shave his head and to divide the hair three ways, symbolic that God would destroy Jerusalem and a third of the people would die of pestilence, a third would be killed, and a third would be scattered all over the world.

    In this book "and ye shall know that I am the Lord" is stated seventy times; "the word of the Lord came to me" is stated forty-nine times; "son of man" is stated one hundred times.

God condemns the accumulation of gold and silver, ". . . They cannot satisfy their appetite . . ." (Ezekiel 7:19). He says ". . . the land is full of bloody crimes, and the city is full of violence" (Ezekiel 7:23). Ezekiel's second vision is of God showing him the sins of Judah and the abominations in the Temple, the marking of the few faithful by an angel-scribe before the slaughter of the sinful and idolators, the destruction of Jerusalem, and the future restoration of those cured and purified. Each chapter describes by illustration in different ways how the people of Judah have sinned, how they have tried the patience of God beyond all reason, and how they will be destroyed if they don't change their sinful ways. Ezekiel tells the stories of his own move, the false prophets, the idolatrous elders, the fruitless vine tree, the adulterous unfaithful wife, the parable of the two eagles. He laments that the soul that sins shall die by individual judgment, laments the coming fall of David's city, and rehearses Israel's continued sins during and since its original captivity in Egypt. In chapter 20, he has his third vision and sees the sword of the Lord, which will cut down Jerusalem; and reiterates Israel's sins over and over. He tells the story of the two adulterous sisters, Oholah (Samaria) and Oholibah (Jerusalem) in chapter 23, and the story of the boiling caldron in chapter 24.

In his fourth vision, Ezekiel's wife dies on the day that the siege of Jerusalem finally begins, and he is silenced about Jerusalem until news is received, three years later, of its final destruction. He probably now starts to prophesy in writing, as he is forbidden to speak. Ezekiel now starts to prophesy as to the destruction of Judah's enemies, who have taken great pleasure in the fall of Jerusalem, and Ezekiel prophesies the doom of Ammon, Moab, Edom, and Philistia.

In his fifth vision, he prophesies the death of Tyre, which took Nebuchadnezzar thirteen years to accomplish. Tyre was a powerful and influential city in trade and commerce—a shipping point from all the inland routes to all the Mediterranean, North African, and Atlantic ports. It was subdued by Nebuchadnezzar, later by the Persians, and then by Alexander the Great. Ezekiel prophesied that it ". . . will never be found again . . ." (Ezekiel 26:21), which is true to this day.

In his sixth vision (and also in another vision sixteen years later, but discussed here for continuity), he predicts Nebuchadnezzar's invasion and defeat of Egypt after the fall of Jerusalem. Egypt up to this time has been a powerful nation, but after subjugation to Nebuchadnezzar for forty years and then under Persian rule, she never regains her strength and the prestige of her former glory. His eighth and ninth visions lament the fate of Egypt and classify her in the realm of the dead.

His tenth and eleventh visions further clarify events after the fall of Jerusalem. His twelfth vision allows Ezekiel to talk again. He says the remaining wicked in Judah will be exterminated. He talks about the future restoration of Israel and its future, and the destruction of Edom. He obeys God's order to tell about the valley of the dry bones and the two sticks to be united, representing the resurrection of the Hebrew people and their union into one great nation again.

In chapters 38 and 39, he hears God's message of Gog and Magog assembling great hordes to conquer Israel after its restoration. Modern interpretation is that Gog represents the hordes of people from Turkey, Armenia, and Russia who plan to conquer Israel. But they will fail, apparently in the Messianic age, and with the help of God and by His will, they will be defeated. The Israelites will ". . . make fires with the weapons . . . for seven years . . ." (Ezekiel 39:9). It will take seven months to bury all the dead.

His final vision gives exact specifications for the rebuilding of the Temple. It could possibly be interpreted as a prediction of the Messianic age. The vision outlines the details of the Temple, the role of the priestly service, the lands for the priests and the prince, and the worship and offerings. The "life-giving stream" (*see* Ezekiel 47:1–12) seems to be a river of the water of life, probably to be interpreted as an ever-widening stream, offered to the whole world as the blessing of God to all nations, with its life-giving qualities and eternal life in heaven.

The final chapter gives final details to the city, the Temple, and the division of all the lands among the twelve tribes, an area of about 400 miles by 100 miles.

DANIEL

Time   606 B.C.–534 B.C., from the third year of King Jehoiakim, king of Judah, to the third year of Cyrus, king of Persia.

Author   Daniel, a prince in the line of David, and kin of Zedekiah. He was taken as a captive at about age eighteen to Babylon and lived there until two years after the Jewish return to Jerusalem. He lived ninety years, seventy-two in captivity in Babylon. There is a minor school of thought which says this book was written by an unknown author about 164 or 165 B.C.

Theme   Daniel was taken to Babylon by Nebuchadnezzar in 606 B.C. His name was changed to Belteshazzar. He rose to be prime minister of Babylon and served both Babylonian and Persian nations under kings Nebuchadnezzar, Belshazzar, Darius, and Cyrus. Chapters 1–6 are narratives about Daniel. Chapters 7–12 are visions of Daniel, and are difficult to understand. They foretell of the Babylonian, Persian, Greek, and Roman empires and the final everlasting Kingdom of God.

    The general purpose of this book is to show God's providential guidance in the lives of men and nations. It shows His foreknowledge and plan, and the power to develop that plan through the forces of nature, history of nations, and lives of men. He does that in this book through the world's mightiest kings and humblest captives. This power and wisdom are revealed in the government of the world to the end of all days.

    When Nebuchadnezzar conquered Jerusalem, he took many youths of the nobility to Babylon, to send them to college for three years, during which time they were to eat the rich food of the king. Daniel (Belteshazzar), Hananiah (Shadrach), Mishael (Meshach), and Azariah (Abednego) refused to eat the rich food. At graduation, they were ten times smarter than the king's magicians and enchanters, and Daniel had developed the ability to understand dreams and visions.

    In Nebuchadnezzar's second year, he had a dream that he could not understand. He demanded that his magicians, enchanters, and sorcerers tell him the dream and its interpretation, or he would have them all killed. They could not do this, so Arioch, the captain of the king's guard, was ordered to have Daniel and his companions kill them. Daniel asked the king to give him time to interpret the dream and to save these men from death. Daniel asked his three companions to help him seek the mercy of God to decipher this mystery, which He gave, and Daniel thanked God for His answer.

David explained to the king that it was his God in heaven who revealed all mysteries. Daniel explained the dream and also the interpretation that the Babylonian empire would fall to the Persians, and they to the Greeks, and they to the Romans, and that Christ's Kingdom would survive as the universal and everlasting Kingdom. The king rewarded Daniel with great power, and at his request appointed his three companions, Shadrach, Meshach, and Abednego to high positions in Babylon.

The king erected a golden idol and decreed that all should bow and worship it. Shadrach, Meshach, and Abednego refused to do so when confronted by the king, who then ordered them burned in the fiery furnace, which was heated seven times hotter than normal. They were bound and thrown into the furnace, which was so hot that it killed the men who threw them in. When Nebuchadnezzar looked in the furnace, he saw four men walking around in the flames, and he called to Shadrach, Meshach, and Abednego to come out. They were unscorched; the king praised God and the angel who delivered them from the fire and issued a decree for all people to respect their God. He promoted Shadrach, Meshach, and Abednego in rank.

Nebuchadnezzar had another dream, and his own wise men could not interpret it for him, so he sent for Daniel. (Actually, history relates that Nebuchadnezzar went insane for three to four years.) He related the dream to Daniel, who interpreted it as the temporary insanity of the king but the ultimate downfall of Babylon. He said that the king should repent. After recovering from his insanity, Nebuchadnezzar praised the God of Daniel to all.

King Belshazzar, son of Nebuchadnezzar, had a great feast (or probably a drunken brawl) for a thousand of his lords, wives, and concubines. He commanded that the gold and silver vessels taken from the Temple in Jerusalem be brought out, so they might drink from them. Immediately the fingers of a man's hand appeared and made a writing on the wall. The terrified king ordered his magicians to interpret the writing, but no one could.

The queen heard of the problem, came to the hall, and told the king about Daniel. The king summoned Daniel and offered him great gifts if he could interpret the writing, which gifts Daniel refused. He told the king that he had defiled God like his father Nebuchadnezzar had, and the writing was "Mene, Mene, Tekel, Upharsin," meaning "God has numbered the days of your kingdom and brought it to an end. You have been weighed and found wanting. Your kingdom is divided and given to the Medes and Persians" (*see* Daniel 5:26–28). Daniel was decorated and made the third ruler of the kingdom. That very night the king was slain, and Darius ruled.

Darius set up 120 governors to rule the kingdom and over them three presidents, of whom one was Daniel, a Jew. The governors were jealous of Daniel and had the king issue an edict that for 30 days no one should pray to any god except the king, or be cast into the den of lions. The law of the Medes and Persians was that no king's edict could be changed. The plotters then found Daniel praying three times a day to the living God and reported to the king. This distressed him greatly, because a king's orders cannot be rescinded. He had no choice except to have Daniel thrown to the lions, but in so doing the king said, ". . . Your God whom you constantly serve will Himself deliver you" (Daniel 6:16).

The king could not sleep and went early to the den of lions. Daniel walked out unscathed and said that God had sent an angel and sealed the mouths of the lions, because Daniel trusted his God. The king ordered Daniel's accusers, their wives, and children cast into the den of lions, and they were all killed at once. The king issued an order to all the kingdom that they should respect the God of Daniel. Daniel prospered under Darius and Cyrus, the Persian.

Daniel had a great vision in the first year of the rule of Belshazzar (chapter 7). He had another vision in the third year of Belshazzar (chapter 8). Daniel presented a great prayer to God for forgiveness of the sins of his people (chapter 9). In the third year of Cyrus, king of Persia, he had another great vision (chapter 10). In the first year of Darius, he had another vision (chapter 11). He had a final vision (chapter 12).

The visions are difficult to understand. The general consensus of most scholars is that they signified that great empires will rise and fall, God will be worshipped by some and ignored by others, and sin and evil will always be among the people. Babylon will fall to Persia; Persia will fall to Greece; and Greece will fall to the Romans. But ultimately, the Kingdom of God will prevail, and the righteous who love and revere God will be saved in eternity.

HOSEA

Time	Sixty years. Between 790 B.C.–697 B.C. Main period, probably 760 B.C.–720 B.C. Before the Assyrian captivity of the northern kingdom of Israel.
Author	Hosea, first of the minor prophets, son of Beeri, prophet to the ten northern tribes called Israel, and sometimes referred to as Samaria and Ephraim.
Theme	A personal object lesson applied to the sins of a nation—unfaithfulness, chastisement, and restoration.

Two hundred years before Hosea's time, the ten northern tribes had seceded from Jerusalem, had adopted the golden calf as their official national god, and were officially known as Israel. This kingdom, ruled mostly by bad kings, had become more idolatrous and morally corrupt with its increased prosperity. Previous prophets had been Elijah, Elisha, Jonah, and Amos. Hosea, talking to Israel, but sometimes to Judah also, was to denounce sin and warn of the consequences.

The first three chapters are a personal object lesson, and the fourth to fourteenth are a message of rebuke, punishment, and ultimate pardon.

Rome and Carthage were founded during this period. Hosea lived during the reigns of Uzziah, Jotham, Ahaz, and Hezekiah—kings of Judah; and Jeroboam II, Zechariah, Shallum, Menahem, Pekahiah, Pekah, and Hoshea—kings of Israel. Hosea foretold the downfall of Israel, the deliverance but ultimate downfall of Judah, and the final restoration of Israel and Judah. He was the poet laureate to kings and God's voice to the people.

In chapters 1–3, Hosea was commanded by God to marry a harlot named Gomer and to have three children. This action is symbolic of Israel's relation with Jehovah. The prophet makes his personal love for the unfaithful wife akin to that of God, who continued to love a wicked and unfaithful Israel. Her desertion and recovery by Hosea in the slave market, and her segregation in his home were symbolic of God's divine love for an unfaithful nation.

In chapters 4–14, Hosea pictures the Lord's controversy with the people—their gross immorality, sanctioned and exampled by the priests. The people have broken their covenant with God, and there is no escape except by reform and repentance. Israel's inner sinfulness and outer decay signify nothing but woe to Israel, because it has turned away from

God. Israel has sown the wind and must reap the imminence of the whirlwind. The stiff-necked people have refused to listen to God, and Hosea pictures them as wanderers among nations. Examples are given of Israel's guilt and punishment. God's love for Israel has never ceased, in spite of her terrible sinfulness. Divine judgment must come to pass, and the people's blood is on their own hands. They have destroyed themselves by going deeper and deeper into sin. Israel shall be destroyed and become desolate, but the door of mercy will still be open.

Apparently the immorality, idolatry, beastliness, corruption, and whoredom of Israel was beyond belief. Hosea worked unceasingly and unsuccessfully to tell the people of the rewards for honoring God and that God still loved them and would eventually redeem them and purify their hearts. Hosea is quoted several times in the New Testament.

JOEL

Time   850 B.C.–838 B.C. Some scholars think about 350 B.C.
Author Joel, son of Pethuel, an inhabitant of Jerusalem, but not a priest.
Theme A plague of locusts is a judgment from God as punishment for the sins of the people. They are urged to turn back to His obedience. This is a warning to foreshadow a coming of the Lord's day and the return of Christ later. The Apostle Peter builds his message on the day of Pentecost on the prophecy of Joel, given hundreds of years previously.

The worst famine in the memory of any living man is caused by a plague of locusts that have eaten everything in sight, and a great drought has dried up the land and streams.

The people are called together to repent, and the Lord delivers them from the curse of destruction and promises an era of prosperity.

Joel interprets these things as enemy nations of Sidonians, Philistines, Egyptians, and Edomites attacking Israel. But in the later book of Acts, Peter interprets Joel's prophecy as a forecast of the Gospel era, of the Holy Spirit, and of the Christian Age, in which God's Word, symbolized in the Gospel of Christ, given to all mankind, will be the sickle for the grand harvest of men's souls.

AMOS

Time 810 B.C. to 785 B.C. or 785 B.C. to 750 B.C. There are differing opinions.

Author Amos, a Judean herdsman and farmer of Tekoa, a village six miles southeast of Bethlehem, sent by God to prophesy to the northern kingdom of Israel during the reign of Jeroboam II. He was a contemporary with Hosea, Joel, and Jonah.

Theme Amos, like Moses and David, could not figure out why God selected him as His mouthpiece, but nevertheless he obeyed. He called a spade a spade and didn't mince words like a politician. During the great prosperity, he ministered to the northern kingdom, but warned Judah, also, of its corruption and prophesied God's judgment against it, but also His eventual forgiveness and blessing. Though Israel was wicked, God was gracious, as He is today.

Amos started his preaching to the crowds at Bethel. He decreed by God's word a general impeachment of the whole area of Syria, Philistia, Phoenicia, Edom, Ammon, and Moab, as well as Judah and Israel. The earthquake mentioned was remembered for 200 years. He decried their cruelty, their luxury, oppression of the poor, lying, cheating, and hypocrisy of worship.

He then reminded the people that the palatial residences in Samaria, the capital, had been built with the blood of the poor with a ruthlessness that would shock the Egyptians and Philistines. Idolatry was intolerable to God, but they would not heed His warning—". . . Yet you have not returned to Me . . ." (Amos 4:8), God warns before punishment. Israel was doomed to be conquered by Assyria, and the captives led away with hooks in their lips. Amos laments the ultimate fall of Israel and makes repeated appeals to the people to abandon their evil ways. They think they can offer sacrifices while continuing their sinful lives. He reminds and compares their luxurious way of life with the intolerable sufferings that are about to befall them.

Amos had three visions: the locusts, who were going to destroy the land, but Amos interceded, and God relented; the fire, which was to devastate the land, but Amos interceded, and God relented; the plumb line measured the walls of the city for destruction. God had decided the Israelites were a sinful, hopeless lot. Amaziah, the priest at Bethel, tried to get King Jeroboam to get rid of Amos. Amos only became bolder and told the priest that his wife would become a harlot and his own sons and daughters, as well as the priest, would be killed. All Israel would end up in exile.

The symbol of the basket of fruit indicated that Israel was ripe for destruction and ruin. Amos made it clear that there was no way to escape the punishment for greed, dishonesty, corruption, idolatry, brutality, and privation of the poor.

His predictions were all fulfilled within thirty years, and Israel ceased to exist. Amos lamented that the ten tribes had broken from the Davidic nation for two hundred years and had lived in sin and idolatry. He held out hope of the resurrection of the kingdom of David and that God's rule would be over all the nations of the world in eternal glory. In a later book of the Acts, James quotes 9:11, 12 as being God's future program.

OBADIAH

Time 586 B.C.–583 B.C.
Author Obadiah. Nothing is known as to whether he was a priest or layman. A contemporary of Jeremiah.
Theme In Genesis it was told how Rebekah, wife of Isaac and mother of Jacob, plotted with Jacob when Isaac was old and blind, to have Isaac give his blessing to Jacob instead of the older brother Esau. Jacob had traded a bowl of stew to Esau for Esau's inheritance. Esau then left the tribe and moved to Edom, an area about 20 miles wide and 100 miles long, south and east of the Dead Sea. He built the City of Petra in the side of a high cliff at the end of a long steep canyon, which gave total protection from all enemies. Here he felt secure. His people made a living by raiding caravans and other countries, especially those of the Hebrews, whom they hated because of Jacob's trickery. King Herod, an Edomite, was ruler of Judah during the Roman rule, when Christ was born. He was the king who ordered all children under two years of age to be killed. Edom was an illustration of the fate of any nation that attempts to divert God's purpose for His people.

Obadiah had a vision and prophesied regarding Edom. Edom sided with Nebuchadnezzar in his conquest and destruction of Jerusalem in 586, in hopes of getting some of the plunder and winning favor with the Babylonians. Obadiah prophesied that Edom would be destroyed and would have the same fate as Israel. God would judge Edom: such evil thinking causes the doom of the proud and rebellious.

Deliverance is for the meek and the humble. ". . . As you have done, it will be done to you . . ." (Obadiah 15). Edom will never recover, but Judah will be in the reestablishment of the Messiah's Kingdom. God will judge Edom. He destroyed Edom by 400 B.C. Today there are more than 300 cities in total ruin, and nothing is known of Edom since A.D. 70. Obadiah prophesied that Edom would never rise again, but Israel had promise. Edom's destruction five years after the fall of Jerusalem was decreed because of its hatred of the Judeans.

"The deliverers will ascend Mount Zion To judge the mountain of Esau, And the kingdom will be the Lord's" (Obadiah 21).

JONAH

Time	Estimated dates vary from 820 B.C.–746 B.C., if written by Jonah, and 400 B.C.–200 B.C., if written by an unknown author.
Author	Most scholars agree on Jonah, son of Amittai, who lived in Gath-Hepher, three miles northeast of Nazareth. He was a famous statesman in Israel and a contemporary of Hosea and Amos. Some scholars say the book was written much later by an unknown author.
Theme	The story seems to be a protest of Jewish exclusiveness (Nehemiah 13:23–27). God cared for all men, and penitent Gentiles could obtain pardon as well as Jews. The book is read in Jewish synagogues on Yom Kippur. It is a story of the redemptive action of God, and a noble missionary act of the Jews. God wanted Jonah to go to Nineveh, but Jonah didn't want to go. Sennacherib, king of Assyria, had made Nineveh the capital of Assyria. A Gentile city containing 120,000 children, Nineveh was located on the Tigris River, 400 miles from the Mediterranean. The city stretched 10 miles wide and 30 miles long, from Calah on the south to Khorsabad on the north. The city proper was 1½ miles by 3 miles, surrounded by five walls and three moats, with walls 100 feet high and wide enough for four chariots abreast. There were great mansions, halls, and a temple built like a pyramid. Archaeologists have found no tablets telling of the conversion of Nineveh *en masse*. Jesus referred to Jonah in Matthew 2:34–42.

God told Jonah to go to Nineveh, to warn the people of their wickedness, but Jonah did not want to do this. He fled from the presence of God by taking passage on a ship from Joppa to Tarshish (Tartessus in Spain). A great storm blew up, and the sailors threw their cargo overboard. They decided to cast lots to see who had brought the curse of God on them; the lot fell to Jonah. They questioned Jonah and discovered that he was fleeing from the presence of God. Jonah said that if they would throw him overboard, the storm would calm. They hesitated, but finally in desperation threw him over. The storm ceased, and the men feared God greatly.

The Lord appointed a great fish to swallow Jonah, and he remained in the belly of the fish for three days and three nights. Jonah prayed to God and promised to obey Him if saved. God had the fish vomit Jonah on the dry land, probably near Joppa and probably witnessed by many people. God again told Jonah to go to Nineveh, which he did immediately. It is possible that the miracle of his rescue preceded him. Jonah arrived at the city and went a day's journey into it.

He prophesied that ". . . Yet forty days and Nineveh will be overthrown" (Jonah 3:4). The people and the king believed and repented, and the king issued a proclamation to all, telling them to fast and to turn from their evil ways in hope that God would repent. God recognized this great change and decided not to destroy them. This embarrassed and angered Jonah, because he felt it made a fool of him. He went from the city and sat in a shelter to wait and see what would happen. God appointed a plant to grow in one day to shade Jonah, and the next day appointed a worm to wither the plant. God caused a warm wind to blow which, together with the hot sun, caused Jonah to wish he were dead. God rebuked him for being concerned with one plant and himself, and not being concerned with a city that contained 120,000 children. ". . . 120,000 persons who do not know the difference between their right and left hand . . ." (Jonah 4:11). This is a story of the redemptive God in action.

For those who have difficulty in believing that God could cause a fish story like this to be factual, they should recall that man in all his weakness and imperfections has now sent a man to and from the moon. If this had been prophesied even twenty-five years previously, probably not one person would have believed it. God created the earth, the moon, and the man.

MICAH

Time 749 B.C.–693 B.C.

Author Micah, a country preacher, native of Moresheth-gath, twenty miles southwest of Jerusalem. A man of strong convictions and great courage, he was filled with the Spirit of the Lord. He was a contemporary of Hosea and Isaiah and seems to have had Amos' passion for justice and Hosea's heart of love.

Theme He pleaded with the country folk in the northern kingdom of Israel and Judah during the days of Kings Jotham, Ahaz, and Hezekiah, before the fall of Samaria to Assyria. He tried to tell the people of the judgment that would befall Israel and Judah because of their sins and prophesied their destruction and final restoration through God's grace. He was greatly concerned with the wealthy landowners taking advantage of the peasants.

Samaria, the capital of the northern kingdom of Israel, is corrupt: The judges and priests accept bribes, and the rich take advantage of the poor. Sin is prevalent, and the people have ignored the teachings and warnings of Elijah, Elisha, and Amos. Micah prophesies that the Assyrians will carry away all of Israel and leave Samaria in a heap. This all becomes reality in 721 B.C.

He denounces the unmerciful actions of the ruling classes in their treatment of the poor by seizing their homes and ejecting women and children. They bribe false prophets to condone their actions. Micah then condemns Jerusalem and its religious leaders and pronounces its doom. ". . . Who abhor justice And twist everything that is straight." (Micah 3:9). In all his condemnation, he prophesies the coming of Christ (Micah 2:12, 13) and God's love and mercy.

Micah tells that God warns before He punishes. The people of Judah will be taken captive to Babylon. This he foretells one hundred years before Babylon conquers Assyria, which at that time is ruling the world. He prophesies Christ's rule of the whole earth and His calling back of His people to Mount Zion. He prophesies that Christ, the deliverer, will be born in Bethlehem. This seven-hundred-year-old prophecy leads the wise men to seek the newborn king (*see* Micah 5:2). The land must first be purged of its lovers of idolatry, sorcery, carnal weapons, and all who do not obey the will of God.

He changes his theme and pictures God as in a lawsuit with His people of Israel. God indicts the accused. The hills and the mountains of the whole earth are the jury. God then addresses His message to the Israelites, reminding them of their deliverance from bondage in Egypt, His other blessings, and His frustration with their worship of Baal. True religion is the only acceptable worship; not offerings or sacrifices, but justice, loyalty, and divine guidance. Micah does not teach salvation by good works, but man's righteousness is the result of forgiveness. He sums up the true Hebrew religion as ". . . do justice, to love kindness, And to walk humbly with your God" (Micah 6:8). He chastens Israel for keeping the statutes of Omri, sixth king of northern Israel, and his son Ahab, who marries the sinful and vicious Phoenician, Jezebel, daughter of the king of Tyre.

Micah confesses for Israel the loss of the godly man, the treachery of all men, their evil ways and lack of trust even of their own friends and relatives. No other god pardons iniquity, passes over transgressions, and does not anger forever. He will again have compassion for His people, cast His memory of their sins into the sea, and show His love of Jacob and Abraham and their people, as He promised in the days of old.

NAHUM

Time   663 B.C.–607 B.C. This prophecy of Nahum about 630 B.C.
Author Nahum, a prophet of Elkosh, a city of Galilee.
Theme Nahum continued Jonah's prediction of the fall of Nineveh, which at that time sounded utterly impossible, because Nineveh was the ultrafortified majestic capital of Assyria and was at the peak of its total worldly power. Nineveh fell in 612 or 607 B.C. A hundred and fifty years earlier, Jonah had prophesied the destruction of Nineveh, but it had repented and had been saved. Nahum now said it was doomed. The Assyrians were an aggressive, warring, brutal people. They built their empire on loot. They skinned prisoners alive, cut off their hands and feet, noses and ears, put out their eyes and pulled out their tongues, burned children alive, and made mounds of human skulls—all to impress the world with their might and to put fear in their hearts. They said they did this in obedience to their god Ashur. God doomed them to perish.

Nahum addresses his vision to Nineveh. God is jealous and avenging, slow to anger, but He is all-powerful and can rebuke the sea or make mountains quake. The guilty cannot defend themselves against His might. He will put an end to those who oppose Him. No matter how strong Nineveh thinks it is, God will destroy it. God will restore His kingdom and His people; Nineveh has plundered and destroyed them.

Nahum tells how a siege will be laid by the Medes, who will have brilliantly painted shields, purple robes, spears, knives, and chariots with flashing knives on their wheels. Too late the drunken rulers will try to rally their warriors to defend the city. The Tigris River will cause a flood, which will wash away most of the wall of the impenetrable fortress, and the Medes will walk into the defenseless city.

The city will be plundered, and the people will cry in dismay, because God will say, "I am against you" (see Nahum 2:13). The Medes' armies will swarm through the city; there will be so many dead bodies that people will stumble over them. God will make such a desolation of Nineveh that nations will look on her nakedness and shame and none will bemoan her fate. God's might and righteousness will prevail.

So complete was the destruction of Nineveh that every trace of its existence was abolished for several hundred years. Alexander the Great fought the battle of Arbela near Nineveh in 331 B.C. and did not know that there had ever been a city there. When Xenophon and his great army passed by two hundred years later, he thought the mounds were the ruins of a Parthian city. It was not until A.D. 1820–1845 that there was an identification of the site by an Englishman by the name of Layard. Later, palaces were discovered and one of the greatest libraries of ancient Babylon was uncovered in this sinful city.

HABAKKUK

Time   625 B.C.–598 B.C. Probably about 607 B.C. during Jehoiakim's reign.

Author   Habakkuk was a little-known prophet, possibly a musician in the Temple, and a contemporary of Jeremiah. He lived in Judah, but seemed to be arguing with God as to why the good and innocent should suffer as much as the wicked.

Theme   Pride and cruelty always bring destruction. The just shall live by faith.

Nebuchadnezzar had already carried off some nobles to captivity, including Daniel. There were two more deportations to follow—in 587 B.C. and 586 B.C.

Habakkuk complained to God. He couldn't understand why God could see all the evil going on in the world and do nothing about it. He could see the doom of Judah, but couldn't understand why a more sinful nation, Babylon, should be entitled to conquer Judah. He acknowledged that Judah was full of lawlessness, was sinful, guilty of oppression of the poor and idolatry—but God was doing nothing to stop it. Habakkuk didn't appoint a task force to study the problem; he talked directly to God.

He then climbs up to the watchtower, to wait for God to answer him. The Babylonians are coming to destroy what is left. God answers him. He admits the wickedness of the Chaldeans and Babylonians, but says that they, in turn, will be destroyed by their own wickedness, and God's people shall yet fill the earth. Pride and cruelty always bring destruction. Men sometimes have to wait to know what God's plan is.

Habakkuk prays to God and admits His greatness and sovereignty over the universe and everything in it. He realizes that God has His own plan and His own timetable. We can only see the small part in front of us, and we must wait for God to pull back the curtain and reveal His total plan at His own appointed time.

Man shall live by faith, and faith is the ability to feel secure in God's care, entrusting our lives to His judgment. God's people have a future. Habakkuk believed this and tried to tell the people, but they would not listen.

ZEPHANIAH

Time 639 B.C.–608 B.C. Probably written about 630 B.C., during the reign of King Josiah (J), one of the few good kings, who had been preceded by Manasseh (J), the worst, who ruled for fifty-five years.

Author Zephaniah, son of Cushi, and directly related to King Hezekiah (J).

Theme Zephaniah seemed to be talking to the whole world, which was not large in his day, as well as to Judah. The northern kingdom of Israel had already fallen to Assyria. He pronounced doom on Judah, but promised a happy restoration, which has not happened to this day; therefore, it must mean when Christ returns to this earth, to reign in power and glory. A temporary reform in 622 B.C. was probably a result of Zephaniah's influence. Judah was captured and desolated twenty years later.

A vision and the word of God came to Zephaniah. God is going to show His vengeance and punishment to every nation on the face of the earth. He condemns Judah and all the other countries surrounding her and all classes of sinners for their idolatry and sinful ways. He condemns Milcom, the Ammonite god, and Mortar, which is probably the marketplace in Jerusalem. The great day of the Lord is near; God is bitter because of man's sinful ways and is going to show His wrath in the form of bitter distress for men.

He outlines all the nations to fall: Gaza; Ashkelon; Ashdod; Ekron; Canaan; Ethiopia, which was southern Egypt; Assyria with Nineveh, its capital, and terror of the whole world, will all be devastated by Babylon. He then reverts to promises of a future restoration of a people who have a new revelation of God and a pure speech, or reform system of thought. This redeemed remnant of Jews will be established with God in their midst, who ". . . will take refuge in the name of the Lord" (Zephaniah 3:12). This is God's promise to Abraham: ". . . I will give you renown and praise Among all the peoples of the earth, When I restore your fortunes before your eyes, Says the Lord" (Zephaniah 3:20).

HAGGAI

Time   520 B.C.–516 B.C. Covers a four-year period around 520 B.C.
Author Haggai, a Levite prophet. He could possibly have been an old man, who had seen the old Temple before it was destroyed. He died and was buried in Jerusalem.
Theme In 536 B.C., 50,000 Jews under Zerubbabel, the governor, returned to Jerusalem from captivity in Babylon. They built an altar, offered sacrifice, started work on the Temple in 535 B.C. and then stopped, partly due to pressure from their enemy neighbors and partly due to their own selfish desires to build fine homes for themselves. As a result of putting their own interests ahead of God's, they had poor crops, drought, failing business trade, and rapid inflation—"wages in a purse of holes." A new king, Darius, ascended to the throne of Persia, and he was kindly disposed to the Jews.

In the second year of Darius, the word of God came to tell Haggai to talk to Zerubbabel the governor, Joshua the high priest, and to all the people. They had sown much and reaped little, clothed themselves but were not warm, drank but could not satisfy their thirst, and ". . . he who earns, earns wages to put into a purse with holes" (Haggai 1:6). In other words, they were deprived by inflation. God said He caused these things to happen because the people neglected God's house and busied themselves with their own.

Then the people heard and feared God. Haggai received word from God that ". . . 'I am with you,' declares the Lord" (Haggai 1:13). Work was started on the Temple in 520 B.C. and it was finished in 516 B.C. Haggai, who had probably seen Solomon's Temple, in all its glory, was disappointed in this new Temple. But God spoke to Haggai, Zerubbabel, and Joshua, and said He was with them.

He said that in a little while He would shake the heavens, the earth, the sea, and all nations, so that the treasures of all nations would pour into Jerusalem and fill the house with splendor (*see* Haggai 2:6, 7). This is interpreted by some theologians to be a Messianic vision of God's eternal Temple, the Church, built of men's redeemed souls. The final Church, of fadeless and brilliant glory and a culmination of God's work, will be the Temple of God. The shakeup eventually yields earthly things for the birth of God's eternal Temple and Kingdom.

In his final vision, Haggai hears God say that He will make Zerubbabel like a signet ring, for he has been chosen by God.

The essence of this book is, do great things for God, and He will be with you. Treat God at least as well as you treat yourself. Every man should leave behind him something that lasts and that will be eternal in God's Kingdom.

ZECHARIAH

Time 520 B.C.–518 B.C., during two to four years of the reign of Darius, king of Persia. Prophecies and visions for two of the four years during the rebuilding of the Temple.

Author Zechariah, son of Berechiah, son of Iddo, a prophet, of the priestly tribe. Born in Babylon in captivity. Lived in Jerusalem, probably to an old age. Returned to Jerusalem with the first group of 50,000 when about two years of age. Was very young, probably eighteen to twenty, during his prophecy.

Theme In the first ten chapters, Zechariah has many visions—all in a single night. They are not easy for us to interpret now. They were not easy for Zechariah to understand, either. He would have the vision, question the meaning, and it would be interpreted to him by an angel. Haggai, who was prophesying at the same time, dealt more with the religious life of the people. Zechariah was more interested in the national, political, and futuristic situations. Some messages were to his priest, Joshua, and some to his governor, Zerubbabel. He urged the people to rebuild the Temple, and to cut out the evils of their day so they would be free. A spiritual change was needed. He envisioned more details than any other prophet of the first coming of Christ, and also of His ultimate return. The words "thus saith the Lord" are used eighty-nine times.

The vision of the horses and the man standing among the myrtle trees represent God's judgment against all nations who have been too severe against Israel. Jerusalem shall again be a great and powerful city. The vision of the four horns probably represents the powers which have and will scatter Israel—Babylon, Mede-Persia, Greece, and Rome—but God is in power even when His people are temporarily conquered.

The vision of the man with the measuring line was probably to forecast the building of the Temple walls seventy-five years later. A wider version would be to the time when ". . . many nations will join themselves to the Lord in that day and will become My people . . ." (Zechariah 2:11). The vision of Joshua, the high priest, and his filthy clothing, represents the sins of the people. Joshua's clothing is removed in one day, symbolic of the coming of Christ, who by His death in one day represented atonement for all men's sins.

The vision of the candlestick and two olive trees is representative of the lustrousness of God's house. The candlestick was in the Temple and the Tabernacle. The two olive trees refer to Joshua and Zerubbabel, especially Zerubbabel.

The vision of the flying scroll, a sheet thirty by fifteen feet, inscribed with the law, and flying over the whole land, cursing those who sin and steal and renouncing sin by removing sinners, meaning judgment before a final blessing.

In the vision of the woman in the ephah (a cooking vessel or a basket holding a bushel), a woman in the ephah symbolically represents religious evil. Two other women, with wings like storks, bear her away to Babylon, the source of the evil. The vision of the four chariots represents the messengers of God administering judgment on Israel's enemies.

There is the vision of the making of the crown for Joshua and his coronation. God gave David the plans for the Temple, which was built by Solomon and later destroyed by the Babylonians. Zerubbabel, who was a direct descendant of David, was now rebuilding the Temple. Joshua was crowned as representing the branch (branch of David's house), symbolic of the future branch, or Messiah, who will be both priest and king of the Kingdom of God.

During the exile in Babylon for seventy years, the Jews had fasted on the fourth, fifth, seventh, and tenth months, mourning the destruction of Jerusalem and their Temple. Their question was: Should these fasts be continued, now that it was assured that the Temple would be rebuilt? Zechariah reminded them that since their return, these religious events were mainly for their own pleasure. He reminded them that although they were only a remnant, existing by permission of the Persian king, they would someday, by God's grace, become a great nation. Their streets would be filled with happy boys and girls and old men and old women, and would be the center of the world's civilization, where people would come to learn about their God.

Chapters 9–11 are difficult to interpret. Judah's struggle with Greece is forecast, as well as that with Alexander the Great, devastating named cities, yet sparing Jerusalem. The continued struggle against the Greek Ptolemies and Seleucids and Maccabeans is forecast. In the midst of this struggle, there is forecast the entry of Christ into Jerusalem, the day of final triumph, the start of the Church of God, and God's ultimate glorious victory. Zechariah prophesies the final gathering of God's people. The parable of the shepherds tells how God's flock has been scattered and slaughtered because the shepherds are false and have rejected the Good Shepherd. This is the betrayal of Christ by Judas Iscariot, as subsequently quoted in Matthew. The rejection of the true Shepherd is an indication of the postponement of the Jews' reunion in the land. They are to be delivered over to the worthless shepherd, thought to be the destruction of Jerusalem by the Romans after the death of Christ.

In chapters 12–14, Zechariah pictures Judah's or God's struggle with all nations, even to the end of time.

He depicts the branch as a member of the house of David, the branch representing Jesus and His death, which is God's source of power against all nations. There will be an eventual removal of all idols and false prophets from the earth. He finally pictures Judah's struggle with all nations, God's victory and ultimate universal reign, the day of the Lord's return, and His everlasting Kingdom.

Zechariah gives a clear forecast of the coming of Christ, and is quoted many times in the New Testament as to his warnings. He tells of Christ's death for the atonement of man's sins, His authority as representative of God, His universal Kingdom, His entry into Jerusalem, ". . . Humble, and mounted on a donkey, Even on a colt, the foal of a donkey" (Zechariah 9:9), and His betrayal for thirty pieces of silver. He pictures the ultimate Kingdom of God ". . . living waters will flow out of Jerusalem . . . it will be in summer as well as in winter" (Zechariah 14:8). "And people will live in it, and there will be no more curse, for Jerusalem will dwell in security" (Zechariah 14:11).

MALACHI

Time Opinions vary, from 470 B.C. to 397 B.C. Probably about 425 B.C., one hundred years after Haggai and Zechariah.
Author Malachi. Nothing is known of a man by the name of Malachi, who is a contemporary of Nehemiah. Malachi means "my messenger," and some scholars speculate that there was no one by that name, but that this book could have been written by Ezra. The book is quoted in Mark, Luke, and Romans.
Theme History was repeating itself for the Jewish people. They were degenerating in all aspects of life and were trying to blame God. Malachi said that the fault was with the people and that God would bless them if they would only obey His laws.

536 B.C.: The captives had returned with Haggai and Zechariah.
520–16 (515) B.C.: They rebuilt the Temple.
457 B.C. (60 years later): Ezra came to reestablish the nation.
444 B.C. (13 years later): Nehemiah came to rebuild the wall.
The Jews had been back one hundred years when Malachi preached.

The book takes a question-and-answer form. The people say to God, "How have you loved us?" and He answers that the Israelites of Jacob have been restored, but the Edomites of Esau have not been, and never will be. He chastens the people for offering diseased and blemished animals for sacrifice, which has been an insult to God. God is particularly displeased with the priests, who have become careless, slovenly, and corrupt, and who are responsible for the attitudes of the people. God criticizes the men for divorcing their wives and marrying heathen women. The people's attitude has been that those who lie, cheat, and are corrupt are more prosperous. They are saying "Why serve God?" Malachi's answer is that the coming day of judgment will show whether it pays to serve God or not.

God took a very angry attitude toward the people, because they were withholding their tithes. He said they were robbing God of money that He had merely entrusted to them. God promised prosperity to those who respected Him, saying, ". . . I will . . . open for you the windows of heaven, and pour out for you a blessing . . ." (Malachi 3:10). A faithful few swore to be true to the Lord. He made a book of remembrance of them and said He would spare them in the final day of judgment, when they would be exalted above the unrighteous.

In closing this book and the Old Testament, Malachi talks about the day of the Lord, telling them to remember the law of Moses. He tells of the day when Elijah will usher in the day of the Lord in the form of John the Baptist, which He did four hundred years later. The Old Testament closes with these words: "Behold, I am going to send you Elijah the prophet before the coming of the great and terrible day of the Lord. And he will restore the hearts of the fathers to their children, and the hearts of the children to their fathers, lest I come and smite the land with a curse" (Malachi 4:5, 6).

SUMMARY OF THE OLD TESTAMENT AS PERTAINING TO THE FORETELLING OF THE COMING OF THE MESSIAH (JESUS CHRIST) 1500 B.C.–400 B.C.

The Old Testament is the story of the beginnings of mankind and the creation of the world. Very quickly it concentrates on the story of the Hebrew nation and man's struggle with himself to obey God. More importantly, it is the weaving of the story of the expectancy of the coming of one majestic person who will come to be known as the Messiah (Jesus Christ).

The first references and hints of this Messiah are very dim and difficult to interpret or understand, except by learned scholars of the Bible. In tracing the earlier part of the story of the predictions of the coming of the Messiah, it is easier to understand the full story, in the brief form of this book, if the reader will relax and accept the statements made, without having to read all the documentation. The Bible has been determined to be factual by scholars who took the time to do the proper research to reach the conclusions that are presented. As the story develops, these predictions become specific, more abundant, and more clearly spoken. By the time all of these threads are woven together, there can be no doubt that the story of Christ has been foretold in detail, in writing, and that the story can refer to no other person in history but the Messiah, Jesus Christ. This summary concentrates on weaving these threads into the tapestry of the picture of Jesus Christ and the new story to be told in the New Testament, of His life and the establishment of His Church.

Genesis. The Hebrew nation was to be founded for the purpose of blessing all nations (Genesis 18:18; 22:18). The setting in Jerusalem for the final scenes of Jesus' life was depicted in the life of Melchizedek (Genesis 14:18–20), as later referred to in Psalms 110:4 and Hebrews 7. The Messiah was first referred to as Shiloh (Genesis 49:10, 11) and was to arise from the tribe of Judah and rule all nations.

Exodus. The Passover (Exodus 12), celebrated for fourteen hundred years before Christ, was an indication of the ultimate death of the Lamb of God.

Numbers. Moses made a serpent of brass, so that whoever looked at it would not die by snakebite (Numbers 21:6–9). This is interpreted (John 3:14) by Jesus to be a picture of Himself on the cross as the Saviour for all who have been bitten by sin, who would look to Him for life and be saved. He is referred to as a Star of David (Numbers 24:17, 19), who will have dominion over man.

Deuteronomy. God will raise up one person, called Shiloh, a star, like Moses, through whom He will speak to all mankind (Genesis 49:10).

First Samuel. David is anointed king of Israel and is a central figure all through the Old Testament. As Abraham was the founder of the Messianic nation, so David is the founder of the Messianic family.

Second Samuel. God says He will establish the throne of David forever in one great king, who will live forever and establish a kingdom of endless duration. This promise of God is repeated over and over (2 Samuel 7:16).

Psalms. Mostly written around 1000 B.C., the Psalms referred to ". . . the Lord and . . . His Anointed" (Psalms 2:2). ". . . blessed are all who take refuge in Him" (Psalms 2:12). His resurrection (*see* Psalms 16:10). His dying words "My God, my God, why hast Thou forsaken me . . ." (Psalms 22:1). The sneers of His enemies, "All who see me sneer at me . . ." (Psalms 22:7). His crucifixion, ". . . They pierced my hands and my feet" (Psalms 22:16). "They divide my garments among them, And for my clothing they cast lots" (Psalms 22:18), as actually happened at His final crucifixion (Matthew 27:35). His betrayal by Judas is foretold (Psalms 41:9), as well as His throne and reign forever and forever (Psalms 6; 7; 8; 11; 17; 19). His method of teaching in parables (Psalms 78:2, quoted in Matthew 13:34, 35). God's promise of the endurance of David's throne under God's firstborn (Psalms 89:3, 4, 27, 28, 35, 36, 37). This eternal kingdom and priesthood is later quoted by Jesus Himself in Matthew 21:42–44 (Psalms 110:1, 4). His rejection by His own people is foretold and referred to by Jesus in Matthew 21:42–44, (Psalms 118:22).

Isaiah. The glory, the magnitude, and the reign of the coming Messiah are foretold by Isaiah (Isaiah 2:2–4). He is referred to as a Branch of the Tree of David, and is a guide and refuge for His people (Isaiah 4:2, 5, 6). The virgin birth and deity by use of the word *Immanuel,* which means "God with us," are later quoted in Matthew 1:23 as referring to Jesus (Isaiah 7:13, 14). The same person previously referred to as Shiloh, the Star, and the Prophet is referred to as Child, Son, Wonderful, Counselor, Mighty God, Eternal Father, Prince of Peace, and Ruler forever. The very spot of His ministry in Galilee is foretold, hundreds of years in advance (Isaiah 9:1, 2, 6, 7) and presents a beautiful picture of the glory of the world to be under the reign of the coming Messiah (Isaiah 11:1–10). The resurrection of Jesus after death (Isaiah 25:8; 26:1, 19) and the Messiah is foretold as a King and as a man (Isaiah 32:1, 2 KJV).

Also foretold are the exact miracles performed by Jesus in His ministry (Isaiah 35:5, 6); and the joy and happiness of the redeemed and ransomed of the Messiah (Isaiah 35:8–10). The glory of Jesus and His tenderness and mercy are portrayed (Isaiah 40:5, 10, 11). The glory of the King and Messiah's rule will be for Gentiles as well as Jews (Isaiah 42:1–11). The sufferings and persecutions of the Messiah for the redemption of man's sins is foretold, together with the ultimate songs of joy of the Christian Era (Isaiah 53; 54; 55; 60; 61). The "light of the world" is foretold, which is the title given to Jesus many times in the New Testament (Isaiah 60:1, 2, 20). The use of the name Christian instead of Israelite is foretold as being used after Christ (Isaiah 62:2; 65:15).

Jeremiah. Jeremiah makes the same predictions as to the use of the word *Branch* of the family of David for a coming King (Jeremiah 23:5, 6).

Ezekiel. The spread of Christianity and effects of the Messiah are compared to a life-giving stream of good water, in which fish will multiply in abundance (Ezekiel 47:1–12).

Daniel. Six hundred years before Christ, Daniel foretold the rise and fall of the four empires of Babylon, Persia, Greece, and Rome and predicted that the Messiah would emerge in the fourth (Roman) kingdom (Daniel 2:40, 44). He also forecast the exact date for the coming of the Messiah and the exact term of His ministry (Daniel 9:24–27). These were amazingly accurate predictions.

Hosea. Hosea repeats that the Messiah's kingdom will include the Gentiles (Hosea 1:10).

Joel. The Messiah will institute the evangelization of the whole world under the leadership of the Holy Spirit (Joel 2:28, 32; 3:13, 14).

Jonah. Jesus compared Jonah's three days and three nights in the fish's stomach (Jonah 1:17) to the miracle of His own three-day resurrection from the tomb (Matthew 12:40).

Micah. Bethlehem shall be the Messiah's birthplace, and His influence shall radiate to the ends of the earth (Micah 5:2–5).

Zephaniah. The Gospel of Jesus Christ is to be a new and pure language for all people, to communicate with God (Zephaniah 3:9).

Zechariah. Zechariah is not only very specific in his prophecies of the Messiah's death for the atonement of man's sins, His deity, and His universal Kingdom, but also in the details of His entry into Jerusalem riding on a colt, His betrayal for thirty pieces of silver, and how His prosecutors would look at His pierced body (Zechariah 3:8, 9; 6:12, 13; 9:9, 10; 11:12, 13; 12:8, 10; 13:1).

Malachi. Malachi foretells the coming of the messenger, John the

Baptist, who will prepare the way for the Messiah (Malachi 3:1; 4:5). Jesus, in Matthew 11:7–14, refers to John the Baptist as prophesied by Malachi.

These writings by different writers, which cover hundreds of years before Christ, are amazing in the way they fit together in detail. They are so accurate that they appear to have been written after Christ, instead of before. Only one God could have been responsible for such a perfect assemblage of prophetic information.

DEVELOPMENTS IN CIVILIZATION
400 B.C.–A.D. 1

The most highly developed and powerful civilization during this period was that of the Romans, who made great advances in every aspect of life.

While the plebeians, or commoners, were struggling for equality with the patricians, or nobility, they were being accepted in the political and religious arenas. They achieved full equality in 287 B.C. The first theatrical performances were staged in Rome, and Roman comedy developed. The first Roman coins were introduced. The Romans continued their policy of military aggression and expansion and conquered much of Italy. The Appian Way, the famous Roman highway that was 356 miles long, was completed. The Romans learned about Greek medicine through prisoners of war. For entertainment, the Romans had ball games, dice games, and board games; also, there was the public combat of the gladiators in Rome. The Venus De Milo sculpture was created (c. 150 B.C.) and the Roman poets Catullus, Virgil and Horace were writing; the best Roman literature was produced during this time. The first Roman prison, Tullianum, was erected.

In the rivalry between Caesar and Pompey for control of Rome, Caesar was the victor. A few years later, Caesar was murdered by a group of conspirators. There was more political intrigue when Mark Antony and Cleopatra committed suicide after their defeat at the famous battle of Actium. Octavian, whose fleets defeated those of Antony and Cleopatra, became the most powerful man in Rome and remained so through Rome's rise to the peak of its empire.

In Greece, Sparta was the supreme military power, while Athens was the leader in culture. Aristotle taught at the time; he laid the foundation for musical theory and founded the Peripatetic School in Athens. At the same time, great progress was being made in Greek sculpture, painting, and the arts.

Between 336 B.C. and 323 B.C. Alexander the Great ruled Greece and expanded its borders. After his death, there were civil wars for several years.

The famous men of this time included Diocles, the physician; Archimedes, the mathematician; Eratosthenes, the scientist; and Apollonius, the mathematician.

After a series of wars, the Romans completed their conquest of all

Greece. Subsequently, the Greek civilization existed under Roman rule for 300 years.

Egypt had deteriorated into a minor entity. This was the time of the Thirtieth Dynasty in Egypt—the last native house to rule there. Persia reconquered Egypt. Alexander the Great founded Alexandria, which served as the capital and, with its famous library and school of medicine, as an important center of Greek culture. Heron, the great mathematician, founded the first college of technology at Alexandria. Cleopatra VII was the last queen of Egypt.

There were many advancements in China. The Great Wall of China, which was 1,500 miles long, was constructed. The Chinese dictionary of 10,000 characters was written. China was expanding; the first Chinese ships reached the east coast of India.

Two of Rome's emperors were born in Spain. The Romans built many cities, roads, and aqueducts in Spain. Christianity was introduced later, while Spain was under Roman rule.

During this time period, the Jews were persecuted, and the Temple at Jerusalem was desecrated. Judea was annexed by Rome and was divided among Herod's sons at his death. In 4 B.C., Jesus Christ was born in Bethlehem. The change from A.D. 1 to 4 B.C. is due to calendar adjustments.

Greek conquerors and Parthians absorbed the Persian culture over a period of 400 years. The history of Babylon came to an end; the Babylonians re-established at the new city of Seleucia. At this time, Antiochus III, the ruler of Persia, was at the peak of his power. Later, he was defeated by the Romans.

Asoka, the Indian emperor, erected columns forty feet high, inscribed with his laws. Bactria, a province of India, broke away from the foreign rule of the Greeks and became independent. Some time later, the Greeks were driven out by India.

In the Scandinavian area, the Goth-Teutonic peoples of central Europe were emerging into a factor in the world civilization. The people of Sweden traded with the Roman Empire; they traded furs and amber for glass, bronze, and silver coins.

Britannia (England) was conquered by the Emperor Claudius, and Rome ruled for 400 years.

The Indian civilization in Mexico came to an end.

The world was growing in knowledge and was becoming more highly developed, and its growing pains included violence and warring. But many important contributions to civilization were made, and the major cultures advanced greatly in their developments; this was an eventful period in history.

CHRONOLOGICAL SUMMARY

GREECE

399 B.C. Socrates died in this year.
395 B.C. The city-states of Athens, Thebes, Corinth, and Argos joined forces against Sparta, but the Spartan general, Agesilaus, defeated the allied troops at Coronea in 394 B.C.
393 B.C. Plato wrote *Apologia*.
384 B.C. Aristotle, the famous philosopher, was born. Demosthenes, the statesman and orator, was also born at this time.
380 B.C. Pioneers settled around the Black and Caspian Seas.
377 B.C. Hippocrates, the Greek physician, died. Catapults were used as weapons of war. While Sparta became the supreme power, Athens led in culture.
356 B.C. Alexander the Great was born.
350 B.C. There was general peace between the Greek states. Philip of Macedonia defeated the Greek states and united them against Persia. Corinthian columns appeared in Greek architecture.
343 B.C. Aristotle laid the foundation for musical theory. Great progress was made in Greek sculpture, painting, and the arts.
339 B.C. Xenocrates became the head of the Athens Academy.
336 B.C. Philip was assassinated and succeeded by Alexander the Great. This was the date of the birth of Zeno, the Greek philosopher who founded the Stoic School.
334 B.C. Aristotle founded the Peripatetic School in Athens.
330 B.C. The Greek explorer, Pytheas of Marseilles, reached Briton.
328 B.C. Alexander married the Bactrian princess, Roxana, and invaded India.
325 B.C. Alexander ordered his general, Nearchus, to explore the Indian Ocean, the Persian Gulf, and the Euphrates River.

323 B.C.   Alexander died in Babylon. His empire was divided among his generals, who promptly started fighting among themselves for additional power and territory.

316 B.C.   Olympias, the mother of Alexander the Great, was put to death by Cassander, who founded Salonika (Thessalonica) and rebuilt Thebes.

311 B.C.   This marked the end of civil wars among Alexander's successors.

291 B.C.   Menander, the master of Greek new comedy, died.

280 B.C.   This time marked the completion of the Colossus of Rhodes, which was built in honor of the sun god, Helios. It was approximately the same size as the Statue of Liberty and made of bronze. The colossus, one of the Seven Wonders of the Ancient World, was destroyed by an earthquake in 224 B.C. Famous men of this time were Diocles, the physician; Archimedes, the mathematician; and Apollonius, the mathematician. There were ball games, board games, and dice throwing.

275–195 B.C.   Eratosthenes, a Greek mathematician, found a way to measure the circumference and the diameter of the earth. He stated that the earth was round and that the sun's rays were parallel. He knew that at noon in Alexandria, Egypt, a vertical post cast a shadow; at the same time, in Syene, a town directly south, a vertical post cast no shadow. He developed the angles of these lines, and by geometry determined that the diameter of the earth was approximately 7,850 miles. The present correct figure is 7,900 miles (Columbus, 1,790 years later, must have known the earth's dimensions and that it was round).

261 B.C.   Athens was captured by Antigonus II, the ruler of Macedonia. (Antigonus I had been one of Alexander's generals and had seized a part of Turkey as his empire when Alexander had died.) Athens was liberated thirty-two years later (229 B.C.).

250 B.C.   Arcesilaus founded the second Academy of Athens.

230 B.C.   Oil lamps were used in Greece.

221 B.C.   Antigonus III of Macedonia took possession of Sparta, and King Cleomenes fled to Egypt.

200 B.C.   During the Second Macedonian War, Attica was ravaged; Philip V of Macedonia was defeated by the Romans.

192 B.C.   There was a war between Sparta and Rome.

179 B.C.   The first stone bridge was constructed in Rome.

172 B.C.   In a war between Rome and Macedonia, the Romans were defeated by Perseus, son of Philip V and the last

king of Macedonia. Four years later, the Romans defeated him at Pydna, and Macedonia was placed under the rule of a Roman governor. This event marked the beginning of Roman world domination.

170 B.C. The earliest-known paved streets appeared in Rome.
159 B.C. The first water clock was introduced in Rome.
147 B.C. Even while Greece was fighting its final death struggle with Rome, Sparta and Archaean League continued to battle each other. The Romans completed their conquest of all Greece. The Isle of Delos became a center of international commerce, but in 88 B.C. Mithridates of Pontus destroyed Delos when he tried to drive the Romans from Greece. The Romans then burned Athens and its shipyards. The Greek civilization spread for 300 years under Roman rule.
146 B.C. The Romans destroyed Corinth.
140 B.C. The Venus De Milo sculpture was created.
88 B.C. There were uprisings against Roman rule in Athens.

ANCIENT ROME

396 B.C. The Romans captured the Etruscan city of Veii.
390 B.C. The Gauls (French) from northern Italy captured Rome, sacked it, and withdrew.
387 B.C. Rome was rebuilt, and walls were built around the city one year later.
366 B.C. The first plebeian was elected to the office of Consul in Rome.
365 B.C. Etruscan actors staged the first theatrical performances in Rome.
350–300 B.C. Northern Italy was subjected to Roman rule.
338 B.C. The first Roman coins were introduced.
300 B.C. Roman comedy developed. Roman plebeians were admitted to the priesthood.
287 B.C. There was full equality between the patricians (nobility) and the plebeians (commoners).
283 B.C. Corsica (west of central Italy) was captured by the Romans.
280 B.C. Pyrrhus, the king of Epirus (in the northwest part of Greece), helped Tarentum defeat the Romans, but he did not exploit his victories; he left in 275 B.C.
275 B.C. Antiochus I, one of Alexander's generals and the founder of the Seleucid Dynasty which was to rule Syria and Mesopotamia, defeated the Gauls.

146 / Chronological Summary

272 B.C. Rome conquered central and southern Italy. The Romans continued the construction (which began in 312 B.C.) of the Appian Way (the first and most famous Roman highway, which is still in use today) from Capua to Beneventum, Tarentum, and Brundisium—333 miles.

265 B.C. First contact of the Romans with Greek medicine, through prisoners of war. There were ball games, dice games, and board games.

250 B.C. The first Roman prison, Tullianum, was erected. There was public combat of the gladiators in Rome. The comedies of the Greek slave, Livius Andronicus, were first performed in Rome (240 B.C.).

239 B.C. The island of Sardinia became part of the Roman empire.

228 B.C. This was the first time Rome had ambassadors to Corinth and Athens.

225 B.C. Quintus Fabius Pictor, the first Roman historian, was born.

222 B.C. Rome conquered most of northern Italy.

220 B.C. Flaminian Way, a great military road which was two hundred miles long, was built from Rome to Ariminum on the Adriatic Sea (the Aemilian Way to Milan was extended in 187 B.C.).

202 B.C. Pictor wrote Roman history in Greek.

183 B.C. Pisa and Parma in northern Italy became Roman.

179 B.C. The first stone bridge was erected in Rome.

170 B.C. The earliest known paved street in Rome.

168 B.C. After the Battle of Pydna, the Macedonians were sold as slaves in Rome—the men for $50 to $75, the women for up to $1,000.

147 B.C. At this time, the Roman Empire consisted of seven provinces: Sicily; Sardinia; Corsica; two Spains (actually Spain and Portugal); Africa (Carthage); and Macedonia (Greece).

133 B.C. Asia Minor became the eighth Roman province.

112 B.C. There was a war in Africa between Rome and Jugurtha, the king of Nunidia (Algeria).

100 B.C. Julius Caesar was born.

90 B.C. There was civil war in Rome; Marius was driven out by Sulla, and Sulla regained control of Italy. Asclepiades, a Greek physician, practiced nature healing in Rome.

87–54 B.C. The Roman poets Catullus and Virgil were writing during this time.

82 B.C. The oldest extant amphitheater was erected at Pompeii.

79 B.C. Lucullus imported the first cherry trees from Asia Minor to Rome.
73–71 B.C. The slaves and gladiators revolted under the leadership of Spartacus, the most famous of all gladiators. He had been born in Thrace, was captured as a soldier, sold into slavery, and forced to become a gladiator.
68 B.C. Crete was captured by the Romans.
65 B.C. Roman poet Horace was born.
63 B.C. Marcus Tullius Tiro, a former slave of Marcus Tullius Cicero, a Roman author, orator, and lawyer, invented a system of shorthand.
62 B.C. The city of Florence was founded.
60 B.C. There were Roman colonies in Switzerland.
58 B.C. Caesar was in Gaul.
54 B.C. Caesar invaded Briton. Cassivelaunus, a powerful tribal leader in southern Briton, agreed to pay tribute to Rome.
54 B.C. The erection of the new forum in Rome began.
50 B.C. There was rivalry between Caesar and Pompey for control of Rome. Rome made expeditions into Germany. The best Roman literature was produced. The earliest form of oboe was known in Rome.
48 B.C. Pompey was defeated by Caesar.
46 B.C. The Julian calendar, devised by the order of Julius Caesar, was composed of 365.25 days. The Senate changed the month of Quinctilis to Julius (July) in honor of Caesar, and made it 31 days long. Later, Augustus, not to be outdone, made his month August and made it 31 days long by taking a day from February. In A.D. 1582, Pope Gregory XIII corrected the calendar with the present Gregorian calendar.
44 B.C. Caesar was murdered by a group of conspirators who were led by Brutus and Caius Cassius Longinus.
43 B.C. This was the time of the Triumvirate of Mark Antony, Marcus Aemilius Lepidus, and Caius Octavius. They pronounced Caius as Julius Caesar Octavianus (Octavian).
42 B.C. Defeated by the new Triumvirate, Brutus and Cassius committed suicide.
34 B.C. Dalmatia (Yugoslavia) became a Roman province.
31 B.C. Mark Antony and Cleopatra committed suicide after their defeat at the famous Battle of Actium. One of the great naval battles of history, it took place off the west coast of Greece. The fleet of Octavian, under the leadership of the Admiral Agrippa, defeated the combined

fleets of Antony and Cleopatra. Octavian subsequently became the most powerful man in Rome. He ruled Rome thereafter, marking the beginning and nearly the peak of the Roman Empire.

30 B.C. The construction of the Pantheon at Rome began. (It was finished in A.D. 124.)

EGYPT

400 B.C. Egypt had deteriorated into a minor entity; the Carthaginians controlled the island of Malta.

396 B.C. The Carthaginians destroyed Messina in Sicily.

380 B.C. This was the time of the Thirtieth Dynasty in Egypt, the last native house to rule Egypt.

350 B.C. The Carthaginians conquered Sicily and Phoenicia, which temporarily became a Greek province.

343 B.C. The Persians reconquered Egypt.

332 B.C. Alexander the Great destroyed Tyre and founded Alexandria two or three years later; it served as the capital and as an important center of culture with its famous library and school of medicine.

314 B.C. The Seleucids of Syria ruled Palestine. Antigonus I ruled Judea.

305 B.C. A new dynasty, under the rule of Ptolemy Soter, one of Alexander's succeeding generals, lasted until the death of Cleopatra (30 B.C.). Manetho, the high priest of Egypt, wrote a history of Egypt in Greek (c. 300 B.C.).

301 B.C. Palestine reverted back to Egyptian rule.

300 B.C. The kingdom of Aksum (or Axum) was founded in Ethiopia.

285–246 B.C. This time period was the reign of Ptolemy II. He built the famous lighthouse Pharos, of Alexandria, one of the Seven Wonders of the Ancient World (c. 280 B.C.).

264–241 B.C. The first Punic (Punic is Latin for Phoenician, and the Phoenicians founded Carthage) War took place between Carthage and Rome for control of the Mediterranean; the Romans won.

246 B.C. Hannibal, the son of Hamilcar Barca, a famous military leader who hated the Romans, was born in Carthage. His father forced him to take an oath to be an enemy of Rome.

239 B.C. Leap year was introduced into the Egyptian calendar.

230 B.C. The Egyptian temple of the sun god Horus was constructed at Edfu.

201 B.C. After his defeat by the Romans, Hannibal was allowed to govern Carthage, but in 195 B.C. he fled to Syria. Later he

Chronological Summary / 149

	fled to Bithynia in Turkey, where he committed suicide in 182 B.C.
189 B.C.	There were insurrections in upper Egypt, due to exorbitant taxes.
123 B.C.	Carthage was rebuilt.
105 B.C.	Heron, the great mathematician, founded the first college of technology at Alexandria.
47 B.C.	Pompey was murdered in Egypt by order of Ptolemy XIII, brother, husband, and coregent of Cleopatra. The library of Ptolemy I in Alexandria was destroyed by fire.
46 B.C.	Africa became a Roman province. Caesar returned to Rome, where he became a dictator.
36 B.C.	Mark Antony returned to Egypt.
30 B.C.	Cleopatra VII, consort of Julius Caesar and Mark Antony, the last queen of Egypt, died.

CHINA

356 B.C.	The first wall of China was built to protect it from the Huns. There were Mongolian and Tartar raids on China. The philosopher Mencius (372 B.C.–288 B.C.) placed people first, God second, and sovereignty third in national importance. This was the end of the feudal period.
343 B.C.	Chu Yuan, the earliest of the important Chinese poets, was born. Iron was used as a working material in China.
221–209 B.C.	Shi Huang Ti was the Emperor of China and founded the Chin Dynasty from which the name of China derives. He established the centralized imperial system that was to govern China during stable periods.
221–206 B.C.	The Great Wall of China was 1500 miles long, 25 feet high, 25 feet thick at its base, and 15 feet wide at the top, with a paved road on top and 35–40-foot-tall towers placed every 200–300 feet.
221 B.C.	All measurements and weights were unified.
202 B.C.	Liu Pang assumed the Imperial title, founding the Han Dynasty (202 B.C.–A.D. 220).
200 B.C.	The use of gears led to the use of the ox-driven water wheel for irrigation.
149 B.C.	Hu Shin wrote the Chinese dictionary of 10,000 characters.
115 B.C.	The Chinese army crossed the Hop Nor Desert, occupied the Tarim Basin, and imposed Chinese authority.
100 B.C.	The first Chinese ships reached the east coast of India.
50 B.C.	This was a brilliant period of Chinese history. The feudal

system—one hundred principalities divided among thirteen provinces and under the jurisdiction of civil governors—was restored. Persia introduced Greek culture through contact with China, through Bactria. Persia introduced art and merchandise from the Roman market.

38 B.C. The Chinese octave was subdivided into sixty notes.

SPAIN

300–250 B.C. During this time, the civilizing and development of the Iberian culture was taking place, due to Greek and Carthaginian influence (the Iberians were early native, primitive immigrants from northern Africa).

238 B.C. Carthage began its conquest of Spain. Hannibal went with his father, Hamilcar, in the conquest of Spain; he became a Carthaginian commander in Spain when he was twenty-five years old.

218–201 B.C. In the Second Punic War, Carthage battled Rome. Hannibal attacked from Spain with 60,000 men. They crossed the Pyrenees, France, and the Alps; he entered Italy from the north. He used elephants like modern-day tanks. By the time he reached Italy, he had 26,000 men, 6,000 horses, and 38 elephants left. He recruited 10,000–15,000 Gauls to help him. He defeated the Romans in each encounter, due to strategy. At Cannae, while greatly outnumbered, he killed 50,000 Romans in one day—the greatest defeat in Roman history. Even with Macedonia, Syracuse, and Sicily as allies, Hannibal could not hold his territory after Rome attacked Carthage and Spain cut off his supplies. He was called back to defend Carthage, but met with defeat in 201 B.C. Two of Rome's emperors, Hadrian and Trajan, were born in Spain. The Romans built many cities, roads, and aqueducts in Spain. Christianity was introduced later, while Spain was under Roman rule.

HOLY LAND

350 B.C. The Jews revolted against Artaxerxes III of Persia.

332 B.C. Alexander conquered Tyre and Jerusalem.

320 B.C. Ptolemy Soter of Egypt invaded Syria, captured Jerusalem.

255 B.C. The Septuagint (the Greek version of the Hebrew writing of the Old Testament by seventy scholars) was written.

Chronological Summary / 151

198 B.C. Antiochus III of Syria took Palestine from Egypt.
168 B.C. Antiochus IV persecuted the Jews and desecrated the Temple at Jerusalem.
164 B.C. Judas Maccabaeus rededicated the Temple after expelling the Syrians.
143 B.C. Judas' successor, Jonathan Maccabee, was assassinated. He was succeeded by Simon Maccabee, who expelled the Syrians from Jerusalem and won Judean independence in 142 B.C.
112 B.C. This time marked the rise of the Pharisees and the Sadducees in Palestine.
63 B.C. Pompey invaded Syria and completed his conquest of Palestine, which he made a part of the Roman province of Syria.
47 B.C. Herod became the governor of Galilee.
40 B.C. Herod at Rome was made the king of Judea.
6 B.C. Judea was annexed by Rome.
4 B.C. Judea was divided among Herod's three sons at his death. Jesus Christ was born in Bethlehem (after the adjustment of the calendar).

PERSIA-BABYLON-ASSYRIA

359 B.C. This time marked the ascension of Artaxerxes III in Persia.
333 B.C. Alexander defeated Darius III at Issus and at Gaugamela in 331 B.C. Persian power was ultimately destroyed, but the culture was absorbed first by Greek conquerors and later by the Parthians for 400 years.
330 B.C. Alexander occupied Babylon, Susa, and Persepolis. Darius III was murdered.
300–250 B.C. This was the end of the history of Babylon. The Babylonians re-established the new city of Seleucia, near Antioch on the Mediterranean Sea. The rule of the Seleucids lasted until the birth of Christ.
209 B.C. Antiochus III, the ruler of Persia, was at the peak of his power.
200 B.C. The Tartar Parthians revolted and started the Parthian Empire southeast of the Caspian Sea. They fought furiously for their independence, especially with Rome, and finally succumbed to Trajan in A.D. 116.
195 B.C. Hannibal fled to Antiochus III of Syria.
192 B.C. Antiochus III, aided by Hannibal, landed in Greece.
191 B.C. Antiochus III was defeated by the Romans at the famous

152 / *Chronological Summary*

189 B.C.   mountain pass of Thermopylae.
189 B.C.   Hannibal was defeated by the Rhodian fleet.
182 B.C.   Hannibal committed suicide in exile to avoid extradition by Rome.
140 B.C.   Crates of Mallus formed his great globe of the world.

INDIA

400–300 B.C.   King Porus was defeated by Alexander (327 B.C.). The Nanda Dynasty of Magadha was in existence.
326 B.C.   Alexander was forced by his generals to turn back.
319 B.C.   Maurya reconquered northern India from the Greeks and founded the Maurya Dynasty. Rain was being measured in India.
250 B.C.   Asoka, the Indian emperor, erected columns forty feet high, inscribed with his laws. Bactria, one of the provinces, broke away from the foreign rule of the Greeks and became independent.
230 B.C.   Greeks from Bactria invaded Pakistan.
185 B.C.   The Shunga Dynasty replaced the Maurya Dynasty.
100 B.C.   The great Stupa Sanchi (a Buddhist memorial mound) was erected. The Greeks were driven out of India by Scythians. The Senual Scythian dynasties followed in the Indo-Scythian Empire.

SCANDINAVIA

113 B.C.   The Cimbri, an ancient German tribe, left Jutland (Denmark) which was devastated by storms and cold weather, and retreated to the Roman province of Noricum Corinthia (Hungarian Alpine country).
103 B.C.   The Cimbri and the Germanic Teutons became allies to invade Italy. They were defeated by Marius in 101 B.C.
72 B.C.   The Suevi (or Suebi), a Germanic tribe, crossed the Upper Rhine and invaded Gaul (France).
50 B.C.   The Goth-Teutonic peoples of Central Europe began to emerge into a factor in world civilization. The people of Sweden traded with the Roman Empire. They traded furs and amber for glass, bronze, and silver coins.

ASIA MINOR–TURKEY

351 B.C.   The Tomb of Mausolus, an official of the Persian empire, was completed, and was one of the Seven Wonders of the

Ancient World. This was the origination of the word *mausoleum*.

250 B.C. Parchment was produced at Pergamum, a Greek city in western Turkey, in commercial quantities.

189 B.C. Armenia became independent from Seleucid rule.

164 B.C. There was a Maccabean revolt against Antiochus IV.

82 B.C. Alexander Poly, a historian of Miletus, wrote a history of the Jews.

BRITON

250 B.C. Briton was invaded by LaTene.

FRANCE

225 B.C. The Gauls were defeated in north central Italy.

51 B.C. The Gauls were subdued by Caesar.

RUSSIA

380 B.C. The Greeks settled around the Caspian and Black Seas.

200 B.C. The Sarmatians settled north of the Black and Caspian Seas (these people were probably of Iranian origin).

OTHERS

400 B.C. This time marked the end of the Indian civilization in Mexico.

300 B.C. The Mexican sun temple, Atetello, was constructed at Teotihuacán.

23 B.C. The first recorded wrestling match was held in Japan.

THE JEWISH NATION BETWEEN TESTAMENTS

536 B.C.–330 B.C.—Restoration

Cyrus the Great, of Persia (553 B.C.–529 B.C.), conquered Lydia, the Medes, and Babylonia, transforming Persia into a vast empire. In 536 B.C., he freed the Jews from Babylonian captivity and helped them return to Israel. He was succeeded by his son, Cambyses, who took Egypt in 525 B.C. Cambyses committed suicide in 522 B.C. Cambyses was succeeded by Darius I (522 B.C.–485 B.C.), who divided the empire into twenty provinces (satrapies) and introduced a common currency, regular taxes, and a standing army.

Xerxes I becomes king (485 B.C.–465 B.C.), and the Persian decline starts. Babylon is destroyed in 479 B.C. Xerxes I is assassinated (465 B.C.) and is succeeded by his son Artaxerxes I (465 B.C.–424 B.C.). Xerxes II becomes king of Persia (424 B.C.); is assassinated two months later; and is succeeded by Darius II, who rules until 405 B.C., when he is succeeded by Artaxerxes III (404 B.C.–359 B.C.), who is assassinated and succeeded by Arses in 338 B.C. Arses is assassinated and succeeded by Darius III (336 B.C.).

This is the period of time in which the Jews return from captivity in Assyria and Babylon, rebuild the Temple, re-establish the nation, and rebuild the walls of Jerusalem. The prophets try to re-establish the obedience of the people to God. Judean law forbids marriage between Jews and aliens.

330 B.C.–321 B.C.—Macedonian Rule

At the age of twenty, Alexander the Great, a Greek (356 B.C.–323 B.C.), expanded his nation by conquest, destroying Thebes, in Greece (335 B.C.). He defeated Darius III at Issus (333 B.C.), Tyre, and Egypt (332 B.C.). He defeated Darius III at Gaugamela (331 B.C.). Babylon, Susa, and Persepolis fell in 330 B.C. Darius III was murdered in 330 B.C. Alexander married a Bactrian (Bactria was a satrapy of Persia), Princess Roxana (328 B.C.). He invaded (326 B.C.) India and quickly controlled all of the nations under the dominion of Persia, Babylon, Assyria, and Egypt. The known world was at his feet. When he invaded Palestine in 332 B.C., he showed great consideration to the Jews at Jerusalem and encouraged them to migrate to his new city of Alexandria. He established Greek cities everywhere, spreading the Greek culture and language. The Jews built synagogues in all the cities where they settled. Alexander died at the age of thirty-three in Babylon (323 B.C.).

Alexander's kingdom was divided among his five top generals. Syria went to Seleucus and Egypt to Ptolemy Soter. Antigonus took Asia Minor, Lysimachus took Thrace and Bithynia, and Antipater took Greece and Macedonia. Alexander's Macedonian empire was short-lived.

321 B.C.–198 B.C.—Egyptian Rule

Palestine, located between Egypt and Syria, went first to Syria but later (301 B.C.) to Egypt, and remained under Greek-dominated Egyptian control until 198 B.C. During this century under Egyptian control, the Jews had peace and prosperity in Egypt, and the cultures of the Greeks and the Jews maintained a peaceful contact. All the Greek kings of Egypt were named Ptolemy. There were seven of them between 323 B.C.–30 B.C. Cleopatra, the last of the Ptolemy monarchs, died in 30 B.C. There was a constant nettling in Palestine between Seleucus of Syria and Ptolemy of Egypt, and the country was often a battleground between the two.

198 B.C.–166 B.C.—Greek-Syrian Rule

The envious Seleucids in Syria finally gained control of Palestine in 198 B.C. Thus, Antiochus the Great became ruler of Palestine. The Syrians were not as tolerant of the Jews as the Egyptians were. They were also losing power in the north and east to the rising power of the Romans. At the battle of Magnesia (190 B.C.), the Romans defeated the Syrians. The Romans demanded tremendous war indemnity. Antiochus seized the treasures of the Jewish temples and synagogues to help pay this tribute, which angered the Jews.

In 175 B.C., the Seleucid throne was assumed by Antiochus IV (175 B.C.–164 B.C.), a son of Antiochus the Great, who gave himself the title Epiphanes, meaning *illustrious*. He proved to be the most vile and outrageous ruler in the history of the Jews. He not only tried to exterminate their literature, but also the Jews themselves. He devastated the Temple and Jerusalem, and history says he offered a sow as a sacrifice on the altar as an act of desecration. He forbade temple worship, circumcision on pain of death, sold the people into slavery, destroyed their scriptures and murdered those having copies of scriptures, and tried by every conceivable means of punishment to force the Jews to abandon their religion. These autocracies led to what became known as the heroic Maccabean revolt in 168 B.C.

166 B.C.–63 B.C.—Maccabean Independence Revolt

The Roman domination of the world was beginning to be well known. The rule of the Greek Seleucids in Syria was declining. In 168 B.C., a godly priest, Mattathias, a Hasmonean, incensed with the cruelty of the Syrians under Antiochus Epiphanes, led a Jewish war of revolt, or war of independence, known as the Maccabean, Asmonean, or Hasmonean period. He and his five sons, Judas, Jonathan, Simon, John and Eleazar, withdrew to Modein, 17 miles west of Jerusalem, to avoid the persecutions of Antiochus. He was pursued by the Greek Hellenizers, who tried to force him to profane the religious rites. He refused and killed the Hellenizer leader and a Jewish traitor.

This started the war. Mattathias and his sons fled and gathered other followers to their cause. Mattathias died (166 B.C.) shortly thereafter, and his third son, Judas Maccabee, took over the leadership. Judas was a military genius. He reconquered Jerusalem by winning many battles (165 B.C.) and purified and rededicated the Temple (164 B.C.). Antiochus died (164 B.C.), without sorrow to Palestine; his successor, Lysias, proposed a conditional peace with Judas, who refused, and in an ensuing battle, Judas was killed (161 B.C.).

Jonathan succeeded Judas, but he was captured and killed (143 B.C.), and Simon took over leadership. He finally declared complete independence from Syria in 142 B.C. Simon was assassinated by his son-in-law, who wanted the leadership (134 B.C.), but Simon's third son, John Hyrcanus, assumed the office of high priest and civil and military leader. He sought a treaty with Rome, but it was busy with other internal affairs, so refused his offer. At his death in 104 B.C., the Pharisees and Sadducees came into being, and each side struggled for power.

Jannaeus, son of Hyrcanus, was angered with the Pharisees, and with the aid of mercenary forces, killed 6,000 Jews, which precipitated a civil war in Judah. This war lasted for six years and eventually resulted in the bloodshed of 50,000 lives. The whole nation was weakened by turmoil, conspiracy, and strife. Finally in 63 B.C., both sides appealed to Pompey, consul of the Romans, to arbitrate the dispute. He did this by entering Jerusalem, killing 12,000 Jews, ending Jewish independence, and converting Palestine to a tributary of Rome, governed by a military garrison. Thus, in 63 B.C., Jewish independence was abolished for 2,011 years, until A.D. 1948.

63 B.C.–A.D. 70—Roman Rule

Pompey, the Roman consul and military general, followed the Roman custom of noninterference with Jewish religious customs. Hyrcanus II, the high priest, exercised full liberty in matters of worship. Antipater, an Idumaean, was appointed ruler of Judea. The Idumaeans were the Edomite descendants of Esau, who lived between Judea and Egypt, east of the Dead Sea, after a division of the territory between Esau and his brother Jacob, who had previously tricked Esau out of his birthright privileges from his father Isaac. Esau's resentment was carried through history by his descendants. This resentment was increased after 129 B.C., when these Idumaeans were captured by the Jews and given a choice of going empty-handed or at least appearing to accept the Jewish religion by being circumcised. They accepted the latter. The Idumaeans were, therefore, delighted to be rulers of the Jews.

Antipater was succeeded by his son, Herod the Great, king of Judea 42 B.C.–3 B.C.), who was an astute politician and who won favor with the Romans by taxing the Jews and bribing governors and emperors until he was appointed governor of Judea in 42 B.C. He was successful in getting Rome to give him the title of king and also to send reinforcements to help drive out the Parthians, who had helped Antigonus, son of Aristobulus, to become king. The Jews preferred Antigonus, because he was a Maccabean. Herod, the unwanted Idumaean, regained control and was reinstated as ruler in 37 B.C. He immediately murdered about one hundred of the most outstanding Jewish citizens, including most of the members of the Sanhedrin.

Herod had ten wives, among whom was his most favored, the beautiful Mariamne, a sister of Aristobulus, who, because of her beauty, aroused the jealousy of Herod's sister Salome. The intrigue in the Roman ruling class was almost beyond belief. Herod had Aristobulus appointed high priest, but his popularity made Herod fearful of his own position, so he had him drowned. Within a few years, he also had executed his mother-in-law, Alexandra; her grandfather, Hyrcanus II; his uncle, Joseph; his wife Mariamne; and two of his sons by her. He was also the ruler who put out the order to slay all children in Bethlehem two years old and under, after he learned from the wise men that a child destined to be king (Jesus Christ) had been born there. In 4 B.C., at the age of seventy, a few days before his death, he had his son Antipater murdered because he had planned to succeed his father. Before he died, Herod gave orders to have hundreds of Jews killed at the same time, to be sure that there were many people mourning at the time of his death. This order was not carried out.

Herod was succeeded by three sons and several other procurators until A.D. 26, when Pontius Pilate was made prefect of Judea (A.D. 26–A.D. 36). The provincial capital was at Caesarea, and Tiberius was the Roman Emperor. Among other things that made him unpopular, he used Temple funds to build an aqueduct to bring water to Jerusalem. He had many Jews wounded and killed for objecting to this. He was deposed after ten years in office.

Such acts by Roman rulers persisted until A.D. 66, when the Jews revolted; but after four years they were destroyed and dispersed. The

Temple and Jerusalem were destroyed in A.D. 70, and the entire country was annexed to Syria. Thus ended the history of Israel and Judea. The Hebrew nation founded by God through Abraham had come to an end by the providence of the same God who had raised her up. The last seventy years are the times of Jesus Christ and the New Testament history of the establishment of the Christian Church.

INTRODUCTION TO THE NEW TESTAMENT

The New Testament is a record of the promises made by God through the teachings and experiences of Christ and His followers. The twenty-seven books were all written in the first century after Christ, in the common vernacular Greek language of the time of Jesus. All of the authors were Jews except Luke, who was a Syrian Gentile.

The order of the books in the New Testament is not the order in which they were actually written. Thus Paul's missionary journeys and most of his letters were written before the Gospel books of Matthew, Mark, Luke, and John were written; therefore, he did not have these written books of Scripture to refer to. In fact, the New Testament Scriptures as we know them today were not assembled as official (Canonical) until about A.D. 300—two hundred fifty years after Paul's missionary work and the writing of his own letters, or epistles. There were many writings available, but they were not all accepted as official.

Apocalyptic types of literature (see definitions), as found in some books, needs a special word of explanation. In the history of the Hebrew people, there were times of great crises and persecution of the Jews. In these times some of their writers revealed their visions, revelations, dreams, references to current events of that day, warnings, and prophecies of the triumph of Israel, in half-hidden or symbolic meanings. Therefore, in some cases the lamb is Christ; the dragon is Satan; the beast is Rome, and so forth. These things were done for safety's sake. Thus there are writings from 587 B.C. to A.D. 100 in Ezekiel, Isaiah, Zechariah, Daniel, and Revelation of this apocalyptic type of writing, which is very difficult for the novice to understand. Basically these writings are both Jewish and Christian and are intended to comfort the faithful in their present state of suffering and reconcile that condition with God's righteousness by forecasting the ultimate triumph of Israel. It is generally a message of triumphant faith in the goodness, justice, and mercy of God. The book of Revelation is written in this type of literature.

The first five books of the New Testament consist of the biography of Jesus and the history of the acts of the apostles. The next twenty-one books, possibly fourteen of which were written by Paul, are teachings in the form of letters written to individuals and to the various new churches, covering Church doctrine, Christian living, and personal behavior. The last book, Revelation, is one of revelation and prophecy as to the hereafter.

The first four books, called the Gospels of Matthew, Mark, Luke, and John, all tell a different version of the same story, the arrival of the Messiah. Throughout the Old Testament there is woven the prophecy of the coming of the Messiah. The meaning in Hebrew is "anointed one"; in Greek the word is *Christ*. These first four books tell the life of Christ as seen by four different authors with different viewpoints and objectives. Matthew, a tax collector, writes primarily to the Jews who are interested in Jesus as the King or Messiah who has been promised to them. The genealogy offered proves that He is the son of David, the son of Abraham.

Mark writes primarily to the Romans, who are interested in deeds. Jesus is presented as a servant doing His work in the form of miracles.

Luke, a physician, writes primarily to the Greeks, with their mythological attitude, and presents Jesus as the perfect man. He is pictured as a gracious yet severe Lord.

John, a fisherman, writes to all who will listen and believe. He tells it factually—Jesus is the Son of God, sent to this earth for the purpose of leading men to Christ, so that all who believe will have eternal life.

These four Gospels tell of the birth of Jesus Christ, His baptism by John the Baptist at the age of thirty, His selection of the twelve disciples, His travels and teachings for three years, and His miracles, parables, and healings of probably thousands of people. During this three-year period of His ministry, He trained His disciples to go out into the world to preach what He taught them. Some of the stories are repetitious.

After the birth of Jesus, He was unheard of for twelve years, until His visit as a boy with the leaders and teachers in Jerusalem. He was then unheard of for eighteen years, except as a carpenter. He took thirty years for His preparation to minister for three years. The legal age under Roman law was thirty. He was baptized by His cousin, John the Baptist, who was six months older, before He was qualified to start His ministry.

Jesus tried to prove His message to His disciples, as well as to all the people: that He was the Christ, sent by God to bring the message to all mankind that His life was to be sacrificed on the cross for the redemption of the sins of those who would confess their beliefs, repent of their sins, and be baptized so that they would be saved and have eternal life in heaven.

He taught the people and His apostles to have faith in their beliefs and in their prayers to God, and that they should love the Lord their God and love their neighbors as themselves. He told His disciples how He would be arrested, crucified, and buried, and on the third day rise from the grave and meet with them in the flesh.

In essence, Jesus Christ, being of sound mind and legal age, and the owner of eternal life, was making His last will and testament, to provide for the inheritance of eternal life by all who would confess Jesus Christ as their Saviour, ask God's forgiveness of their sins, repent, be baptized, and open their hearts for receipt of the Holy Spirit. His apostles were actually executors of His will.

Thus, the New Testament is the story of the birth, life, teachings, death, resurrection, and administration of the will, or testament, of one man for all men.

There are two things to remember that are important as being difficult to understand: (1) We do not earn salvation by deeds, but receive it by the grace of God. (2) Unjust man has always been of a sinful nature, disobedient to the will of God, and has failed to live up to divine requirements, while at the same time, just man has experienced much unmerited suffering.

JESUS CHRIST
AS DESCRIBED BY HISTORIANS

Josephus, the great Jewish historian (A.D. 37–A.D. 100), says, "Now, there was about this time, Jesus, a wise man, if it be lawful to call Him a man, for He was a doer of wonderful works—a teacher of such men as receive the truth with pleasure. He drew over to Him both many of the Jews, and many of the Gentiles. He was [the] Christ; and when Pilate, at the suggestion of the principal men amongst us, had condemned Him to the cross, those that loved Him at the first did not forsake Him, for He appeared to them alive again the third day, as the divine prophets had foretold these and ten thousand other wonderful things concerning Him; and the tribe of Christians so named from Him, are not extinct at this day."

Napoleon, according to tradition, said, "I know men, and I tell you, Jesus is not a man. He commands us to believe, and gives no other reason than his awful word, I AM GOD. Philosophers try to solve the mysteries of the universe by their empty dissertations: fools: they are like the infant that cries to have the moon for a plaything. Christ never hesitates. He speaks with authority. His religion is a mystery; but it subsists by its own force. He seeks, and absolutely requires, the love of men, the most difficult thing in the world to obtain. Alexander, Caesar, Hannibal conquered the world, but had no friends. I myself am perhaps the only person of my day who loves Alexander, Caesar, Hannibal. Alexander, Caesar, Charlemagne and myself founded empires; but upon what? Force. Jesus founded his empire on Love; and at this hour millions would die for him. I myself have inspired multitudes with such affection that they would die for me. But my presence was necessary. Now that I am in St. Helena, where are my friends? I am forgotten, soon to return to the earth, and become food for worms. What an abyss between my misery and the eternal kingdom of Christ, who is proclaimed, loved, adored, and which is extending over all the earth. Is this death? I tell you, the death of Christ is the death of a God. I tell you, JESUS CHRIST IS GOD."

According to tradition, Publius Lentulus, a friend of Pilate, wrote: "In this time appeared a man endowed with great powers. His name is Jesus. His disciples call him the Son of God. He is of noble and well-proportioned stature, with a face full of kindness, and yet firmness, so that beholders both love him and fear him. His hair is the color of wine, straight and without lustre, but from the level of the ears curling and flossy. His forehead is even and smooth, his face without blemish, and enhanced by a tempered bloom, his countenance ingenuous and kind. Nose and mouth are in no way faulty. His beard is full, of the same color as his hair; his eyes blue and extremely brilliant. In reproof and rebuke he is formidable; in exhortation and teaching, gentle and amiable of tongue. None have seen him to laugh, but many, on the contrary, to weep. His person is tall, his hands beautiful and straight. In speaking, deliberate, grave, little given to loquacity; in beauty surpassing most men."

THE BOOKS OF THE NEW TESTAMENT

Biography—The Four Gospels

Matthew   Luke
Mark   John

History—Of the acts of the apostles and disciples in the original establishment of the Church

The Acts

Letters or Epistles	**Written by**	**Written to**
Romans	Paul	Roman church
1 Corinthians	Paul	Corinthian Christians
2 Corinthians	Paul	Corinthian Christians
Galatians	Paul	Christian groups
Ephesians	Paul, Philemon, or Tychicus	Groups of non-Jewish Christians
Philippians	Paul	Christians at Philippi
Colossians	Paul	Philemon and Colossian Christians
1 Thessalonians	Paul	Thessalonian Christians
2 Thessalonians	Paul	Church at Thessalonica
1 Timothy	Paul, or a follower of Paul	Church officers
2 Timothy	Paul, or a follower of Paul	Church officers
Titus	Paul, or a follower of Paul	Church officers
Philemon	Paul	Philemon
Hebrews	Paul, or possibly a teacher	Jewish Christians
James	Probably a teacher	All Christians
1 Peter	Probably Peter	Christians in Asia Minor

Letters or Epistles	Written by	Written to
2 Peter	Unknown	Christians everywhere
1 John	John	Christians in Asia Minor
2 John	"The Elder"	"Elect lady"—the Church
3 John	"The Elder"	"Gaius"—the Church
Jude	Probably James	Quarreling Christian groups
Revelation	John	The seven churches in Asia

MATTHEW

Time A.D. 65, about thirty years after the death of Christ. Opinions vary from A.D. 37–A.D. 80.

Author Matthew. He was one of the twelve apostles and was formerly a tax collector for the Romans, which made him hated by the Jews. He wrote especially to the Jews. He referred to himself as a publican, a collector of toll or tribute. Matthew and John were companions of Jesus.

Theme Matthew was concerned with proving to the Jews that Jesus was the promised King as foretold in the Old Testament. He made more than sixty references to the Old Testament and used the words "to fulfill" many times. He introduced Jesus Christ as the promised King from the line of David and Abraham. Constant references were made to prophecies and quotations in the Old Testament. Christ was born, rejected, crucified, and resurrected, but was still the King. He told of His return, or second coming.

The opening verses trace Jesus' ancestry back to David and Abraham, to prove that He was a Jew of kingly blood, the Messiah who had been foretold all through the Old Testament. The Old Testament anticipates Christ. The four Gospels each tell the story of Christ in a different way. The rest of the Bible explains Him and His teachings. Only Matthew and Luke tell of the birth and childhood of Jesus. Not too much is told about His father, Joseph; His mother, Mary; or His six brothers and sisters.

Jesus' birth took place this way: Mary, His mother, was engaged to Joseph, and before they came together, she was found to be pregnant of the Holy Spirit. Not understanding this, Joseph decided not to marry her, but an angel of the Lord appeared to him in a dream and told him to marry her and name the son Jesus, for He would save the people from their sins. When Joseph awoke, he did as commanded.

After Jesus was born in Bethlehem, in Judea, in the days of Herod the king, wise men seeing His star came from the east to worship Him. Herod, hearing of this, told them to let him know where Christ was after they found Him, so that he could worship Him also; he secretly plotted to kill Jesus. The wise men followed the star, found Jesus, worshipped Him, left their gifts of gold, frankincense (fragrant gum resin), and myrrh (also a fragrant gum resin) and then, having been forewarned in a dream, returned to their own country without telling Herod.

An angel appeared to Joseph and told him to take the child, go to Egypt, and stay there, because Herod was trying to find the child, to destroy Him. Joseph did this and stayed in Egypt probably only for one or two years, until Herod was dead. All of these events were foretold by the prophets. Herod, in attempting to destroy Jesus, killed every male child two years or younger in the region of Bethlehem. When Herod died, an angel told Joseph to return. He heard that Archelaus, son of Herod, reigned in Judea. Having been warned in a dream, Joseph decided to go to Nazareth in Galilee, instead of Jerusalem.

John the Baptist, a relative of Jesus (probably a cousin), was preaching and baptizing in Judea, at the River Jordan. He had foretold how the Messiah would come and baptize in the Holy Spirit. Then Jesus came to John, to be baptized. The Spirit of God descended like a dove on Him, and a voice from heaven said, ". . . This is My beloved Son, in whom I am well-pleased" (Matthew 3:17).

The life, travels, teachings, experiences, stories, death, and resurrection of Jesus, which are told in the Bible, must of necessity be abbreviated in this book.

Jesus was first led by the Spirit into the wilderness, to fast for forty days and nights. He was tempted by Satan to worship Satan, but withstood Satan's offers with, ". . . You shall worship the Lord your God, and serve Him only" (Matthew 4:10).

Jesus' basic theme was, "Repent, for the Kingdom of heaven is at hand." As He traveled throughout the land, He called the twelve apostles to come and follow Him. They were Simon (called Peter); Andrew, his brother; James, son of Zebedee and John, his brother; Philip and Bartholomew; Thomas; Matthew, the tax collector; James, son of Alphaeus; Thaddaeus; Simon the Cananaean; and Judas Iscariot, who was to betray Him.

As He traveled about the area of Galilee, He taught in the synagogues and preached the Gospel to all who would listen, and He healed every disease and infirmity among the people. At the same time, His fame spread in all directions. Great crowds followed Him, and He healed all the sick.

Jesus went up on a mountain with His disciples and a great crowd, and taught them what is known as the Sermon on the Mount. This sermon, of 1,922 words, can be read in thirteen minutes (Matthew 5:3–7:27). This is considered the greatest sermon ever uttered by any man and contains all the wisdom for human conduct. The essence of the whole sermon and the key to life is embodied in seventeen words: "But seek first His kingdom, and His righteousness; and all these things shall be added to you" (Matthew 6:33).

There follow many stories of His teachings, healings, and the faith that people had in His ability as the Son of God. He healed a leper. He healed a paralyzed man. He healed Peter's mother-in-law. He calmed a storm while He and some of the apostles were in a boat on the Sea of Galilee. He cast the demons from two demoniacs into a herd of swine, who rushed into the sea and drowned. He healed and forgave sins. He mingled with sinners and tax collectors and was criticized by the pious Pharisees. He restored life to a ruler's daughter who had died. He restored sight to two blind men.

He gave authority to His disciples to cast out unclean spirits, to heal every disease and infirmity, and to go out to the people to preach and heal as He had done. He confirmed to the disciples of John the Baptist, who was in prison, that He was the Messiah. He rebuked the people of the cities because they did not repent and would not be baptized. The Pharisees criticized Him for gathering grain to eat and for healing a man with a withered hand on the Sabbath.

To the amazement of the people, He healed a blind and dumb demoniac and received more criticism from the Pharisees. He spoke to great crowds and told them parables, the meanings of which were not always clear to His listeners. There are about thirty parables in this book.

There was a basic misconception in the minds of the people, the rulers, the priestly hierarchy, and even the apostles as to the Kingdom to be established by Christ. Everyone, including the apostles, thought He was going to re-establish a political kingdom; that He would be king and that there would be many political plums to be passed out in high appointments. Actually, Jesus came to establish a Kingdom of the reign of God in the hearts of men, as shown by their love of Jesus and one another. Jesus stressed the word *love*.

A great crowd gathered around Him at the sea, and He told parables of the sower, the tares in the field, the net, the mustard seed, the hidden treasure, and the goodly pearl. Jesus went to His own town to preach, but was not well received because the people knew Him as a carpenter's son. His reply was, ". . . A prophet is not without honor except in his home town, and in his own household" (Matthew 13:57). Herod had John the Baptist, who was in prison, beheaded, and his head was delivered on a silver platter to Herodias, wife of Philip, Herod's brother. News of this atrocity grieved Jesus. He took a boat to a lonely spot, but the crowds followed Him. In compassion, He healed the sick and talked to them all day. At evening, He fed 5,000 men, plus the women and children, with five loaves and two fish, and they had 12 baskets of food left over.

He sent the disciples across the sea in a boat ahead of Him and in the night came to them, walking on the sea. The disciples couldn't believe their own eyes, so Peter said, ". . . command me to come to You on the water" (Matthew 14:28). Jesus said, "Come," and Peter did, until his faith failed him, and he began to sink. His reaffirmed faith saved him.

Jesus healed many people at Gennesaret. He was challenged again by the scribes and Pharisees. In the area of Tyre and Sidon, He healed the daughter of a Canaanite woman. Again along the Sea of Galilee, He talked to great crowds for three days and healed all the sick. Then with seven loaves and a few fish, He fed 4,000 men, plus the women and children, and had seven baskets of food left over. He was criticized again by the Pharisees and warned His disciples to ". . . beware of the leaven of the Pharisees and Sadducees" (Matthew 16:6).

Three years of Jesus' ministry passed. Peter called Him Lord at the end of the first year; the Holy One of God six months later. Now, one year later, Jesus asks Peter, ". . . who do you say that I am?" Peter answered, ". . . Thou art the Christ, the Son of the living God." Jesus answers, ". . . upon this rock [this statement of truth] I will build My church . . ." (Matthew 16:15-19). This is the fundamental creed of Christendom, on which the apostles were to build the Church of Christ. From this time, Jesus began to show His disciples that He must go to Jerusalem, be killed, and rise on the third day.

Jesus took Peter, James, and John into the mountain, to see Him transfigured in the presence of Moses and Elijah and to hear a voice from a cloud say, ". . . This is My beloved Son, with whom I am well-pleased; hear Him!" (Matthew 17:5).

Jesus talked to His disciples about many things and then went to Judea, beyond the Jordan, where He discussed divorce, little children, the rich young ruler, the parable of the workers in the vineyard, and told His disciples again of His coming death. The mother of James and John requested a special position for her sons in Jesus' new Kingdom. Jesus answered that this privilege was for ". . . those for whom it has been prepared by My Father" (Matthew 20:23). As Jesus left Jericho to go to Jerusalem, He restored sight to two blind men.

Jesus entered Jerusalem on a Sunday, on the back of an ass, with the crowds shouting and laying their garments and tree branches on the road in front of Him. He entered the Temple and drove out the merchants and money changers, healed many of the sick, the blind, and the lame. That night He stayed in Bethany and returned Monday to the Temple, where His authority was challenged by the Pharisees. He told them the parable of the two sons, the vineyard, and the marriage feast, and answered their questions as to tribute to Caesar. The Sadducees then challenged Him as to the resurrection, and His answer (Matthew 22:29-32) left them astonished. Jesus had hardly stopped the Sadducees when the Pharisees came back. He gave them the great commandment (Matthew 22:37-39) and asked them some questions that they could not answer. In their humiliation, they never asked Him another question. Jesus then reviled the Pharisees before the crowds, because they did not practice what they preached. He left the Temple on Tuesday, never to enter it again.

Jesus talked to His disciples on the Mount of Olives for three days concerning the destruction of Jerusalem forty years later, His second coming, the parable of the ten virgins, the talents, and the story of the final judgment scene.

Caiaphas, the high priest, plotted with his counsel to arrest and kill Jesus. Judas Iscariot, one of the twelve disciples, agreed to betray Jesus to them for thirty pieces of silver. The day before His death, the disciples asked Jesus where they should prepare for the Passover supper. It was arranged at a friend's house, and as they were eating, Jesus told them that one of them would betray Him. He gave instructions for the communion service. Judas slipped out to arrange His betrayal, and the rest went to Gethsemane, to receive final instructions and prayer.

While Jesus was in the garden at Gethsemane, Judas came with the crowd and the chief priests, and they led Jesus away to Caiaphas, the high priest, where by trickery and false witnesses they condemned Him to death. Early Friday they took Him before Pilate. Judas, seeing that Jesus was condemned, returned the thirty pieces of silver to the priests and committed suicide. Pilate could find no fault with Jesus, but under pressure from the crowds, had Him whipped and ordered Him to be crucified. Pilate washed his hands before the crowd and said, ". . . I am innocent of this Man's blood . . ." (Matthew 27:24).

The governor's soldiers abused and mocked Jesus and gave Him His own cross to carry. When He was too weak to carry it, they made a man by the name of Simon carry it for Him. The soldiers put a sign over His head, "THIS IS JESUS THE KING OF THE JEWS," crucified Him, and divided His clothes among them. Bystanders abused and mocked Him. From the sixth to the ninth hour, there was total darkness. The curtain in the Temple was split in two, the earth shook, rocks split, tombs were split open, and many saints arose and appeared to the people. Those who were guarding Jesus said, ". . . Truly this was the Son of God!" (Matthew 27:54.)

A rich man, Joseph of Arimathea, asked Pilate for Jesus' body, wrapped it in linens, put it in his own new tomb, and rolled a great stone to cover the door of the tomb. Mary Magdalene and Mary, the mother of James and Joseph, witnessed the crucifixion and burial.

The chief priests and Pharisees secured permission from Pilate to have the tomb guarded day and night, in order to prevent the disciples from removing the body so that they could claim He arose from the grave on the third day.

Early Monday, Mary Magdalene and the other Mary went to the tomb. There was a great earthquake, and an angel rolled the stone from the door. The guards were terror-stricken. Jesus was gone. The angel told the women to see that Jesus was risen and to go and tell the disciples that

Jesus would meet them in Galilee. The guards reported what had happened, and the chief priests bribed them to say the disciples stole the body while they were asleep.

The eleven disciples met Jesus in Galilee and worshipped Him in awe. Jesus said to them, ". . . All authority has been given to Me in heaven and on earth. Go therefore and make disciples of all the nations, baptizing them in the name of the Father and the Son and the Holy Spirit, teaching them to observe all that I commanded you; and lo, I am with you always, even to the end of the age" (Matthew 28:18–20).

MARK

Time Between A.D. 60–A.D. 85, more probably about A.D. 60–A.D. 65.

Author Written by Mark, especially to the Romans. Mark wrote the story he heard Peter tell many times. He was the son of a woman named Mary, living in Jerusalem, whose home was a meeting place for Jesus and the apostles. He was a cousin and companion of Barnabas and Peter and started the first trip with Paul but didn't finish it. His story probably was written in Rome, primarily for the church in Rome.

Theme Mark presents Christ as a mighty man of action, a man of power. This appeals to the Romans, especially the younger ones. He uses such words as *straightway, forthwith,* and *immediately.* The first nine chapters tell of the beginning of Christ's works; chapters 10–14, His teachings and ministry; chapters 15 and 16, His sacrifice of His life and proof that He is the Messiah.

John the Baptist was at the River Jordan, preaching and baptizing, as prophesied by Isaiah. Jesus came from Nazareth and was baptized by John. The heavens opened and a Spirit descended on Him like a dove; accompanied by a voice saying, ". . . Thou art My beloved Son, in Thee I am well-pleased" (Mark 1:11). Nothing was said in this book about the birth of Jesus or His life up to this point. He was about thirty years of age. He went into the wilderness for forty days and was tempted by, but resisted, Satan and his offers of worldly dominion if Jesus would worship Satan instead of God.

Jesus went to Galilee, where He enlisted Simon, Andrew, and James and John, sons of Zebedee, as disciples. They went to Capernaum, where Jesus taught in the synagogue and cast out an unclean spirit in a man. This started His fame throughout the countryside. Many people came to Him, and He healed all of their diseases and cast out demons. He moved from town to town. A leper was healed. When He returned to Capernaum, there was such a crowd that four men lowered a paralytic through the roof of a house for Him to heal. Jesus healed him and said, "My son your sins are forgiven . . . . rise, take up your pallet and go home" (Mark 2:5, 11). This stunned the crowds and irked the scribes of the Pharisees. He then enlisted Matthew, a tax collector, and ate with a group of tax collectors and sinners. The Pharisees criticized Him for this, and He answered, ". . . I did not come to call the righteous, but sinners" (Mark 2:17).

He was criticized because His apostles plucked some grain on a Sabbath and because Jesus healed a man with a withered hand on the same day. The Pharisees started to plot His death. Great crowds followed Him to the Sea of Galilee, but He went up into the hills with His twelve apostles and instructed them to be with Him, so that they could go out and do the same things He did. Again He spoke to large crowds and told them parables that they did not understand. He explained the parables to His disciples, but not to the crowds.

After talking to the crowds, they took a boat to cross the Sea of Galilee, but a great storm came up, and the disciples were fearful for their lives. They awakened Jesus to save them. He said, ". . . Hush, be still . . ." (Mark 4:39). The storm subsided, and the disciples were amazed. Jesus said, ". . . Why are you so timid? How is it that you have no faith?" (Mark 4:40.) When they arrived on the opposite shore, a crazy man, who lived in the cemetery, ran to Him. Jesus cast the demons out of him and cast the demons into a herd of 2,000 swine, who ran down the hill and into the sea. When the people saw that the crazy man was no longer crazy, they asked Jesus to depart from their neighborhood. The crazy man told everyone what Jesus had done for him, and they all marveled.

Jesus went across the water to another town, where a ruler of the synagogue named Jairus asked Jesus to come and heal his daughter, who was very sick. As they were going, in the midst of a large crowd, a woman who had had a flow of blood for twelve years touched His garment, knowing that she would be healed. Immediately Jesus asked who touched His garment. The woman admitted that she did, and Jesus said, ". . . Daughter, your faith has made you well; go in peace, and be healed of your affliction" (Mark 5:34). She was healed instantly. At that moment someone came from the ruler's house and said that the daughter was dead. Jesus said, ". . . Do not be afraid any longer, only believe." He went into the house with Peter, James, and John and said to the girl, ". . . Little girl, I say to you, arise!" She did. (Mark 5:35–42.)

He then went to His home town of Nazareth, where He taught; and His friends were astonished at His knowledge, but nevertheless took offense at this carpenter's son. Jesus said, "A prophet is not without honor except in his home town and among his own relatives and in his own household" (Mark 6:4). It was time to test His apostles, so He sent them out to the surrounding villages two by two and instructed them to heal the sick and to cast out demons. King Herod was hearing more about Jesus and was concerned.

When the apostles returned, Jesus wanted to go apart with them to talk and rest, but great crowds followed them, like sheep without a shepherd.

Jesus talked to them and taught until it was late. He then fed 5,000 men, besides the women and children, with five loaves and two fish, and gathered up 12 baskets of food left over after all had eaten. To get away from the crowds, He sent His disciples ahead to Bethsaida in a boat on a troubled sea, and came to them later, walking on the water. When they saw Jesus walking on the water, they were terrified. Jesus said to them, ". . . Take courage; it is I, do not be afraid" (Mark 6:50). He entered the boat, and the sea was calmed. As soon as they landed at Gennesaret, great crowds began to gather, bringing their sick to be healed. This happened in all the villages that they visited.

The pious Pharisees and scribes criticized Him and found fault with anything they could think of, in order to discredit Him. He answered them in parables that confounded them. He and His disciples then went to the region of Tyre and Sidon, where He healed the daughter of a Greek woman. He started to return to the Sea of Galilee and, at Decapolis, healed a man who was deaf and had an impediment in his speech. The people were astonished, and His fame spread. Later, He was with a great crowd for three days, and the people were far from their homes with no food. Jesus blessed the seven loaves of bread and a few small fish that His disciples had, and they fed 4,000 people, picking up seven baskets of food that was left over.

The Pharisees never lost a chance to find fault with Him, and Jesus warned His disciples to beware of them and King Herod.

At Bethsaida He restored the sight of a blind man. While they were going to Caesarea Philippi, He asked His disciples, "Who do people say that I am?" They answered that some said He was John the Baptist, some Elijah, and some a prophet. He asked them, "But who do you say that I am?" Peter answered, "Thou art the Christ" (see Mark 8:27–29). He told them to tell no one, then told them that He must be rejected by the elders and chief priests, that He would be killed, and that He would rise again after three days. He continued to preach to the people and to His disciples.

Jesus then took Peter, James, and John with Him into a high mountain, to be alone, where He was transfigured (transformed) before them. His garments became dazzling white. Elijah and Moses appeared to them and talked to Jesus, and a voice from heaven said, ". . . This is My beloved Son, listen to Him!" (Mark 9:7.)

When they returned from the mountain, they were met by the other disciples and a large crowd. A man had brought his son to the disciples to be healed of a spirit that had thrown his son into convulsions since he was a child, but the disciples could not heal him. Jesus commanded the unclean spirit out of the child and said, ". . . All things are possible to him who believes" (Mark 9:23).

They all returned to Galilee, and Jesus talked to His disciples many times about His impending death, but they couldn't seem to understand. They were thinking in terms of a political kingdom, while He was talking about a spiritual Kingdom. They traveled to Judea, where He talked to crowds everywhere, and there were always the hypocritical Pharisees to heckle Him.

Jesus talked to the people about marriage and divorce and about little children. As they were leaving a village, a rich man approached Jesus and asked what he should do to inherit eternal life, and Jesus responded that he should keep the commandments, give his wealth to the poor, and follow Him. The man had great possessions, and went away dismayed. Jesus said to His disciples, "It is easier for a camel to go through the eye of a needle than for a rich man to enter the kingdom of God" (Mark 10:25). Jesus taught them many spiritual things, and they were constantly amazed.

They were on the road to Jerusalem when James and John asked Him if they could sit one on His right and one on His left in His glory, much to the indignation of the other disciples. Jesus answered, "But to sit on My right or on My left, this is not Mine to give; but it is for those for whom it has been prepared" (Mark 10:40).

As they came to Jericho, a blind man shouted to Jesus to have mercy on him. Jesus restored his sight and said, ". . . Go your way; your faith has made you well" (Mark 10:52). As they came near Jerusalem, Jesus sent two of His disciples into the village, to borrow a colt. He mounted the colt and started for Jerusalem as people spread their garments before Him, scattered leafy branches on the road, and cried "Hosanna." He entered the Temple and then left for Bethany, to spend the night.

The next day Jesus and the disciples returned to the Temple, where He overturned the tables of the money changers and drove out those who bought and sold merchandise. Then He preached to all, and they were amazed at His wisdom, but the chief priests and the scribes sought a way to have Him killed.

The next day, when they were returning to the Temple, Jesus talked to His disciples about faith in prayer saying, ". . . Have faith in God. Truly I say to you, whoever says to this mountain, 'Be taken up and cast into the sea,' and does not doubt in his heart, but believes that what he says is going to happen, it shall be granted him" (Mark 11:22, 23). As He entered the Temple, the chief priests, scribes, and elders attempted to trap Him with trick questions, but Jesus would not be trapped. He told them the parable of the vineyard.

He told the Pharisees to ". . . Render to Caesar the things that are Caesar's, and to God the things that are God's" (Mark 12:17). The Sadducees, who denied that there was any resurrection, also tried to trap

Him with questions about life in heaven. The scribes asked Him what the greatest commandment was, and Jesus said, ". . . LOVE THE LORD YOUR GOD WITH ALL YOUR HEART, AND WITH ALL YOUR SOUL, AND WITH ALL YOUR MIND, AND WITH ALL YOUR STRENGTH" (Mark 12:30). He taught the crowds and cited the widow who put the two copper coins in the church treasury as having contributed "out of her poverty" (see Mark 12:44). He foretold the total destruction of the Temple.

As they sat on the Mount of Olives that evening, Peter, James, John, and Andrew asked Him about this. Jesus warned them that persons would come as pretenders of Christ; that there would be great suffering before the Temple was destroyed (A.D. 70); and that there would be great catastrophes and suffering before His return and the day of judgment, when God would send His angels to gather the ones chosen to inherit the Kingdom of heaven.

It was two days before the Passover, and the chief priests and the scribes were plotting to have Jesus killed before then. Jesus' death, crucifixion, burial, and resurrection were approaching.

Judas Iscariot, apparently realizing that the Kingdom was not a political one for gain, went to the chief priests to betray Him. Jesus instructed His disciples about how to find a room to prepare for the feast of the Passover. That evening, as Jesus was eating with the twelve disciples, He said, ". . . one of you will betray Me . . ." (Mark 14:18). He taught them the communion service of the breaking of the bread and drinking of the cup in memory of Him.

They then went to the Mount of Olives, and Jesus told them He would be killed and they would all run away. Peter denied this, and Jesus told him that Peter would deny Him three times before the cock crowed. This proved to be true. In the Garden of Gethsemane, Jesus prayed. Judas then came with the chief priests and the scribes and a mob, seized Jesus, and led Him before the high priest, where they tried to condemn Him by false witnesses. They then took Him before Pilate, who could find no fault in Him; but to please the mob, he had Him beaten and delivered to be crucified.

The soldiers mocked Him as King of the Jews, beat Him, spit on Him, and led Him away to be crucified, where they divided His clothes by lot. They even mocked Him while He was dying on the cross with two thieves.

In the ninth hour, Jesus died, and the curtain in the Temple was split in two, from top to bottom. Joseph of Arimathea, a member of the council, asked Pilate's permission to bury the body. He put it in a tomb hewn out of the rock and rolled a stone over the door. Mary Magdalene and Mary, the mother of James, witnessed Jesus' crucifixion and the burial.

When the Sabbath was past, these women went to the tomb, to put spices on the body and anoint it. They wondered who they would get to roll the rock from the entrance to the tomb, but it was already rolled back. A young man in a white robe in the tomb told them that Christ was risen and that they should go tell the disciples that Jesus would meet them in Galilee.

LUKE

Time
: A.D. 60–A.D. 75. Before Paul's death, about A.D. 68. Probably while Paul was in prison.

Author
: Luke was a physician, but this is never stated as a fact in the Bible. Luke was not one of the apostles, but was a companion with Paul on many of his travels. He never saw Jesus, but he talked with others who did. He was a Greek Gentile and wrote especially to the Greeks. He addressed his work to Theophilus, a high Roman government official.

Theme
: Luke wrote what he heard Paul tell from one end of the Roman empire to the other. He told the Gospel for the outcasts on earth, as well as for the weak and suffering. He told of the beauty and perfection of Jesus, the ideal and universal man. Luke may have talked to Jesus' mother, Mary, in person. He had the benefit of reading Matthew and Mark before writing his book. He and Matthew both told the story of Jesus' birth.

In the days of Herod, a priest named Zacharias, who had married Elizabeth, was in the Temple when Gabriel, an angel of the Lord, appeared to him and told him that his wife Elizabeth would have a son. Zacharias and his wife were old; she was barren, and they had no son. Gabriel told Zacharias that because he doubted, he would be unable to speak until the child was born. In the sixth month of Elizabeth's pregnancy, the angel Gabriel went to Nazareth and appeared to a virgin whose name was Mary and said, ". . . you will conceive in your womb, and bear a son, and you shall name Him Jesus" (Luke 1:31). Mary went to visit Elizabeth, and as she entered the house, the babe in Elizabeth's womb leaped for joy, and Elizabeth called Mary blessed. When the child was born, they named him John and knew that he came for a great mission for the Lord. (He was later known as John the Baptist.)

Caesar Augustus decreed that all in the world be enrolled, primarily for tax purposes; Joseph, in the lineage of David, took Mary, his betrothed, to Bethlehem, to be enrolled. While they were there, she gave birth to her baby in a manger, because there was no room in the inn. An angel of the Lord appeared to some shepherds in a field and told them of the birth of Christ the Lord. They went with haste and found the babe in the manger, and they told everyone of the angel's message. At the end of eight days, the babe was circumcised and named Jesus, the name given by the angel. When the time came for the rite of purification, they took Jesus to Jerusalem, where an old man named Simeon had been told by the Holy Spirit that he would not die before he saw the Christ. He took the child in his arms and blessed Him.

When Jesus was twelve years old, His parents went to Jerusalem for the Passover. When they were leaving, they missed Jesus, so they returned to Jerusalem to find Him. After three days, they found Him in the Temple, talking with great wisdom to the teachers. When they admonished Him, He said, ". . . Did you not know that I had to be in My Father's house?" (Luke 2:49.)

In the fifteenth year of Tiberius Caesar, the word of God came to John, the son of Zacharias, to preach and baptize. John the Baptist said to the people that he baptized with water, but one who was coming would baptize with the Holy Spirit and with fire. Herod had him put in prison.

After he baptized Jesus, the Holy Spirit descended on Jesus as a dove, and a voice from heaven said, ". . . Thou art My beloved Son, in Thee I am well-pleased" (Luke 3:22). Jesus' ancestry was traced directly to Adam as the son of God. He started His ministry at age thirty, which at that time was the legal age.

After being baptized, Jesus was led by the Holy Spirit into the wilderness for forty days, to be tempted by the devil, but He resisted all his offers to sin against God. He then went to His hometown of Nazareth, where He was rejected.

Capernaum was selected for His headquarters for His preaching. Jesus cast a demon out of a man. All were amazed, and His fame started to spread. He healed the fever of Simon's mother-in-law and all others who came to Him. He preached throughout Judea, and while at the lake at Gennesaret, a great crowd gathered, so He had to get in a boat to talk to them. When He finished, He told Simon, whose boat He had used, to cast out his net to catch some fish. Simon replied that they had fished all night and had caught none, but threw the net out and caught so many fish that he had to call for another boat to carry all the fish. Simon and James and John, sons of Zebedee, who had helped, were all amazed and afraid. Jesus said ". . . Do not fear, from now on you will be catching men" (Luke 5:10). They all left everything and went with Jesus.

While He was in one of the cities, He healed a man of leprosy, who said, ". . . Lord, if You are willing, You can make me clean." Jesus answered, ". . . I am willing; be cleansed" (Luke 5:12, 13). Healing like this caused great multitudes to gather wherever He went.

One day when Jesus was teaching, there were scribes and Pharisees in the crowd, who had come from all over Galilee. Some friends who had brought a paralyzed man on a bed could not get through the crowd, so they lowered him down in front of Jesus through the roof. When Jesus saw their faith and said, ". . . Friend, your sins are forgiven you," the scribes and Pharisees said, ". . . Who can forgive sins, but God alone?" Jesus said, ". . . rise, and take up your stretcher and go home," which the man did (Luke 5:20, 21, 24). After that He saw a tax collector, Matthew, called Levi; He said, "Follow me," and Matthew did. Levi then arranged for a feast with many other tax collectors, and when Jesus ate with them, the Pharisees criticized Him, but He replied, "I have not come to call righteous men, but sinners to repentance" (Luke 5:32).

They also found fault with Him because His disciples feasted instead of fasted. He told them the parable of the wedding guests and the patching of the old garment with the new cloth and putting new wine in old wineskins. The Pharisees were constantly trying to find ways to criticize Jesus. They did so when His disciples gathered grain on a Sabbath to eat and when, on the Sabbath, Jesus healed a man who had a withered hand. The Pharisees were now plotting to find a way to kill Him.

At one time He went into the hills and prayed all night for guidance the next day, to select the twelve apostles from all His disciples. He then came to a place where a great crowd, from all over Judea, Jerusalem, the coast of Tyre, and Zidon, was assembled. He healed all the sick and gave them the great sermon of the Beatitudes, which is commonly called the Sermon on the Mount. He urged all to practice what was taught.

After this, He went back to Capernaum. A centurion (a Roman soldier who had one hundred men in his command), who had built a synagogue for the Jews, had a slave who was very sick, so he had the elders ask Jesus to come and heal him. Jesus went to heal him and was met by friends of the centurion with the message that he was not worthy, but that if Jesus would say the word, his slave would be healed. Jesus said, ". . . I say to you, not even in Israel have I found such great faith" (Luke 7:9). The slave was healed.

Jesus went from village to village, preaching, teaching, and healing. At Nain, He resurrected the dead son of a widow. He praised John the Baptist. He dined with a Pharisee. He forgave the sins of a very sinful woman. He told the parable of the sower and explained it to His disciples, but not to the crowds. He calmed a storm at sea. At the country of the Gerasenes, He cast the demons from a crazy man into a herd of swine, which plunged down a bank into the sea and drowned. The people were amazed and afraid. He crossed back over the sea, where He was met by crowds and where He healed a woman who had had a flow of blood for twelve years. He resurrected a twelve-year-old girl.

Jesus then called the twelve apostles together, gave them power and authority over all demons and the ability to cure diseases, and sent them out to preach the Kingdom of God to all the villages and the countryside. Later, when they returned, He went with them to Bethsaida, where He talked to a great crowd. They fed 5,000 men, plus the women and children, with five loaves and two fish, and gathered 12 baskets of food left over. He then told His disciples that He must suffer many things, must be rejected by the chief priests and scribes, must be killed, and on the third day would be raised.

A few days later He took Peter, James, and John with Him into the mountains to pray. As He was praying, His countenance was altered; His clothing became dazzling white (the transfiguration), and Moses and Elijah appeared and spoke of His departure from Jerusalem. A cloud overshadowed them while a voice declared, ". . . This is My Son, My Chosen One; listen to Him!" (Luke 9:35).

The next day, when they came down from the mountain, Jesus healed a boy with a demon that convulsed him. The disciples had not been able to cast the demon out, and Jesus said, ". . . O unbelieving and perverted generation . . ." (Luke 9:41). He again told His disciples of His impending death, but they did not understand. Many people halfheartedly wanted to join Him, but He said, ". . . No one after putting his hand to the plow and looking back, is fit for the kingdom of God" (Luke 9:62).

Jesus appointed seventy others to go two by two into all the villages where He was about to come, to prepare the way. They were to carry no money or clothes and were to bestow peace upon any household that would take them in. As the seventy returned, they reported that even the demons were subject to them in Jesus' name.

A lawyer tested Jesus by saying, ". . . what shall I do to inherit eternal life?" Jesus said, ". . . What is written in the Law? . . ." The man replied, ". . . YOU SHALL LOVE THE LORD YOUR GOD WITH ALL YOUR HEART, AND WITH ALL YOUR SOUL, AND WITH ALL YOUR STRENGTH, AND WITH ALL YOUR MIND; AND YOUR NEIGHBOR AS YOURSELF." Jesus answered, ". . . You have answered correctly; DO THIS, AND YOU WILL LIVE." The lawyer answered, ". . . who is my neighbor?" (Luke 10:25–29.) Jesus answered by telling him the story of the good Samaritan, and then said, ". . . Go and do the same" (Luke 10:37).

There is then the story of Martha and Mary, her sister, who sat at Jesus' feet, and the story of how Jesus taught His disciples to pray (known as the Lord's Prayer). He talked with crowds everywhere; some praised Him; and some tested Him in order to condemn Him, but He always answered them and told them parables, because He came to save men, not to condemn them.

A Pharisee invited Him for dinner and then condemned Him because He did not wash His hands, and Jesus answered, ". . . Now you Pharisees clean the outside of the cup and of the platter; but inside of you, you are full of robbery and wickedness" (Luke 11:39). He also reproached a lawyer for criticizing Him.

He talked to crowds of thousands about God's love for His people and why, with faith, they need not worry, saying, ". . . do not be anxious for your life . . . Consider the lilies, how they grow; they neither toil nor spin; but I tell you, even Solomon in all his glory did not clothe himself like one of these" (Luke 12:22, 27). He told the stories of and explained about the unpardonable sin, the rich fool, treasures in heaven, the faithful servant, fire upon earth, signs of the times, settlement out of court, the Galileans' blood, the barren fig tree, the healing on the Sabbath of the bowed woman, the mustard seed compared to the kingdom of heaven, and heaven compared to leaven.

As He traveled toward Jerusalem, He preached and taught in the towns and villages and continued with His illustrative stories and parables about the love of God and the Kingdom of heaven. He urged the people to cease their sinfulness and to abide by God's commandments. He told the story of the narrow door, the honored seats, feasts for the poor, the excuses of many, and the task to be a follower. He called Herod a fox and healed a man with dropsy on the Sabbath.

He was criticized constantly by the hypocritical Pharisees. In a large gathering, He told the stories and parables of the finding of the lost sheep and the lost coin, as compared to saving one sinner who repents; the famous story of the prodigal son; the unjust steward (no servant can serve two masters); divorce creates adultery; the rich man and Lazarus the beggar; constant forgiveness; and the power of faith. The apostles asked Jesus to increase their faith and He said, ". . . If you had faith like a mustard seed, you would say to this mulberry tree, 'Be uprooted and be planted in the sea'; and it would obey you" (Luke 17:6).

Continuing on the way to Jerusalem to His destiny, He healed the ten lepers; only one praised God. He answered the Pharisees' question about when the Kingdom of God was coming and told the parables and stories of the judge and the widow, the Pharisee and the tax collector, children and the kingdom of heaven, and the rich young ruler. Jesus said, ". . . it is easier for a camel to go through the eye of a needle, than for a rich man to enter the kingdom of God" (Luke 18:25). But He also said, ". . . The things impossible with men are possible with God" (Luke 18:27).

Jesus took the twelve apostles to one side and told them that they were going into Jerusalem, where everything that had been written and prophesied would be accomplished. He said that He would be delivered to the Gentiles, mocked, shamefully treated, spit upon, scourged, and killed; and that on the third day, He would rise. They had no idea as to what He was talking about. As they approached Jericho, He healed the sight of a blind man, saying, ". . . your faith has made you well" (Luke 18:42). In Jericho He stayed with Zaccheus, a rich chief tax collector who had climbed up a tree to see Jesus as He passed by. He then told the crowd the parables of the pounds.

When He came near Bethany at the Mount of Olives, He sent two of His disciples into the city, to get a colt to ride into Jerusalem. He rode into the city with the crowds throwing their garments and branches in the road ahead of Him. In the Temple, He drove out the merchants and preached daily. The chief priests and scribes were plotting constantly to trick Him into saying something that would help them convict Him and have Him killed.

He told the parables of the vineyard and answered their question of tribute ". . . render to Caesar the things that are Caesar's, and to God the things that are God's" (Luke 20:25). He answered a question of the Sadducees by ending, ". . . He is not the God of the dead, but of the living; for all live to Him" (Luke 20:38). He denounced the scribes, praised the widow who put two copper coins into the church treasury, and prophesied the destruction of the Temple and the final day of judgment.

As the day for the feast of the Passover approached, Judas Iscariot, one of the disciples, plotted with the Pharisees to betray Him. On the day of the Passover, Jesus sent Peter and John to find a place and prepare the feast. This was called the Last Supper in the upper room, where Jesus instructed the disciples in the communion service of breaking the bread and drinking the wine in remembrance of Him. Peter told Jesus that he would go to prison or die for him, but Jesus said, ". . . the cock will not crow today, until you have denied three times that you know Me" (Luke 22:34).

Jesus went to the Mount of Olives at Gethsemane to pray, where Judas, the traitor, brought the soldiers to arrest Him. One of the disciples took a sword and cut off the ear of a slave of the high priest, but Jesus touched it and healed it back again. The soldiers and chief priests led Him away, to the high priest's house. Peter followed with the crowd near Jesus; as he mingled with the crowd, three different people accused Peter of being a follower of Jesus. As he denied these things the third time, the cock crowed, and Jesus looked around toward Peter, who wept and ran away from the crowd.

The people holding Jesus mocked Him, reviled Him, and the next morning delivered Him before the Jewish council, where they were determined, regardless of any evidence, to have Him crucified. They took Him before Pilate, then Herod, and then back to Pilate. Neither of them could find any fault with Him, but the mob kept screaming, "Crucify Him," so Pilate finally granted their demand. They led Him away and had a man by the name of Simon of Cyrene help carry Jesus' cross.

Jesus was crucified with two common criminals, one of whom said to Him, ". . . remember me when You come in Your kingdom!" Jesus answered, ". . . today you shall be with Me in Paradise" (Luke 23:42, 43). From the sixth hour to the ninth hour, there was total darkness. The curtain in the Temple was torn in two, and Jesus cried, ". . . Father, INTO THY HANDS I COMMIT MY SPIRIT," and died (Luke 23:46). Many people mourned, and others were ashamed. Joseph, a goodly man from the town of Arimathea, requested Jesus' body from Pilate, wrapped it in a linen shroud, and put it in a new tomb.

The women from Galilee prepared spices and ointments on Friday, did nothing on the Sabbath, and early Sunday, went to the tomb. The sealing rock was rolled back, and the body was gone. Two men were there in dazzling apparel. They reminded the women that Jesus had said He would be delivered into the hands of sinners, He would be crucified, and He would rise on the third day. The women, Mary Magdalene, Joanna, Mary, the mother of James, and others, ran to tell this to the disciples, who did not believe.

That same day, two of the disciples going to Emmaus, about seven miles from Jerusalem, met Jesus but did not recognize Him, even after He told them of the prophecies of the Scriptures. They urged Him to stay with them, and at supper Jesus broke bread with them. When they recognized Him, He vanished.

They returned at once to Jerusalem and found the disciples, who reported that Jesus had appeared to Simon, also. At that moment Jesus appeared to them and they were startled and afraid. He ate with them, invited them to feel His body, and said, ". . . These are My words which I spoke to you while I was still with you, that all things which are written about Me in the Law of Moses and the Prophets and the Psalms must be fulfilled" (Luke 24:44). Then He opened their minds by saying, ". . . Thus it is written, that the Christ should suffer and rise again from the dead the third day; and that repentance for forgiveness of sins should be proclaimed in His name to all the nations, beginning from Jerusalem. You are witnesses of these things. And behold, I am sending forth the promise of My Father upon you; but you are to stay in the city until you are clothed with power [the Holy Spirit] from on high" (Luke 24:44–49).

He then led them out of the city as far as Bethany, where He blessed them and disappeared. They returned to Jerusalem with great joy and expectation.

JOHN

Time   A.D. 80–A.D. 100. John was probably ninety-five when he wrote this book. Jerusalem had been destroyed (A.D. 70).

Author   John was the brother of James. He and James were the sons of Zebedee, and were partners with Peter as fishermen. Jesus called these strong-willed, violent-tempered, and vehement Galilean men "Sons of Thunder." John was the youngest apostle and the last to die. He had been a disciple of John the Baptist and referred to himself as the "disciple whom Jesus loved." His mother was Salome, sister of Mary, the mother of Jesus. His family lived in a good neighborhood and was considered well off because it had servants. John wrote the three books of John, plus Revelation.

Theme   The writings cover a period from John the Baptist to the last appearance of Christ—probably five years. John probably wrote this for the church at Ephesus, but it was intended for all the known world and was concerned primarily with Jesus' Judean ministry. Jesus' ministry covered about three and one half years, starting in the Fall of A.D. 26 and ending in the Spring of A.D. 30. Jesus was thirty (born 4 B.C.—modern calendar) when He started His ministry. John gave no account of Jesus' birth, His boyhood, temptation or transfiguration. He did not write about the appointment of His apostles, and there are no parables and no ascension. This book is considered by many people to be the most important single writing of all mankind.

Matthew, Mark, and Luke told about the miracles of Jesus to demonstrate His compassion for men. John told of the miracles to prove the divine power of Jesus, to prove Christ was God, and to use this proof as an inducement for men to have faith in Him, His teachings, and in God. John wrote to prove to the Jews that Jesus was the Christ, the promised Messiah, and to prove to the Gentiles that He was the Son of God. John wrote to lead all believers into a divine fellowship with Him. John told of seven witnesses to prove that "Jesus is the Christ, the Son of God." He told of seven miracles that proved that He was God. And he used seven statements made by Jesus to prove His deity in the form of "I am." John established His deity in every one of the twenty-one chapters in this book.

The seven witnesses are:
  John the Baptist, ". . . this is the Son of God" (1:34)
  Nathanael, ". . . You are the Son of God . . ." (1:49)
  Martha, ". . . I have believed that You are the Christ, the Son of God . . ." (11:27)
  Peter, "You are the Holy One of God" (6:69)
  Thomas, "My Lord and my God" (20:28)
  John, "Jesus is the Christ, the Son of God" (20:31)
  Christ, "I am the Son of God" (10:36)
The seven miracles are:
  Turning the water into wine (2:1–11)
  Healing of the nobleman's son (4:46–54)
  Healing the man at Bethesda, who had been sick thirty-eight years (5:1–9)
  Feeding the 5,000 (6:1–14)
  Walking on the water (6:16–21)
  Healing the blind man (9:1–41)
  Raising of Lazarus, who had been dead four days (11:1–44)
The seven *I ams* are:
  ". . . I am the bread of life . . ." (6:35)
  ". . . I am the light of the world . . ." (8:12)
  ". . . before Abraham was born, I AM" (8:58)
  "I am the good shepherd . . ." (10:11)
  ". . . I am the resurrection and the life . . ." (11:25)
  ". . . I am the way, and the truth, and the life . . ." (14:6)
  "I am the vine, you are the branches . . ." (15:5)

John opens his book like Genesis: "In the beginning was the Word, and the Word was with God . . ." meaning that Jesus is the Word and that He was God and is God's message to mankind.

John the Baptist was prophesying the coming of the light, the Christ, and was baptizing with water in the Jordan River. One day John saw Jesus coming toward him, and he said, "Behold, the Lamb of God who takes away the sin of the world!" (John 1:29.) John saw the Spirit descend as a dove from heaven, remaining on Jesus, and John remembered the words, ". . . 'He upon whom you see the Spirit descending and remaining upon Him, this is the one who baptizes in the Holy Spirit'" (John 1:33).

Two of John's followers, John and Andrew, went with Jesus. He also selected Simon Peter (Peter), whom Jesus called Cephas, which means Peter. At Galilee He selected Philip and Nathanael.

There was a marriage feast at Cana in Galilee, and Jesus and His mother Mary were invited. They ran out of wine. Jesus had the servants fill six stone jars, each holding twenty to thirty gallons, with water and then serve from the jars. The steward said to the bridegroom, ". . . you have kept the good wine until now" (John 2:10). This was Jesus' first sign, and His disciples believed.

At the time of the feast of the Passover, Jesus went to Jerusalem. Finding the Temple being used as a marketplace, He made a whip of cords and chased out the money changers and those who sold oxen, sheep, and pigeons, saying, ". . . stop making My Father's house a house of merchandise" (John 2:16). He also said, ". . . Destroy this temple, and in three days I will raise it up" (John 2:19). Jesus meant His body, but the Jews said that it had taken forty-six years to build the Temple, so how could He rebuild it in three days?

A Pharisee by the name of Nicodemus, a member of the Sanhedrin court, came secretly to Jesus, to talk to Him. Jesus told him many things, but basically that man must be born anew (again) in the spirit. Nicodemus could not understand, but he always defended Jesus in the court, even at great peril to his own life.

Jesus went to Judea to baptize, and John the Baptist continued to preach and baptize near Salim. After Jesus' reputation for teaching, preaching, and healing spread to the Pharisees, Jesus left Judea, to go to Galilee.

As Jesus and the disciples passed through Samaria, they stopped at Jacob's well, where Jesus asked a Samaritan woman to give him a drink. (The Jews of Judea literally despised the Samaritans of northern Israel because of their mixed marriages, idolatry, corruption, and sinful disobedience to God.) She said, ". . . How is it that You, being a Jew, ask me for a drink since I am a Samaritan woman?" (John 4:9.) He talked to her about living water, and told her that she had been married five times and was not married to the man she was living with then. She said, ". . . Sir, I perceive that You are a prophet . . . I know that Messiah is coming (He who is called Christ); when that One comes, He will declare all things to us" (John 4:18, 25). Jesus answered, ". . . I who speak to you am He" (John 4:26). She rushed to the village to tell the people, and they came and asked Him to stay. They believed Him and said to the woman, ". . . we have heard for ourselves and know that this One is indeed the Savior of the world" (John 4:42).

Jesus went to Galilee and then on to Capernaum, where there was an official whose son was ill. The official said to him, ". . . Sir, come down before my child dies." Jesus answered, ". . . Go your way; your son lives" (John 4:49, 50). The man believed. As he was returning home, his servant met him and said his child was well. They determined that he was healed the same hour that Jesus said he would live.

Jesus then went to Jerusalem, where He saw a man who had been ill for thirty-eight years, at the pool of Bethesda. He said, ". . . Do you wish to get well?" The man said yes. Jesus said, ". . . Arise, take up your pallet, and walk" (John 5:6, 8). This he did, and the Jews criticized him for carrying his pallet on the Sabbath. He told them that Jesus told him to do this, which was why the Jews tried to persecute Him whenever they could. This gave Jesus the opportunity to tell them that He was the Son of God, sent by God to save men's lives. Many of the people believed, but those of the priesthood refused and intensified their efforts to kill Him.

After this, Jesus went to the other side of the Sea of Galilee, to Tiberias, where He talked to a great crowd who believed in Him because they had seen Him heal the sick and diseased. Late in the day He blessed five loaves and two fish and distributed them among 5,000 men. After they had all eaten, they gathered up 12 baskets of fragments. The people marveled and said, ". . . This is of a truth the Prophet who is to come into the world" (John 6:14).

Jesus and the disciples had to retreat to the hills to get away from the crowds, and after dark the disciples went down and got into a boat, to cross to Capernaum. After they were out about three or four miles in a strong wind, Jesus came toward them, walking on the water. They were frightened, but Jesus said, ". . . It is I; do not be afraid" (John 6:20). The sea calmed, and they landed.

The next day the crowds followed Him, to learn how to get this free bread and what they must do to do the works of God. Jesus counselled them not to labor for food that perishes, but for food that endures to eternal life. He said, ". . . I am the bread of life; he who comes to Me shall not hunger, and he who believes in Me shall never thirst . . . For this is the will of My Father, that every one who beholds the Son, and believes in Him, may have eternal life . . ." (John 6:35, 40). The Jews found fault with this because He was a carpenter's son. Jesus answered, ". . . the bread also which I shall give for the life of the world is My flesh" (John 6:51). They didn't understand, and He explained again, but even many of His followers couldn't understand His saying, ". . . the words that I have spoken to you are spirit and are life" (John 6:63). Jesus asked if the twelve wanted to desert Him, also. Peter answered, ". . . You are the Holy One of God." Jesus answered, ". . . Did I Myself not choose you, the twelve, and yet one of you is a devil?" (John 6:69, 70.)

The Jews sought to kill Jesus, so He would not go with His disciples to Judea to the feast of the Tabernacle. Later He went alone and, in the midst of the feast, went into the Tabernacle and taught openly. The people asked many questions, and some tried to entrap Him. Some believed Him and others didn't. The Jews wanted to arrest Him, but even the officers said, ". . . Never did a man speak the way this man speaks" (John 7:46). Nicodemus defended Him and was criticized for it. The Pharisees finally took up stones to throw at Him, but He escaped and went out of the Temple.

As He passed by, He saw a man blind from birth. His disciples asked Him, ". . . who sinned, this man or his parents, that he should be born blind?" Jesus answered, "It was neither that this man sinned, nor his parents; but it was in order that the works of God might be displayed in him," and healed the man's blindness, on a Sabbath day (John 9:2, 3). The Pharisees condemned Jesus for doing this on the Sabbath. They debated this miracle with Him but refused to listen and believe anything He said. They finally tried to arrest Him, but He escaped. He went across the Jordan, to where John the Baptist first baptized, where many heard Him and believed.

Lazarus, the brother of Mary and Martha, all of whom Jesus loved, became very ill, and they sent for Jesus to come and heal him. Jesus delayed two days and told His disciples that they would go, but that Lazarus was already dead. Lazarus had been in his tomb for four days when Martha met Jesus; she said, ". . . I know that whatever You ask of God, God will give You" (John 11:22). Jesus said, ". . . Remove the stone . . . ." Martha said, "Lord, by this time there will be a stench; for he has been dead four days." Jesus answered, ". . . Did I not say to you, if you believe, you will see the glory of God?" (John 11:39, 40.) He then cried with a loud voice, ". . . Lazarus, come forth" (John 11:43).

The dead man came out, with his hands and feet bound and his face wrapped with a cloth. Jesus said, ". . . Unbind him, and let him go" (John 11:44). Many Jews believed in Him, but some went to the Pharisees and told them what had happened. The chief priests and the Pharisees gathered the council, and Caiaphas decreed, ". . . it is expedient for you that one man should die for the people, and that the whole nation should not perish" (John 11:50). From that day on, they plotted His death.

Later, as the time for the Passover neared, many went to Jerusalem, hoping to see Jesus. The chief priests had put out orders to watch for Him, so that they might arrest Him. Six days before the Passover, Jesus came to Bethany, about one and one-half miles from Jerusalem, and stayed with Lazarus, Mary, and Martha. The news spread quickly, and a great crowd gathered to see Jesus and also to see Lazarus, whom Jesus had resurrected from death.

The next day, the crowd spread branches of palm trees in the road as Jesus entered the city on the colt of an ass; all cried, "Hosanna! BLESSED IS HE WHO COMES IN THE NAME OF THE LORD, even the King of Israel" (John 12:13). This made the Pharisees even more desperate to kill Him.

Some Greeks had come to celebrate the Passover, and they asked Philip if they could see Jesus. Jesus answered, ". . . The hour has come for the Son of Man to be glorified" (John 12:23). Jesus said, "Father, glorify Thy name . . . ." Then a voice came from heaven, saying,

190 / John

". . . I have both glorified it, and will glorify it again" (John 12:28). Some said it was thunder, and others said it was the voice of an angel, but all heard it. Many Pharisees believed, but were afraid to say so, lest they be put out of the synagogue.

Before the feast of the Passover, while Jesus was with His disciples, He bathed all their feet and said, ". . . He who has bathed needs only to wash his feet, but is completely clean; and you are clean, but not all of you" (John 13:10). He was referring to Judas, who was to betray Him. He also said, ". . . he who receives whomever I send receives Me; and he who receives Me receives Him who sent Me" (John 13:20).

Judas left the group, to betray Jesus. As Jesus talked, Peter said that he would lay down his life for Him, but Jesus said that Peter would deny Him three times before the cock would crow. As Jesus talked of His leaving, the disciples could not understand. He explained many things to them and said, "A little while, and you will no longer behold Me; and again a little while, and you will see Me" (John 16:16). He was referring to His death and resurrection on the third day, but they still could not comprehend. Jesus tried to re-explain many things to them and then prayed to the Father, after which they went to the garden of Gethsemane.

Judas led a group of soldiers, officers of the high priests, and Pharisees to where Jesus was; they seized Him and led Him away to the home of Annas, father-in-law of Caiaphas, who was the high priest. It was Caiaphas who said that it was expedient that one man should die for the people. Peter denied that he knew Jesus when a woman asked him if he was a disciple. They questioned Jesus, then bound Him and took Him to Caiaphas. A man asked Peter if he was one of the disciples, and as he moved among the crowd, another man asked him, but Peter denied both times that he knew Jesus; at that time, the cock crowed.

They then took Jesus to Pilate, who questioned Him and could find no fault with Him, but the Jews had the mob rehearsed to cry, "Crucify. Crucify." Pilate tried to reason with the priests, but they made so much noise that he finally relented and gave Jesus over to them, to be crucified. They made Him carry His own cross to the hill called Golgotha, where they crucified Him with two others. The soldiers divided His garments and cast lots for His tunic.

Standing by were His mother, His mother's sister, Mary, the wife of Clopas, and Mary Magdelene. When Jesus saw His mother and the disciple John, he said, "Woman, behold, your son!" And then he said to John, ". . . Behold, your mother! . . ." (John 19:26, 27.) Later He bowed His head, saying, "It is finished!" and died.

Joseph of Arimathea asked Pilate for Jesus' body, that he might bury Him. Nicodemus helped him put spices of myrrh and aloes on the body, wrap it in linen cloths, and place it in a new tomb. On the day after the Sabbath, Mary went early to the tomb and saw that the stone had been rolled back. She ran to Peter and John and said, ". . . They have taken away the Lord out of the tomb . . ." (John 20:2). Peter and John ran to the tomb and saw the linens, but no body, and left. Mary wept at the tomb. Two angels said to her, ". . . Woman, why are you weeping?" She said, ". . . Because they have taken away my Lord . . ." (John 20:13). She turned around and Jesus was standing there. He said, ". . . Stop clinging to Me; for I have not yet ascended to the Father; but go to My brethren, and say to them, 'I ascend to My Father and your Father, and My God and your God' " (John 20:17).

Jesus appeared to the disciples in a closed room that evening and said, "Receive the Holy Spirit. If you forgive the sins of any, their sins have been forgiven them; if you retain the sins of any, they have been retained" (John 20:22, 23). Eight days later, Jesus appeared to them again in the closed room and said to Thomas, who was not present before, ". . . Reach here your finger, and see My hands; and reach here your hand, and put it into My side; and be not unbelieving, but believing" (John 20:27). Thomas answered, "My Lord and my God!" Jesus did many other things in the presence of the disciples that are not written in this book, but these are written that you may believe that Jesus is the Christ, the Son of God, and that believing, you may have life in His name.

Jesus revealed Himself at the Sea of Tiberias to Peter, Thomas, Nathanael, James, and John, and two others. They had been fishing all night and had caught nothing. As day was breaking, they saw Jesus on the shore. He told them to cast their net on the other side of the boat, which they did, and it was so full of fish that they could not haul it in. When they landed, they ate breakfast with Jesus. Jesus said to Peter, ". . . Simon, son of John, do you love Me?" (John 21:16.) and Peter said yes. Jesus said, ". . . Tend My lambs" and ". . . Shepherd My sheep," and ". . . Tend my sheep" (John 21:15–17).

John's enduring words are, "And there are also many other things which Jesus did, which if they were written in detail, I suppose that even the world itself would not contain the books which were written" (John 21:25).

TERRITORY COVERED IN CHRIST'S MINISTRY

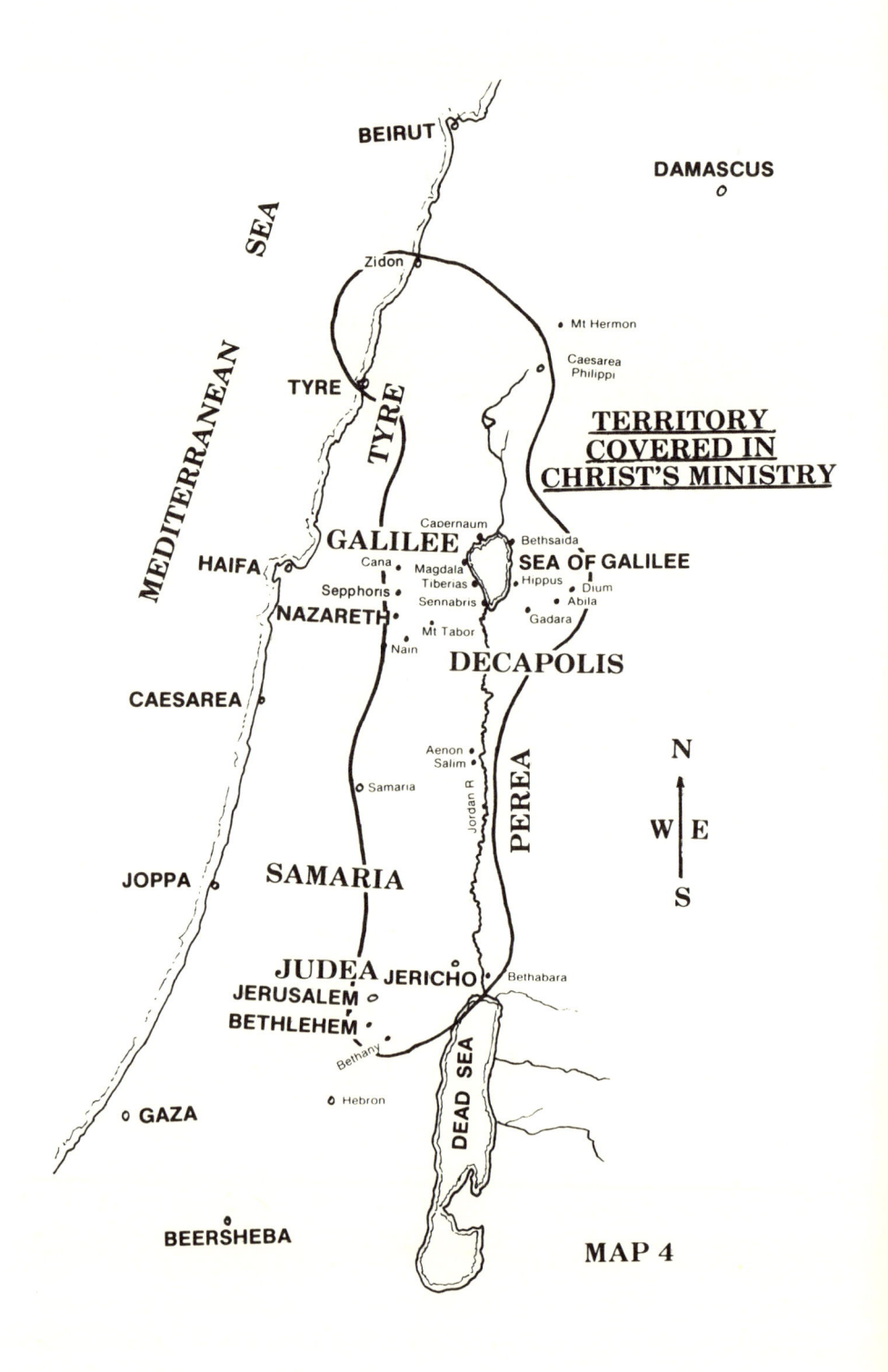

MAP 4

DEVELOPMENTS IN CIVILIZATION
A.D. 1–A.D. 100

During this period of time, the most prominent culture was that of the Romans. Rome was the focal point of authority in the world, and would remain so for 400 years. There was, basically, peace and prosperity because the Romans ruled with strict discipline and an iron fist, which, together with high taxes, earned them a universal hatred.

The Roman empire covered an area nearly five-sevenths the size of the United States, and consisted of several dominant civilizations. Egypt, which had reached its peak 2500 years previously, was at this time a province of Rome. Greece, which had risen to great heights of learning in all of the arts, as well as in crafts, sciences, literature, mathematics, medicine, and astrology, had fallen under Roman rule, never to rise again.

Alexandria, Carthage, and northern Africa, all had passed their peaks of glory. Spain, France, Germany, Britain, and the Scandinavian fringes had not progressed as much in their civilizations as the Mediterranean areas had; they also were under Roman domination.

Babylon, Assyria, Persia, and Turkey had risen to the zenith of their power and development, only to fall. All but the Parthians were under Roman domination.

The Chinese, Indians, and Mongolians had been progressing for 2000 years in their growth, stability, and ruling leadership. They were trading with western countries at this time.

This was the world into which Jesus Christ was born and subsequently baptized by John the Baptist. This was the period of all of the books of the New Testament. After beginning at the age of thirty (the legal age at that time), Jesus preached and taught for three years. He was crucified at the age of thirty-three and rose from His grave after three days. He instructed His twelve apostles to establish the Church of Christ throughout the world, and to teach brotherly love, forgiveness of sins, salvation, and God's love. This was the world in which these twelve men went forth to establish the Church of Christ.

CHRONOLOGICAL SUMMARY

ROME

A.D. 14 The Roman Empire was at the zenith of its power at this time; cosmopolitanism and prosperity flourished.
A.D. 42 Founding of the Christian Church by St. Peter.
A.D. 50–100 During this period, the Christians were persecuted.
A.D. 50 Romans learned the use of soap from the Gauls.
A.D. 64 Nero rebuilt Rome, following the Grecian pattern, after the fire.
A.D. 65 St. Linus became the second Pope.
A.D. 67 St. Peter died a martyr in Rome, and was buried on the site of the present St. Peter's Basilica in Rome. The Roman army leaders were in control of the government.
A.D. 68 Nero committed suicide.
A.D. 75–79 Flavius Josephus wrote *History of the Jewish War*.
A.D. 79 Pompeii was destroyed by the eruption of Mount Vesuvius.
A.D. 88 Clement became the third Pope. Emperor Titus was responsible for the conquest and destruction of Jerusalem (A.D. 70). The Arch of Titus, located on Sacred Way by the Forum, was built to honor this feat.
A.D. 98 Trajan became emperor. Under his leadership, the Roman Empire reached its greatest geographical extent.

GREECE

A.D. 16 The first definite reference to diamonds was made.
A.D. 40 One of the earliest Christian churches was erected at Corinth.

PERSIA-BABYLON-ASSYRIA

A.D. 45 St. Paul set out on his missionary travels.

ASIA MINOR-TURKEY

A.D. 50 St. Paul established the first Christian churches.

CHINA

A.D. 58 Ming Ti, the new emperor of China, introduced Buddhism.

GERMANY-SCANDINAVIA

A.D. 50 The Goths set up a kingdom in Poland on the Vistula River. The Teutonic civilization was in its primitive, pastoral stage.

BRITON

A.D. 43 This marked the Roman invasion of Briton. Emperor Claudius conquered Britania (England), and Rome ruled for 400 years. The city of London was founded.

A.D. 98 The city of Gloucester was founded.

FRANCE

A.D. 51–58 Julius Caesar conquered all of Gaul (France). Gaul prospered under Roman rule.

HOLY LAND

A.D. 6 Judea became a Roman province.
A.D. 27 Jesus Christ was baptized in the Jordan River.
A.D. 30 Probable date of crucifixion of Jesus Christ.
A.D. 70 The Jews revolted against Rome. Jerusalem was captured and destroyed.

OTHERS

A.D. 1 Bantu-speaking Negro farmers used iron. They made one of the greatest migrations in history when they moved from Cameroon into the sparsely populated forests of Central Africa. These people introduced farming and the use of tools.

A.D. 1 The Mayan Indians in Mexico are recorded from approximately A.D. 1. They probably originated in Asia and crossed from Siberia to Alaska. The Mayas built a civilization in Central America. They had a calendar and a numbering system, and they used bark for cloth.

THE TWELVE APOSTLES

The twelve apostles were a motley group of inexperienced men who became the most successful sales force the world has ever known. It is their continuing influence that has made the Bible the world's best seller for more than five hundred years, ever since the invention of the printing press in A.D. 1440. Nothing like this has happened again in the history of mankind.

Peter, the rock (Simon, Simeon), was a Galilean fisherman, son of Jona, meaning dove. He was married. He went to Rome in A.D. 61. According to tradition, his wife was crucified in Rome. Later Peter was crucified, upside down, at his own request.

John, called "son of thunder," was the son of Zebedee and brother of James. A hot-tempered Galilean fisherman, he was in partnership with Peter. John and James were always together in company with Peter. John was a disciple of John the Baptist. John, James, and Peter were closest to Jesus. John was ambitious and intolerant and was compared to a bow unstrung. He took care of Mary after Jesus' death. He lived to an old age and died at Ephesus around A.D. 100, the only apostle to die a natural death.

Andrew was a Galilean fisherman from Bethsaida, who formerly was a disciple of John the Baptist. He was the first to join Jesus, and he brought Peter, his brother. He was a self-effacing, salt-of-the-earth type of person, who was willing to take a back seat. He was an optimist and devout disciple. He worked in Cappadocia, Bithynia, Galatia, Byzantium, and Scythia (Turkey, Greece, and Russia). He was crucified in Patros, Achaia, Greece, on an X-type of cross, because he did not think he was worthy of the same type of cross as Christ.

Thomas was the doubter. His name is Didymus in Greek and Thomas in Aramaic; both mean twin. He was always a pessimist, until convinced, and then became a fierce, faithful, courageous believer. He preached among the Parthians and Persians in India and as far away as China. He died in India.

Matthew, also called Levi, was the tax collector. He was the brother of James and the son of Alphaeus. He was a publican, who was universally hated. Tax collectors were classified with harlots, criminals, murderers, and adulterers. He lived at Capernaum and worked in Judea. He and John were the only disciples who could write. He was a most unlikely disciple, but as far as we know, he was one of the best. Tradition says he was martyred in Ethiopia, where he had gone as a missionary.

Judas Iscariot was the betrayer. He was the trusted treasurer of the group and a Judean, the only non-Galilean. He was supposedly more level headed than the flighty, emotional Galileans. He betrayed Jesus to the high priests for thirty pieces of silver, about fourteen dollars, or the price of a slave, and committed suicide.

Philip. He was Philip the apostle, and not the Philip of the seven. He came from Bethsaida, as did Peter and Andrew; therefore, he is presumed to have been a fisherman. He was the first to answer Jesus' words "Follow Me." He forthwith went to tell Nathanael. He was the disciple who asked Jesus to show the apostles the Father, and Jesus answered, "He that hath seen Me hath seen the Father." Tradition says that he was martyred at Hieropolis, Phrygia (Turkey).

Simon was the Zealot. The Zealots were a fanatical Jewish nationalist group. They hated the Romans and were willing to die in defense of their cause. When Jerusalem finally fell in A.D. 70 to the Romans, the surviving Zealot men murdered their own wives and children before committing suicide. At Masada, 960 perished. They would assassinate any Jew who cooperated with the Romans. Simon preached and was martyred in Persia.

James was the brother of John. The first of the twelve to become a martyr in A.D. 44, he was murdered by the sword on orders from Herod. James and John, sons of Zebedee, were inseparable. Together with Peter, they formed the inner circle with Jesus. They were typical quick-tempered Galilean fishermen. James and John were ambitious for power seats in Christ's Kingdom, but James died young in his fidelity to Christ.

Bartholomew (some think he is also Nathanael) was possibly of royal blood, of the Ptolemy kings of Egypt. Nothing was told about him in the Bible. He was a friend of Philip. Nathanael came from Cana, close to Nazareth in Galilee. After Philip was called, he ran to get the skeptical Nathanael, who was considered a "doctor of law." He was the one who said, "Can any good thing come out of Nazareth?" Later he said, "Thou art the Son of God, Thou art the King of Israel." He was a searching student and a prayerful man. He was a missionary to Mesopotamia, Persia, Egypt, Armenia, and possibly India. Legend says he was martyred in Ablonopolis, Armenia.

James was sometimes thought to be James the less and brother of Jesus. He was thought by others to be a brother of Matthew. He was probably a fanatical Zealot in company with Simon, the Zealot; Thaddaeus (Judas); and Judas Iscariot. If he was a brother of Matthew, they undoubtedly hated each other until reconciled to Jesus, which would prove that Jesus came to reconcile men to God, and also to each other. James presided over the affairs of the church of Jerusalem. Tradition says that he made a public declaration of his faith, was hurled from one of the temple ramparts, and then was stoned to death.

Thaddaeus, called Lebbaeus and Judas, was the son of James. He was a Zealot, like Simon. He was anxious for Jesus to establish His material kingdom on earth and throw out the Romans. He was probably discouraged at first to learn that Jesus was saying that material and physical power are not the substitutes for the way of a loving heart and a life surrendered to God. Tradition says he traveled and preached in Arabia, Syria, Mesopotamia, and Persia and was martyred in Persia with Simon, the Zealot.

THE ACTS

Time   A.D. 63. Written to Theophilus, a high Gentile official who was a Christian, but actually addressed to all people. Probably written while Paul was in prison in Caesarea and before his death in A.D. 68 in Rome. Covers a period of about thirty-three years, from Christ's ascension to Paul's two-year imprisonment in Rome, A.D. 30–A.D. 63.

Author   Luke, a physician. A Greek and the only apostle who was a Gentile, he probably was born in Antioch or Philippi. He was a man of culture and scientific education and a master of Hebraic and classical Greek.

Theme   The story of the birth of the Church of Christ on Pentecost, 50 days after the redemption of the world by Christ's death and resurrection, when the Holy Spirit descended on 120 disciples, an act which was witnessed by a large throng. This is the beginning of the history of the Church. It tells what Jesus did through consecrated men and women under the direction of the Holy Spirit (*see* definition of *Holy Spirit* in appendix), and how the Holy Spirit works through men. Salvation is by grace through faith, and not by works. The Church is missions, and missions to others is the Church. This is the book of Church organization, mission, and procedure. Christ spent 40 days with the disciples after His resurrection and was seen 10 or 11 times.

This book tells how the power of the Holy Spirit came to the disciples and apostles, their witnessing for Christ in Jerusalem, Judea, Samaria, and then into all the known world at that time. Peter is the central figure in the first twelve chapters and Paul in the last sixteen chapters. It tells of the extension of the Gospel to the Gentiles, whereas the Old Testament was exclusively for the Jews.

Jesus had died, had risen, and had been with the disciples several times during the forty days of His time on earth after His resurrection. He had told them to go to Jerusalem and wait for the promise of the Father, "for John baptized with water, but you shall be baptized with the Holy Spirit not many days from now" (Acts 1:5). After three years, the disciples still did not understand that Jesus was talking about a spiritual Kingdom rather than a political kingdom. Jesus said to them, ". . . you shall receive power when the Holy Spirit has come upon you; and you shall be My witnesses both in Jerusalem, and in all Judea and Samaria, and even to the remotest part of the earth" (Acts 1:8). As He said this, He was lifted up into a cloud out of their sight, and two men in white robes appeared beside them, saying, ". . . This Jesus, who has been taken up from you into heaven, will come in just the same way as you have watched Him go into heaven" (Acts 1:11).

The disciples returned to Jerusalem, where they had been staying (there were about 120 of them). Peter told them that they should elect a member to take the place of Judas, and that he should be a person who has been with them from the beginning of John the Baptist until Jesus rose into heaven. They picked two candidates, Joseph, called Barsabbas, and Matthias; after praying, they cast lots to enroll Matthias with the other 11 apostles. On the day of Pentecost, when the disciples were together, a great sound arose, and tongues of fire touched each of them. They were filled with the Holy Spirit, and each began to speak in foreign languages.

At the time of Pentecost, devout Jews from every known nation came to Jerusalem. When they heard each apostle speaking in their own language, they were amazed and wondered what it all meant. Some people, probably the Pharisees, accused them of being drunk. Peter, with great courage and stature, talked to the crowds and reminded them that Jesus came to live with them to save them, but they crucified Him. He rose again. This had all been foretold in the Old Testament. The people were moved to ask, "What shall we do?" Peter answered, ". . . Repent, and let each of you be baptized in the name of Jesus Christ for the forgiveness of your sins; and you shall receive the gift of the Holy Spirit" (Acts 2:38). About 3,000 people were baptized that day. Many others sold all their possessions, gave to the poor, and were baptized and saved.

Peter and John were going up to the Temple when they saw a man, lame from birth, being carried to the gate to beg alms. Peter said to him, ". . . I do not possess silver and gold, but what I do have I give to you: In the name of Jesus Christ the Nazarene—walk!" (Acts 3:6.) The man leaped up and walked and went with them to the Temple, where Peter rebuked the people for crucifying Christ. He urged them to repent and to accept Christ as their Saviour and be saved, resulting in about 5,000 being saved. The Sadducees priests and captain of the Temple arrested them and took them before Annas, the high priest, Caiaphas, John, and Alexander, who questioned them but were amazed at the boldness of these uneducated Galileans, Peter and John. They could not deny the healing of the lame man, because all of the people had seen and heard it; therefore, they released Peter and John, telling them to preach no more in the name of Jesus. Peter and John reported to the other ten apostles, and they all prayed to God for guidance. The building they were in was shaken, and they were filled with the Holy Spirit.

They shared their possessions among the believers and sold what they had for the welfare and support of all. Ananias and his wife Sapphira sold a piece of property, but agreed between themselves to hold back part of the proceeds. Peter accosted Ananias for lying to the Holy Spirit, and Ananias dropped dead. Three hours later Peter accosted Sapphira and told her she would lie by her husband, and she dropped dead. This put great fear and respect into the hearts of all who heard. The apostles, in the name of God, created many signs and wonders and healed all who came from near and far.

The high priest and Sadducees were filled with great jealousy. They arrested all the apostles and had them put in prison, but an angel of the Lord released them, so they were in the Temple the next morning, preaching. When the council convened, they sent for the apostles. The guards were on duty and the doors were locked, but the apostles were not inside. The council ordered them rearrested and plotted to have them all killed. One Pharisee on the council, named Gamaliel, stood up and explained that if these men were fakes or false prophets, they would die and their followers disappear. But if these men were of God, the council would be guilty of opposing God. They took his advice, whipped the apostles, and turned them loose, warning them not to preach any more. Gamaliel was the most famous rabbi of his day. Saul (Paul) received much of his tutoring from him and could possibly have been present at this council meeting (the Bible does not say so). The apostles ignored the threats and continued to teach and preach Jesus as the Christ.

After a while, there were so many disciples that the Hellenistic Jewish disciples complained to the native disciples that their widows were neglected in the daily distributions. Led by the twelve, they decided to appoint a group to administer to all of them, so that the disciples could devote their time to prayers and preaching. They selected seven dedicated men, headed by Stephen.

Stephen, a dedicated disciple, worked great wonders and signs among the people. Some of those in the synagogue who could not match his wisdom plotted to have him arrested and brought false witnesses against him before the council. As he stood before the council, his face shone like that of an angel while he reviewed the history of the Jewish people for them—from Abraham to the murder of Jesus, their own Messiah, by the very court before which he stood. He ended by saying, ". . . Behold, I see the heavens opened up and the Son of Man standing at the right hand of God" (Acts 7:56). This infuriated them. They cast him out of the city and had him stoned to death, while he prayed, ". . . Lord Jesus receive my spirit! . . . Lord, do not hold this sin against them!" (Acts 7:59, 60.) A young man named Saul watched and consented to

202 / *The Acts*

Stephen's death. (This was the Saul who later became Paul after his conversion, and became the greatest of all the disciples.)

This murder set a horrible example of persecution against the Christians, and Saul was a leader in their persecution and in the imprisonment of many. Saul, the persecutor of the Christians, was to become the greatest of all men, except Christ, in the establishment of the Church of Christ. This period probably marked the turning point in the history of mankind. To avoid persecution, the apostles scattered to other places for their preaching. Philip went to Samaria, where he converted many, including a man named Simon, who had previously practiced magic. Philip then started toward Gaza, where he joined an Ethiopian eunuch, the treasurer of Candace the queen, who had been to Jerusalem to worship and was returning home. The eunuch was reading from Isaiah the prophet and asked Philip to explain what it meant. Philip told him the Good News of Jesus, and when they came to some water, the eunuch asked Philip if he would baptize him. They both went down into the water, and Philip baptized the eunuch, then disappeared.

Fervent in his persecution of the Christians, Saul secured permission from the high priest to go to Damascus, seek out any Christians in the synagogues, and bring them, bound, to Jerusalem for punishment. As he approached Damascus, a light from heaven flashed about him. As he fell to the ground, he heard a voice saying, ". . . Saul, Saul, why are you persecuting Me?" (Acts 9:4.) Saul said, ". . . Who art Thou, Lord?" The voice said, ". . . I am Jesus, whom you are persecuting, but rise, and enter the city, and it shall be told you what you must do" (Acts 9:5, 6). The men with Saul were astounded. Saul arose, but he was blind, so they led him to Damascus, where he remained blind and neither ate nor drank.

The Lord spoke to a disciple named Ananias in Damascus, saying, ". . . Arise and go to the street called Straight, and inquire at the house of Judas for a man from Tarsus named Saul, for behold, he is praying, and he has seen in a vision a man named Ananias come in and lay his hands on him, so that he might regain his sight" (Acts 9:11, 12). Ananias protested that Saul was evil, that he had persecuted the disciples in Jerusalem, and was in Damascus to do the same. But the Lord said to him, ". . . Go, for he is a chosen instrument of Mine, to bear My name before the Gentiles and kings and the sons of Israel; for I will show him how much he must suffer for My name's sake" (Acts 9:15, 16).

Ananias obeyed, entered the house, and placed his hands on Saul, saying, ". . . the Lord Jesus . . . has sent me so that you may regain your sight, and be filled with the Holy Spirit" (Acts 9:17). Immediately, something like scales fell from Saul's eyes. He regained his sight, was baptized, and took food. He appeared with the disciples in the synagogues and proclaimed, ". . . He is the Son of God" (Acts 9:20). He was so fervent in his conversion, proclaiming that Jesus was the Christ, that some of the Jews plotted to kill him. Some of the disciples let him down over the wall in a basket, so he escaped to Jerusalem, where he joined the apostles and preached openly. The Hellenists plotted to kill him, so he escaped to Caesarea and then to Tarsus.

Peter went to Lydda and healed Aeneas, who had been paralyzed for eight years, and many people turned to the Lord. There was a good disciple named Tabitha at Joppa, near Lydda, who died; they prepared her for burial and sent for Peter. Peter put all the mourners outside and said to Tabitha, ". . . Tabitha, rise . . ." (Acts 9:40). She did, and the miracle became known throughout Joppa.

At Caesarea, a centurion (a Roman officer having one hundred soldiers under his command), who was a man of God, had a vision of an angel who told him to send for Peter. As his soldiers and messenger approached Joppa, Peter was on the rooftop, where a vision appeared to him that he did not understand, and the Spirit told him to go down to meet these messengers. The next day Peter went with them to Caesarea, accompanied by some of the brethren of Joppa, to meet Cornelius, who had assembled his kinsmen and friends. Cornelius fell down at Peter's feet, but Peter lifted him, saying, ". . . Stand up; I too am just a man" (Acts 10:26). Peter explained that it was prohibited for Jews to mingle with Gentiles, but God had shown him that no man was unclean. He asked why they had sent for him. Cornelius answered that a man in a vision had told him to send for Peter to tell Cornelius and his people about Jesus Christ.

Peter related to them the story of Jesus, from the beginning with John the Baptist to His death, resurrection, appearances to His disciples, and His instructions to them. While Peter was talking, the Holy Spirit fell on all who heard his words, both Jews and Gentiles, and they spoke in tongues and exalted God. He baptized them in the name of Jesus Christ. This was the time in history when it was determined and shown by God that salvation through Christ was not just for the Jews, but for all who would accept Him as their Redeemer. When Peter returned to Jerusalem, he was criticized by his people for his actions with Cornelius, but he related the whole story of what happened. They then said, ". . . then, God has granted to the Gentiles also the repentance that leads to life" (Acts 11:18).

Some of the disciples who were scattered when Stephen was killed had gone to Phoenicia, Cyprus, and Antioch, and talked only to the Jews. But some of the men of Cyprus and Cyrene who came to Antioch spoke to the Gentile Greeks, also. News of this reached Jerusalem; Barnabas was sent to Tarsus to get Saul and go to Antioch, where they both preached for a year. This was the first time that the disciples of Christ were called Christians. A prophet named Agabus came to Antioch and foretold of a famine in all the world, causing the people of Antioch to assemble a relief offering, to be taken by Barnabas and Saul to Jerusalem.

Herod had James, the brother of John, killed. He arrested Peter and had him imprisoned and guarded by four squads of soldiers till after the Passover. The people of the Church prayed earnestly to God for Peter's release. That night an angel of the Lord appeared to him, released his chains, led him past the soldiers, opened the iron gate, and led him into the city. Then the angel disappeared. Peter went to the house of Mary, mother of Mark, told them what had happened, and then went to Caesarea to hide. Herod ordered all the guarding soldiers put to death.

Herod permitted an audience with the people of Tyre and Sidon and spoke to them in a great oration. The people shouted, ". . . The voice of a god and not of a man!" (Acts 12:22.) An Angel of the Lord smote him instantly because he glorified himself instead of God. He was eaten by worms and died.

The Word of God grew, and the believers multiplied. Accompanied by Mark, Saul and Barnabas returned to Antioch. At Antioch the Holy Spirit decreed that Saul, Barnabas, and John should go out to spread the Gospel. They went to Cyprus and proclaimed the Word of God in the synagogues throughout the island. At Paphos they met the proconsul (a Roman governor), Sergius Paulus, who was advised by a magician and false prophet named Bar-Jesus. Paulus wanted to hear of the Word of God, but the envious magician tried to dissuade the proconsul, so Saul, who was now called Paul, caused him to become blind. The proconsul believed and was astonished with the teachings.

Paul and Barnabas then went to Perga in Pamphylia, where John left them to go to Jerusalem. They then went inland to Pisidia (Turkey), where the people were receptive to hearing Paul tell the whole story of the Jews and salvation through Jesus. On the next Sabbath, the whole city turned out to hear them, but this created jealousy among some of the Jews, and they reviled Paul and Barnabas, so Paul said that they would preach the Good News of Jesus to the Gentiles. The Jews created so much dissension that Paul and Barnabas went to Iconium, where they converted many believers, but some of the Jews and Gentiles plotted to stone them, so they went on to Lystra and Derbe, cities of Lyconia.

At Lystra, there was a man with crippled feet from birth who believed in what Paul was saying. Paul said, ". . . Stand upright on your feet," and he did and walked (Acts 14:10). The people were so impressed that they wanted to offer oxen as sacrifices, but Paul and Barnabas urged them to turn to the living God. They made so many converts that Jews from Antioch and Iconium came and stoned Paul and dumped him out of the city, thinking he was dead. When his disciples gathered around, he arose and went with them to other cities and preached, establishing churches and appointing elders. He finally returned to Antioch.

Some men from Judea were telling the Gentiles that they had to be circumcised like the Jews to receive the grace of God and be saved. Paul and Barnabas went to Jerusalem and met with the men of the church where this matter was debated. It was decided that the grace of the Lord and the gift of the Holy Spirit was available to Jews and Gentiles alike, if they would obey the laws of God. Circumcision had nothing to do with spiritual matters with the Gentiles. Paul and Barnabas, accompanied by Judas and Silas, brought this good news back to Antioch, and this matter was settled once and for all.

After spending some time in Antioch, strengthening the Church and winning many brethren to God, Paul and Silas went to Syria, and Cilicia, while Barnabas and Mark went to Cyprus to visit all the churches. Paul went to Derbe, Lystra, Iconium, Phrygia, Galatia, and Mysia to strengthen the churches and to increase the numbers of Christians. (These were all cities along the Mediterranean, from Syria into Turkey.) A vision of a man appeared to Paul, saying, ". . . Come over to Macedonia [a Roman province north of Greece] and help us" (Acts 16:9). They went to Philippi, a principal city of Macedonia, and on the Sabbath spoke to many people. One of whom was Lydia, a seller of purple goods from the city of Thyatira (the famous royal-purple dye was made from tiny mollusks found along the Phoenician coast), who, with her household, was baptized. She asked the disciples to stay with her as her guests.

One day, as Paul and Silas were going to the place of prayer, they cast a demon from a slave girl who was selling her services as a soothsayer for her master, which made the master very angry. He had the magistrates arrest them, beat them terribly, and throw them into prison.

About midnight, Paul and Silas were praying when an earthquake broke open all the doors and broke the chains of all the prisoners. The jailer thought his prisoners were gone and was going to commit suicide, but Paul called to him, ". . . Do yourself no harm, for we are all here!" (Acts 16:28.) The jailer knelt before them and said, ". . . what must I do to be saved?" They answered, ". . . Believe in the Lord Jesus, and you shall be saved . . ." (Acts 16:30, 31). The jailer took them to his home and bathed their wounds, and they baptized him. The next day, the magistrate sent word to release them, but Paul answered that they were Roman citizens, unjustly beaten in public, and that they must be released publicly. The magistrate apologized, released them, and asked them to leave the city. The church at Philippi turned out to be one of the best in the New Testament.

Paul and Silas went to Thessalonica, where they preached and won many Jews, Greeks, and leading women to God. Some of the jealous Jews told the city authorities that they ". . . all act contrary to the decrees of Caesar, saying that there is another king, Jesus" (Acts 17:7). Paul and Silas quickly left and went by night to Berea and talked in the synagogue. They were received with eagerness by Jews, Greeks, and many women, until some of the people from Thessalonica came down and stirred up a riot among the people. Paul left by sea for Athens, but Timothy and Silas stayed.

At Athens, a city where many philosophical men spent their time learning and exchanging viewpoints, Paul noticed many idols. Some of the philosophers invited him to speak at the Areopagus and tell them of this new teaching. He told them he had noticed an idol with an inscription "to an unknown God." He then told them of Jesus, the Christ and living God, who had been unknown to them but was available to every man. ". . . in Him we live and move and exist" (Acts 17:28). Some could not understand the resurrection of Christ, but many did.

Paul went to Corinth, where he was met by Silas and Timothy. He made friends with Aquila and his wife Priscilla, Jews who were recently exiled from Rome by orders of Claudius, and at their invitation lived with them, as they were also tentmakers like Paul. Later, some of the Jews opposed and reviled him because he taught that the Christ was Jesus. At this point, Paul said, "Your blood be upon your own heads! I am clean. From now on I shall go to the Gentiles." Many Corinthians, including Crispus, the ruler of the synagogue, believed Paul and were baptized. The Lord appeared to him in a vision and said, "Do not be afraid any longer, but go on speaking and do not be silent; for I am with you, and no man will attack you in order to harm you, for I have many people in this city." He stayed there a year and a half.

Some time later the Jews tried to get Gallio, the proconsul of Achaia, to prosecute Paul, but Gallio would pay no attention to them. Paul stayed there for some time and then went to Syria, taking Aquila and Priscilla with him. He then went on to Ephesus, where he left them, and he went to Caesarea and on to Antioch. He then went from city to city through Galatia and Phrygia, preaching to the Jews and Gentiles and strengthening the disciples. A native Jew of Alexandria named Apollos came to Ephesus to help Priscilla and Aquila in the other cities around.

It was at Ephesus that Paul learned that the disciples had not received the Holy Spirit. They were baptizing to believe in the one who was to come. Paul baptized them in the name of the Lord Jesus, laid hands on them and they received the Holy Spirit. There were about twelve of them, so baptized. Paul preached in the synagogues and the hall of Tyrannus for two years, and the word of the Lord spread throughout Asia to the Jews and the Greeks.

God performed extraordinary miracles with the hands of Paul, healing the sick and casting out evil spirits. The Spirit of God prevailed so much that exorcists and magicians burned their books in the public square at a cost of 50,000 pieces of silver (could have been $250,000), and the Word of the Lord spread mightily.

Paul planned to go to Macedonia, Achaia, to Jerusalem, and then to

Rome. He sent Timothy and Erastus ahead to Macedonia. About that time, a silversmith named Demetrius started a great resistance to Paul. The silversmith craftsmen of Ephesus and other cities of Asia did a big business in making idols of Diana and Artemis. Paul taught the people to worship the living God, not idols (Artemis was the Goddess Diana, and her temple in Ephesus was one of the Seven Wonders of the Ancient World and a great tourist attraction). Therefore, Demetrius gathered the people together, fearful that Paul's teachings would ruin their idol business. Finally, the town clerk prevented a riot and killing by telling the people that no crime had been committed and that if they had a grievance, they must revert to the courts of law.

Paul then went to Macedonia, Greece, Troas, Philippi, Assos, Mitylene, Chios, Samos, and Miletus. At Miletus, Paul sent for the elders of Ephesus, so that he could bless them and strengthen them in their spirit. He bid them farewell and prayed with them, because they would see him no more. He then set sail for Jerusalem, stopping at various cities to encourage the elders and disciples, who all warned him not to go to Jerusalem, because they feared he would be killed because of his teachings to the Gentiles.

Paul met with the disciples in Jerusalem. They warned him of the zealous attitude of the Jews for the law of Moses, saying it was well known throughout the land that Paul had told the Gentiles it was not necessary for them to be circumcised in order to be baptized and be saved. When Paul went into the Temple, a great crowd of Jews saw him and dragged him from the Temple. They were trying to kill him when he was rescued by the Tribune of the cohort (a Roman commander of 500 soldiers), who rushed to the scene of the riot. He arrested Paul and asked what the charge was against him, but everyone shouted a different answer, so he started to take him to the barracks. Paul asked the Tribune, in Greek, if he might speak to the people. Paul was standing on the same steps where Jesus was led before His crucifixion. He talked to the people in their Hebrew language.

Paul reviewed his whole life. He explained that he was a Jew, born in Tarsus, educated in Jerusalem under Gamaliel, and as zealous for God as they were on this day. He had persecuted to death nonbelievers, had been a member of the council, had gone to Damascus to persecute the Christians, and had been struck blind by God. He told them he had been given his sight back by Ananias, had been baptized, had returned to Jerusalem, and had witnessed Stephen being stoned to death. He said he had received word from God, saying, ". . . Go! For I will send you far away to the Gentiles" (Acts 22:21).

At this point the crowd burst into an uproar, and the Tribune had him brought into the barracks and bound. Paul told the centurion who was binding him, ". . . Is it lawful for you to scourge a man who is a Roman and uncondemned?" (Acts 22:25.) This was against the Roman law. The centurion reported this to the Tribune, who had Paul unbound, but the next day he had Paul appear before the Jewish council and high priests. Paul addressed the court and, noting that part of it was Pharisees and part Sadducees (the Pharisees believed in a life hereafter, but the Sadducees believed that there is no resurrection nor angel nor spirit), said, ". . . I am a Pharisee, a son of Pharisees; I am on trial for the hope and resurrection of the dead!" (Acts 23:6.) This caused a violent disagreement among the members of the council, which was composed of Pharisees and Sadducees. The Tribune ordered Paul to be brought to the barracks for his own protection.

The following night, the Lord stood by Paul and said, ". . . Take courage; for as you have solemnly witnessed to My cause at Jerusalem, so you must witness at Rome also" (Acts 23:11). The next day, 40 Jews made a vow not to eat or drink until they had killed Paul. They plotted with the council to ask the Tribune to send Paul to them for questioning, which would give them the opportunity to seize and kill him. The son of Paul's sister heard the plot and told Paul. Paul asked the centurion to allow the boy to talk to the Tribune, who listened appreciatively because he found no fault in Paul. The Tribune told the boy to tell no one of their conversation and then ordered two centurions to gather 200 soldiers, 200 spearmen, and 70 horsemen. They were to take Paul to Caesarea in the middle of the night and deliver him safely to Felix the governor. He would also send a letter saying that Paul was a Roman citizen and that though the Tribune could see no merit in the Jews' accusations, they could come before Felix and present their case.

Five days later, the high priest Ananias and some elders presented their case before the governor. Paul was given the opportunity to present his defense. He said he worshipped the same God as his accusers, but he accepted Jesus as the Christ, as foretold in the Scripture. He said that He died and rose again, and that salvation through Him was available to the Gentiles, as well as to the Jews. Felix had an accurate knowledge of all matters and told them he would consult with Lysias, the Tribune, and decide later. In the meantime, he decreed that Paul should have some liberty and that none of his friends should be prevented from seeing him.

Felix and his wife Drusilla, a Jewess, talked to Paul many times about his faith in Jesus Christ. Actually, Felix was hoping that Paul's friends would pay him some money, but they didn't. Two years went by, and Felix was succeeded by Porcius Festus, who was immediately confronted by the council to give an answer about Paul. They presented their false accusations again, and Paul answered that they had proved nothing, that he was innocent, and that as a Roman citizen, he had the legal right to appeal to Caesar in Rome. Festus answered, ". . . You have appealed to Caesar, to Caesar you shall go" (Acts 25:12).

Some time later Agrippa, the king, and Bernice arrived at Caesarea to welcome Festus, who told them of Paul's case. Agrippa wanted to hear Paul, so the next day Paul was presented to him and Bernice with great pomp and ceremony. Festus explained that he found it difficult to send a man to Caesar when he actually could find no legal charge against him. Paul presented his life story, ending, "And so, having obtained help from God, I stand to this day testifying both to small and great, stating nothing but what the Prophets and Moses said was going to take place; that the Christ was to suffer, and that by reason of His resurrection from the dead He should be the first to proclaim light both to the Jewish people and to the Gentiles" (Acts 26:22, 23). Festus said to Paul, "You are out of your mind" but Paul replied that he was speaking the truth. Paul asked Agrippa if he believed the prophets, and the king replied, ". . . In a short time you will persuade me to become a Christian" (Acts 26:28). Paul replied, "I would to God, that whether in a short or long time, not only you, but also all who hear me this day, might become such as I am, except for these chains" (Acts 26:29). After Paul was withdrawn, Festus and Agrippa agreed that Paul had done nothing wrong and could have been released, if he had not appealed to Rome.

Paul was entrusted to a centurion named Julius, to be taken to Rome by boat together with other prisoners. Julius treated Paul very kindly. After they set sail, they had much difficulty. After many days, Paul said, ". . . Men, I perceive that the voyage will certainly be attended with damage and great loss, not only of the cargo and the ship, but also of our lives" (Acts 27:10). He was ignored. They encountered constant storms and finally threw all the cargo and gear overboard. They were all desperate, but Paul said, ". . . now I urge you keep up your courage, for there shall be no loss of life among you, but only of the ship . . . . an angel of the God to whom I belong and whom I serve stood before me, saying, '. . . God has granted you all those who are sailing with you,' . . . But we must run aground on a certain island" (Acts 27:22–26).

After 14 more days of storm and distress, they all ate some food and threw everything else overboard, finally running the ship aground. There were 276 persons on board, and all either swam or floated with planks to shore—all were saved. The island was Malta, and the natives, who were friendly, built a fire to dry the men. Paul gathered some firewood with a snake hidden in it, which bit him on the hand. Everyone expected him to die, but when he didn't die or even swell up, they said he was a god. The chief of the island, named Publius, had a father who was very sick with fever and dysentery. Paul healed him and then healed many people who were brought to him. After three months, they boarded another ship with gifts from the natives and later arrived in Rome, where Paul was met by friends and was allowed to live in his own quarters with a soldier.

After three days, he called together the local Jewish leaders and told them why he had been arrested and that no charge had been placed against him by the Romans. They came to him in great numbers, and he preached to them as he had done to all others. Some believed, and others didn't. He finally said, "Let it be known to you therefore, that this salvation of God has been sent to the Gentiles; they will also listen" (Acts 28:28).

Paul lived in Rome for two years at his own expense, welcoming all who came to him, preaching the Kingdom of God, and teaching about the Lord Jesus Christ quite openly and unhindered. Thus ends the Book of Acts.

The Bible does not say so, but tradition says that Paul was acquitted about A.D. 63. He probably went on to Spain, Greece, and Asia Minor about A.D. 65–A.D. 67. He was arrested again, and was taken back to Rome and beheaded about A.D. 67.

Paul spent about thirty-two years of his sixty-five years in missionary work.

THE MAN PAUL

Special attention and mention must be given to Paul (original name Saul). He was not one of the twelve apostles, but he was an apostle of God and probably the most influential of all of them. He wrote fourteen of the twenty-seven books of the New Testament.

Paul's name was Saul. He was a Jewish Roman citizen born in Tarsus, a Pharisee, and a descendent of the tribe of Benjamin. He had knowledge of the law, the prophets, Aramaic, Hebrew, and Greek languages, and Greek culture. As a youth, he learned the art of weaving the famous goat's-hair cloth called *cilicium* and its use in making tents and sails, which gave him a means of making a living in his ministry and allowed him always to be self-supporting.

At about twenty years of age, he went to the school of the Pharisees in Jerusalem under the famous Gamaliel, where he joined the student fanaticism in the stoning to death of Stephen. This seemed to increase his prestige with the high priests, and he became a leader among the fanatics. His specialty was persecution of the Christians. Armed with letters of recommendation and endorsement from the high priests, he started for Damascus, to begin a roundup of Christians to be brought to Jerusalem.

As he approached Damascus, suddenly a light from heaven (Acts 9:1–19) flashed about him. He fell to the ground and heard a voice saying to him, "Saul, Saul, why are you persecuting Me?" And he said, "Who art Thou, Lord?" The voice said, "I am Jesus whom you are persecuting, but rise, and enter the city, and it shall be told you what you must do." Saul arose blind. After Saul entered Damascus, the Lord sent Ananias, one of the men Saul was going to arrest, to Saul, to heal him so that he would be filled with the Holy Spirit.

He was immediately baptized, and he preached in the synagogues in Damascus (A.D. 31–A.D. 32). The Jews hated him because of his conversion and plotted to kill him. At Jerusalem the disciples were afraid to trust him, but Barnabas finally convinced them of his conversion, and they eventually helped him escape to Tarsus about three years after his conversion. Saul, the most zealous persecutor of the Christians, became the most ardent supporter of the building of the new Church of Christ.

At Tarsus he talked to people and studied and preached in the local communities for another ten years before his first missionary journey.

This first journey was to Cyprus, the home of Barnabas, and was led by Barnabas, with Paul as the second member and John Mark as assistant (A.D. 45–A.D. 48). They converted the proconsul, Sergius Paulus, which marked the beginning of their concentration on the Greek-Roman Gentile world and which so inspired Saul that thereafter he was called Paul. From this point on, Paul became the leader of these journeys. They proceeded to the Asia Minor mainland, where Paul became sick with malaria, which affected him for eight years. They talked and preached anywhere and everywhere that people would listen, and at Lystra the Jews from the synagogues of Antioch and Iconium stoned Paul, giving him a taste of the treatment he had helped administer to Stephen. Timothy, his secretary, born of a Jewish mother and Greek father, was converted at Lystra and joined him there.

At a meeting of the church council in Jerusalem (A.D. 50), Paul was largely responsible for recognition by the Church that Gentiles did not have to conform to Jewish Mosaic law to become Christians. He made a second (A.D. 50–A.D. 53) and third (A.D. 54–A.D. 57) missionary journey, establishing many churches and writing many letters.

While Paul was in Corinth, he wrote two letters (A.D. 52) to the church in Thessalonica, which are 1 and 2 Thessalonians, books of the Bible.

While on this third journey, Paul wrote four letters which are now books of the Bible: Romans, written from Corinth (A.D. 57) to the church of Rome; Galatians, written from Corinth (A.D. 57) to a group of churches in Galatia; 1 Corinthians, written from Ephesus to the church in Corinth (A.D. 59); and 2 Corinthians, written from Macedonia to the church in Corinth (A.D. 60).

He was eventually arrested, imprisoned, and sent to Rome (A.D. 60). While in prison in Rome (A.D. 60–A.D. 63), he wrote four letters which are books of the Bible. Colossians was written to the church in Colossae near Ephesus (A.D. 62). Philippians was written to the church in Philippi (A.D. 63). Philemon was a letter to a rich man in Colossae named Philemon, whose slave had stolen some money from him, fled to Rome, and met Paul. Paul was asking for his pardon (A.D. 64). Ephesians was a letter written to the church in Ephesus (A.D. 62). The book of Hebrews may have been written by Paul to a group of Jewish Christians (A.D. 63–A.D. 68).

After Paul's release from prison, he wrote a letter from Macedonia to Titus, his faithful helper in Crete, which is the book of Titus (A.D. 65).

During his second imprisonment, Paul wrote two letters, the books of 1 and 2 Timothy, in the form of letters to Timothy (the first could have been written from Macedonia before his imprisonment), his beloved and trusted helper. The first (A.D. 65) was a letter of instruction, and the second requested Timothy to come and see him in Rome.

He was considered the most dynamic and influential of all the apos-

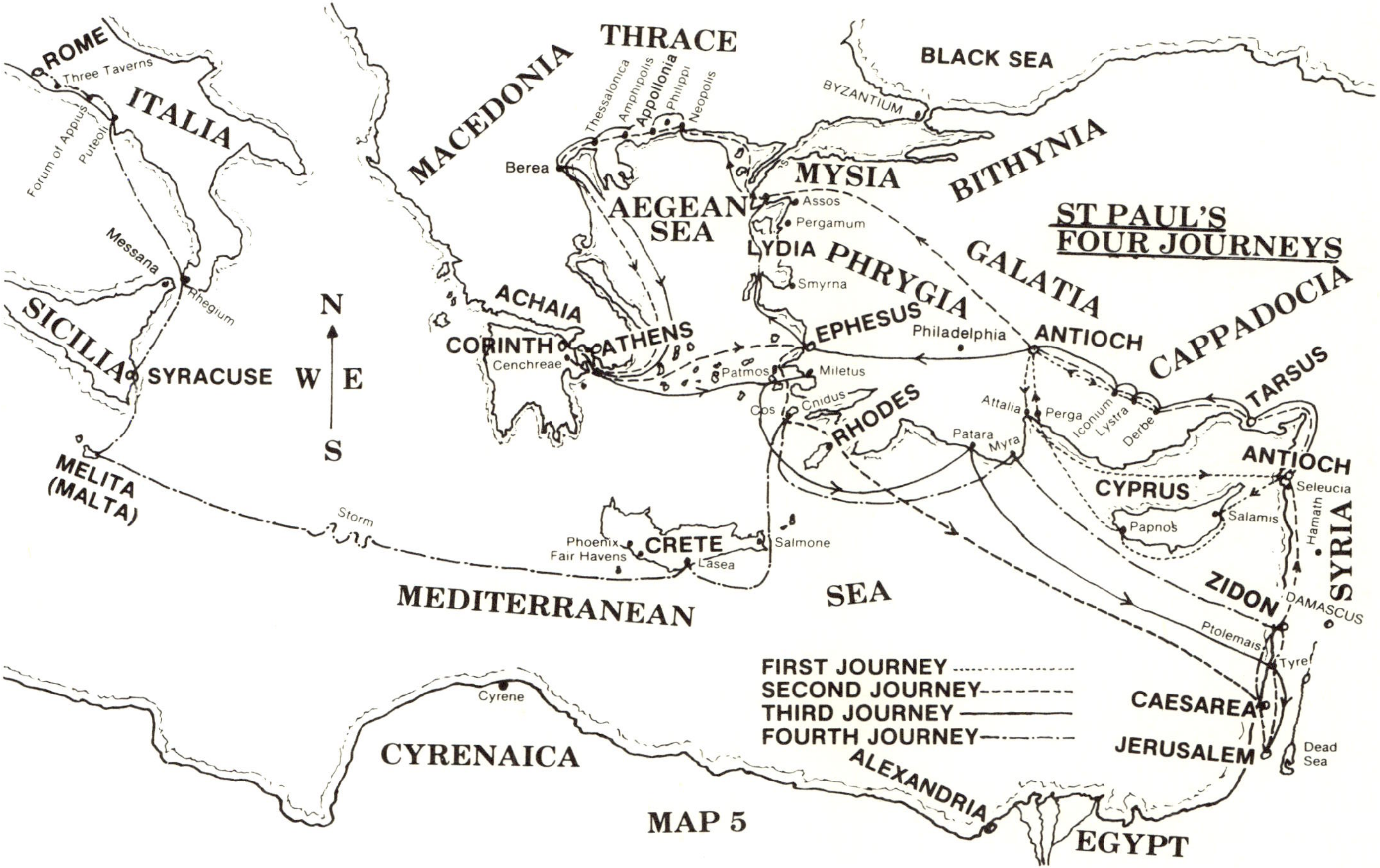

ST PAUL'S FOUR JOURNEYS
ROME
Three Taverns
Forum of Appius
Puteoli
ITALIA
Messana
Rhegium
SICILIA
SYRACUSE
MELITA (MALTA)
N
W
E
S
Storm
MACEDONIA
THRACE
Thessalonica
Amphipolis
Appollonia
Philippi
Neopolis
Berea
AEGEAN SEA
ACHAIA
CORINTH
Cenchreae
ATHENS
Phoenix
Fair Havens
CRETE
Lasea
Salmone
MEDITERRANEAN
SEA
BLACK SEA
BYZANTIUM
BITHYNIA
MYSIA
Assos
Pergamum
LYDIA
PHRYGIA
Smyrna
EPHESUS
Patmos
Miletus
Cos
Cnidus
RHODES
Philadelphia
GALATIA
ANTIOCH
CAPPADOCIA
Attalia
Perga
Iconium
Lystra
Derbe
TARSUS
Patara
Myra
ANTIOCH
Seleucia
CYPRUS
Papnos
Salamis
Hamath
SYRIA
ZIDON
DAMASCUS
Ptolemais
Tyre
CAESAREA
JERUSALEM
Dead Sea
FIRST JOURNEY
SECOND JOURNEY
THIRD JOURNEY
FOURTH JOURNEY
Cyrene
CYRENAICA
ALEXANDRIA
EGYPT

MAP 5

tles. Many books have been written about Paul. There has probably never been a man more poorly equipped physically to undertake a mission than Paul.

"A man little of stature, thin haired upon the head, crooked in the legs, of good state of body, with eyebrows joining, a nose somewhat hooked, full of grace; for sometimes he appeared like a man, and sometimes he had the face of an angel" (*Anonymous*).

He was sick, he was working with nonbelievers, constant oppression, and abuse, and dissent among some of his own people. He was constantly escaping to avoid persecution. He was engaged in riots, stoned, and beaten several times, arrested, threatened with lynching, shipwrecked, imprisoned, and was probably finally beheaded.

Yet no man in the history of mankind, except Jesus Christ, has been more influential in the lives of others than Paul. His life was one of total dedication. In modern-day language, it could be said that he was history's greatest salesman.

ROMANS

Time   A.D. 57.
Author   Paul, whose name was Saul before his conversion in A.D. 35, an apostle.
Theme   This letter was written to the Church and Christians in Rome. Paul was in Corinth and wrote in anticipation of going to Rome. The letter was carried by Phoebe, who was going to Rome from Cenchreae, a suburb of Corinth. There was no postal service in those days. Paul was on his way to Jerusalem at the end of his third missionary journey, and from there planned to go to Rome, but he had warnings that he would be killed by the Jews In Jerusalem. His letter could have been preparation for meeting the people in Rome, or if he never got there, he would have gotten his message to those people by letter.

    In this letter, Paul presents his subjects almost as a case in law, sometimes asking questions and then answering them. He presents man's spiritual needs; the method of remedy; the ultimate results and victories as a result of the death of Jesus Christ; and man's salvation as a son of the living God, helped and comforted by the Holy Spirit and finally rewarded with eternal life by his faith and love of God. This book is almost a constitution of Christianity.

    Paul introduces himself as an apostle and servant of Jesus Christ, concerned with God's work. He somewhat apologizes for not getting to Rome sooner, and tells the people of his plans to visit Rome to help them spread the Gospel to ". . . Greeks and to barbarians, both to the wise and to the foolish" (Romans 1:14). He actually reaches Rome three years after his letter. He says, "For I am not ashamed of the gospel, for it is the power of God for salvation to every one who believes, to the Jew first and also to the Greek. For in it the righteousness of God is revealed from faith to faith; as it is written, 'But the righteous man shall live by faith' " (Romans 1:16, 17).

    He laments the terrible sinfulness and depravity of Rome (it sounds like the front page of any newspaper today) when God's grace is available to all, both Jew and Gentile alike. He points out that judging others does not forgive a man for his own sins. There will be tribulation and distress for those who do evil, but glory, honor, and peace for those who do good. God will judge each person by what is in his heart, not by the impression he tries to convey. The law of the Jews by Moses is not the way to salvation. The Jews and Gentiles alike are guilty of sin, since all have sinned and fall short of the glory of God. They receive justification (*see* definitions) by God's grace as a gift, through redemption of sins, which is in Christ Jesus, who was sacrificed by His blood on the cross, to be received by faith. This is to prove God's righteousness and that He justifies he who has faith in Jesus.

He answers the question that probably has come up before: Must the Gentiles be circumcised before they can receive the grace of God? He tells how Abraham received the promise before he was circumcised. Therefore, heirs to the promise are those who have the same faith. The main thing in Abraham's life was his faith, not his circumcision.

Adam was the origination of all men. Adam sinned, and the rest of mankind were born sinners without choice. Adam did not start with a sinful nature. Paul explained the atonement of sins by one man's death by saying that Adam—one man—was responsible for all men being sinners. Therefore, Christ—one man—can be responsible for the forgiveness of all men's sins.

Adam was the head of the human race. Christ is the head of the spiritual race. What one man can do, another man can undo. Therefore, Christ's death is sufficient for the redemption of the sins of all men who will believe.

Paul explains that when man is baptized into Christ, he is baptized into Christ's death, and as Christ was raised from the dead, he shall be united with Him in a new life and resurrection like His. This destroys the sinful body in death and resurrects the new life to live for God. Man, therefore, is dead to sin and alive to God. If we are no longer under the law of Moses, and if Christ has forgiven our sins, why can't man go on sinning? He answers this: There are two ways of life; the way of Christ and the way of sin. We have a free choice. We can go one way or the other, but not both. Christ is the law of God and eternal life and peace for man. The law was given to make man know the difference between right and wrong, and to see the need of a saviour to save him from wrong.

When we give our lives to Christ, we receive a new inner life, a new birth—a life filled with the Spirit of God, called the Holy Spirit. We may not be totally aware of it, but it is there. We receive a natural life in the flesh from Adam. We receive a new spiritual life from Christ. We accept this fact by faith. This Holy Spirit (*see* definition) is the new life that is ever loving, working quietly within us, never wearied, never exhausted, with control of our whole being. This is the life that will eventually blossom into our eternal life with God. We are not released from living by the laws of man. We must live right and not submit to the temptations of the flesh. The minor sufferings of the present life are not to be compared to the glory of God's completed redemption. "For in hope we have been saved, but hope that is seen is not hope; for why does one also hope for what he sees? But if we hope for what we do not see, with perseverance we wait eagerly for it" (Romans 8:24, 25).

The Holy Spirit within us intercedes to God for us and comforts us. The Spirit never wearies, never sleeps, and never dies. The indestructible love of Christ has forgiven us of our sins and given us this Spirit.

Paul says, "For I am convinced that neither death, nor life, nor angels, nor principalities, nor things present, nor things to come, nor powers, nor height, nor depth, nor any other created thing, shall be able to separate us from the love of God, which is in Christ Jesus our Lord" (Romans 8:38, 39).

Paul bemoans the fact that the Jews have been his worst stumbling block. Many became Christians, but Israel as a nation was not only unbelieving, but antagonistic. It was always the Jews who gave Paul problems, stoned him, beat him, and even planned his death. He grieves for them and quotes Isaiah, ". . . Though the number of the sons of Israel be as the sand of the sea, it is the remnant that will be saved . . ." (Romans 9:27). He quotes again, ". . . he who believes in Him will not be disappointed . . ." (Romans 9:33). ". . . Whoever will call upon the name of the Lord will be saved" (Romans 10:13). He indicates that in God's plan, the envy of the Jews for the Gentiles may be the motivating factor to ultimately bring them to full appreciation of God's desired love for them.

Each individual's work and attitude is important. Paul stresses this in detail, a part of which is, "Let love be without hypocrisy. Abhor what is evil; cling to what is good. Be devoted to one another in brotherly love; give preference to one another in honor; not lagging behind in diligence, fervent in spirit, serving the Lord" (Romans 12:9–11). He stresses humility in all deeds.

The laws of men in the form of governments are for man's protection, but these are instituted by God; therefore, obedience to the law is obedience to God. All laws and commandments are summed up in one sentence. ". . . You shall love your neighbor as yourself" (Romans 13:9).

Men should not judge one another by the foods they eat or the days they keep for the Lord. Let the Jews have their Sabbath and festival days and let the Gentiles have theirs, "for the kingdom of God is not eating and drinking, but righteousness and peace and joy in the Holy Spirit. For he who in this way serves Christ is acceptable to God and approved by men" (Romans 14:17, 18).

Throughout his writings, Paul continually urges cooperation and love between the Jews and Gentiles, and he repeats many times that the

218 / Romans

grace of God for salvation through Jesus Christ is available to all. He tells them that he hopes to see them soon and then go on to Spain, where there is need for his missionary work.

Paul ends this letter with greetings to many friends in Rome, many of whom are influential women. He warns them to beware of those who would try to destroy their efforts to build the Church of Christ and ends, "to the only wise God, through Jesus Christ, be the glory forever. Amen" (Romans 16:27).

FIRST CORINTHIANS

Time   A.D. 57–A.D. 59. Written at Ephesus during Paul's third journey.
Author   Paul.
Theme   Paul had established the church in Corinth about three years previously, on his second journey, and was planning to be there again in about six months. He had spent one and one-half years in Corinth. Several problems had arisen in the meantime, and Paul had learned of them by rumor, by travelers, and by a special delegation that had come to see him to get answers to some questions. He had probably written other letters, but they have been lost.

Corinth was a large city of 400,000–700,000 population and was surpassed only by Rome, Alexandria, and Antioch. It was a commercial trading center between east and west, with many ships coming and going. There were many rich people, and the city was corrupt, with every known type of sin and immorality. Here was the great temple of Aphrodite, known to Romans as Venus, the goddess of physical love and beauty, where 1,000 public prostitutes, or priestesses, lived, who were available for the local people as well as for foreign travelers. Much time was spent at tournaments and speeches on philosophy. There were schools of languages and philosophy, there was art and much culture, but pursuing the lust of the flesh was probably the most popular pastime. This was the setting in which Paul was trying to establish a Chruch of love and discipline. The conflicts and temptations created many problems and questions in basic life-styles. These were the problems Paul tried to deal with in his letter.

In Paul's time there were no church buildings, except the Temple in Jerusalem, and the word *church* meant "those who believed in Christ." They met in homes or wherever they could, but they were small groups. This was one of the problems. These small groups were beginning to be the "group of Paul," "the group of Apollo," or "Cephas" (Peter), or "Christ," and each was developing a personality of its own, as well as quarreling with the others. Paul's answer was that they were not baptized in the name of Paul, but in the name of Christ. The Greeks were steeped in wisdom and philosophy, but they were putting their personal egos ahead of the wisdom of God. He said, "Because the foolishness of God is wiser than men, and the weakness of God is stronger than men" (1 Corinthians 1:25). ". . . Let him who boasts, boast in the Lord" (1 Corinthians 1:31).

Paul, who was a well-educated person, ridiculed those who pretended to be so full of wisdom and said that he approached everyone in utter humility, with plain words, so that their faith might not rest in the wisdom of men, but in the power of God. He explained that the rulers of the age didn't have much understanding, or they would not have crucified Christ. The Holy Spirit in men gives them the mind to understand the gifts of God.

Paul talked of the Corinthians' immaturity, saying that they were men of the flesh; he started their spiritual growth on milk and not solid food. As long as they quarreled among each other, they were still immature. He said, "I planted, Apollos watered, but God was causing the growth" (1 Corinthians 3:6). He compared his work to a building. He laid a foundation, and others built on it. Let the building be spiritual, not material. ". . . for the temple of God is holy, and that is what you are" (1 Corinthians 3:17).

Some of the people in the new church apparently had become arrogant in their new-found knowledge and became "puffed up." Paul reminds them of his own and the other apostles' lives of humility; living almost like beggars, but rich in the Spirit. He admonishes them, not to make them ashamed, but because he loves them as a father would.

He talks about immorality, idolatry, reviling, drunkenness, and robbery. He has heard that a man in the Church is cohabitating with his father's wife (his own stepmother), and that some members approve. He says that the man should be removed from the Church and delivered to Satan, in order that his soul may be saved in the day of the Lord Jesus Christ. He says that a person cannot live in this world and avoid being around sinners, but he should not associate with a brother if he is guilty of being a sinner. God judges those outside the Church. ". . . Remove the wicked man from among yourselves" (1 Corinthians 5:13).

The members of a church should suffer wrong, or even be defrauded, rather than to get into a lawsuit with one another and be judged by the unrighteous nonbelievers. Paul explained, "Do you not know that your bodies are members of Christ? . . ." (1 Corinthians 6:15.) "But the one who joins himself to the Lord is one spirit with Him" (1 Corinthians 6:17). ". . . your body is a temple of the Holy Spirit who is in you, whom you have from God . . . therefore glorify God in your body" (1 Corinthians 6:19, 20).

Apparently Paul had received a letter inquiring about relations among the married and unmarried. He openly discussed these questions regarding actions and attitudes of marriage, divorce, singles, widowhood, and circumcision among Christians. He advised marriage for those who desired it, but did not seem too enthusiastic about marriage. "Only, as the Lord has assigned to each one, as God has called each, in this manner let him walk" (1 Corinthians 7:17).

He warned against eating meat that had been offered as a sacrifice to false idols. Not that the meat itself was bad, because idols have no real existence, but to be seen eating with idol worshippers might set a bad example for others not as strong in the faith.

Another question was presented regarding payment of ministers and apostles. Paul's position was that a minister was entitled to the same pay as anyone else who worked, which was in agreement with the opinion of the Corinthians. What they couldn't understand was why he would not accept pay. He contended that this was his way of honoring the Lord. He worked as a tent- and sail-maker to earn a living and worked for the Lord because he loved Him. "And I do all things for the sake of the gospel, that I may become a fellow-partaker of it" (1 Corinthians 9:23).

The members were reminded of the Hebrews going out of Egypt. Some of them indulged in immorality, and 23,000 died in a single day; some were destroyed by serpents, and some who grumbled were destroyed. He told them, ". . . God is faithful, who will not allow you to be tempted beyond what you are able, but with the temptation will provide the way of escape also, that you may be able to endure it" (1 Corinthians 10:13).

In a city as corrupt as Corinth, where there were many prostitutes, Paul said that Christian women should be very careful in their actions and dress, to avoid giving approval to such corruption. He particularly warned the women to veil their faces and to cover their heads at worship, because the prostitutes did not do these things. The communion service at church had deteriorated in some groups to a feast or an occasion for drunkenness. Paul said, "Therefore whoever eats the bread or drinks the cup of the Lord in an unworthy manner, shall be guilty of the body and the blood of the Lord" (1 Corinthians 11:27).

Paul explained the working of the Holy Spirit in the lives of his people by comparing them to the members of the body. The Spirit manifests itself in one man by wisdom, in another by knowledge, in another by gifts of healing, in another by the ability to heal, and in another by the gift of foreign tongues. All are inspired by the same Spirit. Just as the body has hands, feet, eyes, and ears, none can exist alone; all are part of the same body. The same is true with Christ: "For by one Spirit we were all baptized into one body, whether Jews or Greeks whether slaves or free, and we were all made to drink of one Spirit" (1 Corinthians 12:13).

Regardless of how the Spirit represents itself in each man, there is one ingredient that is necessary in all men. That is love. Paul's definition of love is one of the most beautiful parts of the Bible and is quoted here completely:

> Love is patient, love is kind, and is not jealous; love does not brag and is not arrogant, does not act unbecomingly; it does not seek its own, is not provoked, does not take into account a wrong suffered, does not rejoice in unrighteousness, but rejoices with the truth; bears all things, believes all things, hopes all things, endures all things. Love never fails; but if there are gifts of prophecy, they will be done away; if there are tongues, they will cease; if there is knowledge, it will be done away. For we know in part, and we prophesy in part; but when the perfect comes, the partial will be done away. When I was a child, I used to speak as a child, think as a child, reason as a child; when I became a man, I did away with childish things. For now we see in a mirror dimly, but then face to face; now I know in part, but then I shall know fully just as I also have been fully known. But now abide faith, hope, love, these three; but the greatest of these is love.
>
> 1 Corinthians 13:4–13

Many of the members had been speaking in (foreign) tongues. They felt that this gave them prestige and honor among the others. Paul admonished them against self-adoration and said, "I thank God, I speak in tongues more than you all; however, in the church I desire to speak five words with my mind, that I may instruct others also, rather than ten thousand words in a tongue" (1 Corinthians 14:18, 19).

The final reminder in this letter is that Christ died for our sins, was buried, was raised on the third day, and appeared to Cephas, and then to the twelve. Then He appeared to more than five hundred people at one time. This was twenty-seven years previous, and at least half of those people were still alive to testify that they saw Him. Then He appeared to James, to all of the apostles, and last of all, to Paul himself. If one does not believe that Christ was resurrected from the dead, there is no reason for the existence of Christianity. The resurrection is one of the most important and best-documented facts in history. Paul adds, "Therefore, my beloved brethren, be steadfast, immovable, always abounding in the work of the Lord, knowing that your toil is not in vain in the Lord" (1 Corinthians 15:58). He mentions that he will visit the Corinthians shortly, that Apollos is unable to come now, and that Timothy will visit them, also. He closes, "My love be with you all in Christ Jesus. Amen" (1 Corinthians 16:24).

SECOND CORINTHIANS

Time A.D. 57.

Author Paul. This letter was sent to Corinth after Paul received word from Corinth by Titus, who met Paul in Macedonia. This letter was intended to be circulated to all churches in Achaia (Greece).

Theme Paul had written his first letter to the churches in Corinth and had received word by messengers that there were still some problems. He made a quick trip from Ephesus to Corinth and back to Ephesus. Then he started to Corinth by way of Macedonia, where he met Titus (probably in Philippi), who shared the good news that his previous letter had a good effect, but that there was still some criticism of Paul. Much of this letter was in self-defense, as a means of proving his apostleship. He reminded them that he founded the church itself.

Through his messenger Titus, Paul receives the good news that his first letter has had good results, but in spite of his previous short visit, there were still some problems. He urged the Corinthians to have compassion, to forgive, and to comfort the man who repented of his sin of living with his mother-in-law. He reminded them of his own great suffering and near death in Ephesus and his disappointment in not meeting Titus in Troas; therefore, he had hurried on to Macedonia.

Some said that Paul had no letters of commendation from Jerusalem, but his answer was, why should he have letters to a church that he founded? The accusers were the chief troublemakers. He compared their deeds with his: his Gospel in men's hearts versus theirs of law written on stone; his teachings of the spirit versus theirs of the letter; his interpretation of life, theirs of death, and so on. He reminded them that he preached Jesus Christ as Lord and himself as servant for Jesus' sake.

He reminded them of his sufferings of the flesh in order to preach the things of the Spirit. He did not list these sufferings, but they included plots to kill him in Damascus, Jerusalem, and Antioch; being stoned several times; being beaten with rods, being put in stocks; being driven out of several cities, and being harassed almost constantly. This had gone on for about twenty-five years. Death was at work with him, that he might bring life to others. This momentary affliction is preparing us for an eternal weight of glory beyond all comparison.

Paul said that God had given him the strength and courage to carry out his mission. He compared the life on earth with the life at home with the Lord after death, and said that all must appear before the Lord for judgment, to receive good or evil, according to what they have done on earth in the flesh. Through Christ, God forgave men's sins and entrusted the apostles to be ambassadors to tell this Good News to all, so that all men might become the righteous of God.

He repeated again the personal sufferings he had been through almost constantly, in an effort to vindicate himself from those who were accusing him of being false. He urged the believers not to be associated with nonbelievers, saying, ". . . what partnership have righteousness and lawlessness, or what fellowship has light with darkness? Or what agreement has the temple of God with idols? . . ." (2 Corinthians 6:14, 16.) He reminded them of God's many promises of salvation, urged them to cleanse their bodies of every defilement and to make themselves pure and perfect in the fear of God.

Paul expressed again his great pleasure with the news brought by Titus, which comforted him and made him feel that his persecution and suffering were worth the effort. He did not regret that his letter had made the Corinthians sorry, or that they were grieved, because godly grief produces a repentance that leads to salvation and brings no regret, but worldly grief produces death. He expressed great faith, pride, and confidence in them for their renewed zeal in learning.

In planning his return to Jerusalem, Paul was arranging with all the churches for a combined contribution, which he was taking with him, for the poor saints in Jerusalem. He hoped that the believers in Corinth would contribute as generously as the churches in Asia Minor and Macedonia had done. He sent his trusted messengers ahead of him, to help the people arrange their gifts before he arrived. He reminded them that he who sows sparingly will reap sparingly; he who sows bountifully will also reap bountifully, but each must give as his own conscience dictates and not out of compulsion, because God loves a cheerful giver.

Apparently some of those who opposed Paul made remarks that he was meek, humble, and unimpressive. Paul explained that he did not like to boast about himself, but he reminded them that he spent his time building the Church of God, instead of trying to tear down others' work. He was capable of destroying false arguments and any obstacle that kept the knowledge of God from them. "But he who boasts, let him boast in the Lord," he said (2 Corinthians 10:17).

He said he felt like a fool to have to defend himself and boast about his accomplishments and tell of his privations, but if he must, he would do whatever necessary to promote the will of God. He reminded them that they paid him nothing. He was an Israelite, a Hebrew, a descendent of

Abraham. Five times he had received thirty-nine lashes; three times he had been beaten with rods; once he had been stoned; three times he had been shipwrecked. He had spent a night and a day adrift at sea; had been endangered by rivers at flood, robbers, and beasts in the wilderness. He had spent sleepless nights; had suffered hunger and thirst, cold and exposure, and the constant concern for all his churches. "Who is weak without my being weak? . . . The God and Father . . . knows that I am not lying" (2 Corinthians 11:29, 31).

He tells that he knew a man in Christ who was taken up to the third heaven and borne into Paradise and who heard things that cannot be told, which man may not utter. He does not explain this. He tells how he has borne a thorn in the flesh (probably an illness or weakness of his eyes), probably to keep him from being too elated. He had prayed for relief, and God had answered, ". . . My grace is sufficient for you, for power is perfected in weakness" (2 Corinthians 12:9). For the sake of Christ, then, he says he is content with weaknesses, insults, hardships, persecutions, and calamities. For when he is weak, he is strong.

Paul tells of his love and hope for the people of Corinth. He also says, for the benefit of the nonbelievers, that they had better have two or three witnesses to prove their statements, because he will not spare them, as he has Christ speaking in him, who was crucified in weakness but lives by the power of God. He prays that they may do what is right, asks them to mend their ways, heed his appeal, agree with one another, and live in peace. He prays that the love of God will be with them.

GALATIANS

Time A.D. 57.
Author Paul. Written from Ephesus, Macedonia, or Corinth, to the church in Galatia while on the latter part of his third journey, but before he wrote his letter to the Romans.
Theme The Galatians were originally Gauls (French), who came into Asia Minor after they conquered Rome in 390 B.C. They moved through Italy, Greece, Macedonia, and into Asia Minor about 200 B.C., so they had been in Galatia for about two hundred fifty years before Paul. They had been under Roman domination for approximately one hundred fifty years. They were warm-hearted, impulsive, generous, fickle, flighty, argumentative, courageous, and could be warlike. They accepted Paul's teaching readily, but after listening to some Jewish antagonists, turned on him and stoned him almost to death. Paul had started the churches in Galatia (a Roman Province in the interior of Turkey, between Ephesus and Tarsus), but after he left, the Jews told these Gentiles that they must live by the Hebrew law and be circumcised to be eligible to become Christians. The Galatians believed the Jews as readily as they had believed Paul, and this resulted in wholesale circumcision. These events distressed Paul, and he gave rather stern instructions in his letter to stop these incorrect views.

Paul addressed the problem abruptly: ". . . if any man is preaching to you a gospel contrary to that which you received, let him be accursed" (Galatians 1:9). There is no Gospel contrary to what Paul preached. There is only one Gospel—the Gospel of Christ. He reminded them that the Gospel he preached came from God—a direct revelation from Jesus Christ—not from man. He reviewed his whole life for them, saying he had been a devout Jewish Pharisee and had persecuted the Christians until he was converted by God directly through Jesus Christ. He had meditated in Arabia for three years before returning to Jerusalem, and had only conferred with Cephas (Peter) and James (Jesus' brother) for fifteen days before going to Syria and Cilicia for fourteen years. The Jews in Jerusalem glorified God because of Paul's work.

After the incident at Antioch, he returned to Jerusalem with Barnabas, a Jew, and Titus, a Gentile, who was not circumcised. They joined with Peter, James, and John in persuading the Church to agree that the Gentiles did not have to conform to Jewish law to become Christians. Paul said to Cephas, who ate with the Gentiles, except when other Jews were around, ". . . If you, being a Jew, live like the Gentiles and not like the Jews, how is it that you compel the Gentiles to live like Jews?" (Galatians 2:14.) "I have been crucified with Christ; and it is no longer I who live, but Christ lives in me; and the life which I now live in the flesh I live by faith in the Son of God, who loved me, and delivered Himself up for me" (Galatians 2:20). If acceptance or justification is through the law, rather than the Spirit, then Christ died for no purpose.

Paul reminded the Galatians that they received their first awakening to salvation by faith, and not by the law, and the miracles he performed for them were from the Spirit, and not from the law. He reminded them of God's promise to Abraham, ". . . All the nations shall be blessed in you" (Galatians 3:8).

Therefore, all men of faith are blessed with Abraham, who had faith. Why then the law? Paul states, ". . . the law has become our tutor to lead us to Christ, that we may be justified by faith. But now that faith has come, we are no longer under a tutor" (Galatians 3:24, 25).

Paul represents Christianity as the freedom comparable to the freedom of a former slave. When men did not know God, they were in bondage to beings. Knowing God, they are free. In Christ Jesus neither circumcision or uncircumcision is of any avail; only faith, working through love. Paul expresses his confidence in the Galatians and reminds them that the new freedom is not to be used for permissive sins, but for love. They must be servants to one another, for the whole law is, in one sentence, ". . . You shall love your neighbor as yourself" (Galatians 5:14).

The works of the flesh are plain: immorality, impurity, licentiousness, idolatry, sorcery, enmity, strife, jealousy, anger, selfishness, dissension, envy, drunkenness, carousing, and the like. The fruit of the Spirit is love, joy, peace, patience, kindness, goodness, faithfulness, gentleness, and self-control.

Paul concludes, "For the one who sows to his own flesh shall from the flesh reap corruption, but the one who sows to the Spirit shall from the Spirit reap eternal life" (Galatians 6:8). Paul addresses this problem in a stern and uncompromising attitude, because with him the issue is acceptance or rejection of Christ; as always, his attitude is one of self-sacrifice, love, and compassion for all of God's people.

EPHESIANS

Time A.D. 59–A.D. 61.

Author Paul. Written in Rome while Paul was in prison. Addressed to the Ephesians, but probably used as a circular letter to all of the churches in Asia Minor in the area of Ephesus. This letter, as well as Colossians and Philemon, were carried by Tychicus, a beloved brother and faithful servant in the Lord, who had accompanied Paul on some of his journeys.

Theme This appears to be a circular letter because it lacks the personal greetings to close friends which he generally included in his letters. His deep concern was to unite the Gentile Christians and the Jewish Christians and eliminate their prejudices. He had taken a great offering of money from the Gentile Christians at the end of his third journey, which he gave to the poor in the mother Jewish church in Jerusalem as a demonstration of their love, so that the Jews would feel more kindly toward the Gentiles. This letter was to the Gentiles, and attempted to explain the oneness of all in the body of Christ. To Paul, Christ was the something that could bring all into unity and harmony with God and with one another.

Paul praises God for having sent Christ into the world and for having made available every spiritual blessing in all heavenly places to all who believe. This has always been God's plan for eternity, to unite all things in Him, in heaven and on earth.

This includes Jews who have hoped for Christ's coming and Gentiles who have heard the word of truth and the Gospel of salvation, have believed, and have had that belief sealed with the promised Holy Spirit, which is the guarantee of eternal inheritance until we actually acquire possession of it. He elaborates on the tremendous power and sovereignty of God, the Father of Jesus Christ.

All men were dead in sin and lived in the passions of the flesh, following the desires of body and mind. God, in His great mercy, out of His love for mankind, made all who would accept Jesus Christ alive through Christ. This was the gift of God, not something earned by works. The Gentiles at one time did not have that privilege and were labeled or branded uncircumcised, but now in Jesus Christ these laws of the flesh are abolished. All mankind is united into one, reconciled by God through the giving of His Son on the cross. All men are saints and members of the household of God, which was built upon the foundation of the preaching of the apostles and prophets, with Jesus Christ as the cornerstone.

Paul explained how these things had been revealed to him, by God's grace, to be preached and revealed to all men, both Jew and Gentile, that all might realize God's plan in Jesus Christ. Even though he was in prison, Paul prayed for them, that they might be strengthened in their faith.

He urged them to practice in their daily lives all that they had been taught, by putting aside their former lives of lust and corruption and assuming their new nature, created after the likeness of God. This they could do by always speaking the truth, by not being angry with one another, by not stealing, by letting no evil talk come out of their mouths, and by being tender-hearted and forgiving of one another, as God in Christ forgave them.

Paul then outlined many guidelines for Christian conduct, urging the people to be imitators of God and to love as Christ loves them. Let there be no immorality, covetousness and filthiness, and do not associate with people who reject God's forgiveness. Do not indulge in drunkenness, but be filled with the Spirit. He urged singing as a tribute to the Lord. Wives should be subject to their husbands, and husbands should love their wives. Children should obey their parents, but parents should not be too strict.

Half the population of Rome was comprised of slaves, and slavery was a common practice throughout the Roman Empire. Even slaves should be obedient to their masters as doing the will of God, knowing that in God's Kingdom they will be rewarded. Masters should be tolerant of their slaves the same way they should expect God to be tolerant of them in His Kingdom.

Paul summarized by telling them to put on the whole armor of God; to stand firm for the truth; to take the Gospel of peace, the shield of faith, the helmet of salvation, and the sword of the spirit, which is the Word of God; and to pray at all times.

PHILIPPIANS

Time   A.D. 63–A.D. 64.
Author   Paul. The church at Philippi, which had been founded by Paul in A.D. 51, heard of Paul's imprisonment in Rome and sent an offering to him, to comfort him. This is Paul's thank-you note, sent to them by Epaphroditus, the messenger who had brought the gift to Paul.
Theme   A letter of affection and love for the people of Philippi, and also for all who find life in Christ. Paul had no admonitions for these people; therefore, we can assume that this church was doing well and that there were do divisions or controversies. Philippi was the city where Paul and Timothy were wrongfully imprisoned and beaten, but God's power and delivery were demonstrated to the people by an earthquake, which broke the chains and the gates to the prison. Paul said he was sending Timothy to them and planned to visit them later himself. Luke had been the pastor of this church for six years.

Paul sends his greetings and thanks, together with Timothy's, for the gift of money, but especially for their love, prayers, and steadfastness of living in righteousness to the glory of God. He tells about how his imprisonment has helped him to spread the Gospel to the guards, and even to others of higher rank, so that many are now unafraid to speak out for Christ. Whether he lives or dies is unimportant to him, because "For to me, to live is Christ, and to die is gain" (Philippians 1:21). If he lives, he will have ample cause to glory in Jesus, because he will be able to come to see them.

He urges them to continue with their humility and help for one another. He uses the example of Jesus, who is God, but while in the flesh was humble and obedient to God His Father, to the extent that He gave His life in obedience. He was rewarded and exalted by God, to the extent that every tongue would confess that Jesus Christ is Lord, to the glory of God the Father. He urges them to live their lives in accordance with God's desires, so that they will stand out in a corrupt world like beacon lights. He wants to continue to be proud of them and to know that his labors were not in vain. He tells how Epaphroditus, who brought their gift, became ill and almost died, but was now able to travel and return with this letter, all of which he did in the work of Christ.

He warns them, in their fruitful progress, to be alert for the evildoers who would preach that a person must be circumcised to be eligible for acceptance by Jesus Christ. He reminded them that he was a Jew and was circumcised, but he counted that as a loss because of the advantage of knowing Christ Jesus his Lord. He would sacrifice his life for his Lord, if necessary. He urged them to be equally dedicated, because of the reward of life in heaven with Jesus.

Again he tells them to rejoice in the Lord, to put their lives in His hands, and to let their requests be made known to God. He humbly uses himself as an example for their gift and tells them that, ". . . I have learned the secret of being filled and going hungry, both of having abundance and suffering need. I can do all things through Him who strengthens me" (Philippians 4:12, 13).

COLOSSIANS

Time A.D. 62.

Author Paul. Written to the people of Colossae, a city about 100 miles from Ephesus. This church was not established by Paul, but probably by Epaphras, who was also in prison in Rome. This letter was carried by Tychicus and Onesimus, the runaway slave of Philemon who was returning to Philemon.

Theme A letter of warning and a statement of the total preeminence or loftiness of the position of Christ as the supreme head of the Church and the central focal point in every person's life. Paul warns against being gullible to false teachings, ritualism, worshipping angels, false mysticism (a vague, baffling, or mysterious belief without foundation), asceticism (self-torture or self-denial, designed to produce a high state spiritually), vile sins, and even respectable sins. He urges instruction in Christian virtues for masters, all classes of Christians, and all people. He stresses three words—*faith* in Christ, *love* toward others, and *hope* of eternal life in heaven.

Paul starts his letter by saying how thankful he is for the Christians of Colossae, whose church was founded by Epaphras, who is a faithful fellow minister. He tells them of his constant prayers for them. He outlines how God has placed us in the Kingdom of His Son Jesus Christ, who is the head of our universe as our Saviour, whom we can approach directly, without going through any intermediaries, weird philosophies, or rituals of self-torture. He is our wisdom, our life, and our hope. Our lives should be centered in Him, in loving Him and in living in Him. He is sufficient for every man's life here on earth, and each person's redemption and eternal perfection in heaven.

He points out to them his own dedication to see that the Gospel was preached to the whole world, and how happy he is that he has been able to do that. The things that have been taught to them should become deep-rooted and stronger, and should not be uprooted by false philosophy and empty deceit. In Christ we dwell; therefore, we must walk with Him and express this life; grow with Him and show the power

He has given us; and build with Him, to develop our character fully, in order to be Christlike.

Paul tells them to put aside the earthly things of immorality, impurity, passion, evil desire, and covetousness; anger, wrath, malice, slander, and foul talk. All men are free to live in Christ, and, as God's chosen ones, they should show compassion, kindness, lowliness, meekness, patience, and forgiveness, as God has forgiven man of his sins. They should do everything in the name of the Lord Jesus and give thanks to God the Father through Him. He encourages wives to be subject to their husbands and husbands to love their wives and to be patient with their children. He tells slaves to obey their masters, because all will receive from the Lord their eternal inheritance as their reward.

The churches in those days were in homes, and Paul sends personal greetings to many who have used their homes as meeting places. He praises all of the good workers who are working with him for the glory of God.

FIRST THESSALONIANS

Time   A.D. 52.

Author   Paul. Written from Corinth, to the Christians in Thessalonica and in Macedonia, located about one hundred miles west of Philippi on the road to Corinth. Paul had founded this church, but had been there for a very short time, possibly a month, and had been driven from the city by foes of his thinking. Timothy and Silvanus (Silas) had been with him. This was Paul's first letter. The city was named, about 315 B.C., after Thessalonica, sister of Alexander the Great and wife of Cassander.

Theme   Paul had founded the church at Thessalonica in a very short time, but had received better and faster reception there than from any other city. The reaction had been just as swift by the Jews, who opposed him and accused him of "turning the world upside down," and drove him out of the city. He went to Berea, about fifty miles southwest, and then on south to Athens, where he sent Timothy back to Thessalonica to see how the people were doing. By the time Timothy returned, Paul had gone on to Corinth, where Timothy found him. He stayed in Corinth about one and one-half years. Timothy reported great faith and progress in the new church, in spite of continued opposition, but there was some moral laxity. There was some concern as to what happens to those who have already died when Jesus comes again.

Paul says he gives thanks to God for the church in Thessalonica, because the news of the peoples' acceptance of Jesus Christ and the changes in their way of life has spread, not only throughout all of Macedonia and Achaia (Greece), but throughout their known world, and has made the work of the disciples easier. He and Silvanus and Timothy had lived among them, living clean lives, working day and night to earn their own living. They had not sought glory for themselves while preaching the Word of God, and had set an example of a true believer's conduct. The Thessalonians had responded beautifully, and Paul was pleased that they imitated the disciples in their conduct.

He complimented them for being able to realize and accept the teachings he brought to them as being the Word of God, and not of selfish men, in spite of sufferings imposed on them by nonbelievers. He reminded them that the church in Judea rose in spite of the fact that the Jews killed Jesus Christ, and salvation would come to the Gentiles who believed in spite of all opposition. God's wrath has come on the opposition.

Paul explained that his love and concern for them had caused him to send Timothy to them, to be sure that the "tempters" had not turned them. Timothy's answers had brought Paul great joy. He longed to see them, and had tried twice, but Satan had stopped him.

He urged them to continue to imitate his life of obedience and to abstain from all immorality. He advised that each man should take a wife, and that they should not live by passion of the flesh, because the Lord is also an avenger.

In answer to their question concerning what will happen to those who are already dead when Christ comes, he explained: As Jesus Christ died and rose again, so also will those who are now dead. Those who are alive when Christ comes will not precede those who are dead. When Christ comes, the archangel will call, and the dead in Christ will rise first, then those who are alive will be caught up together with them, to meet the Lord in the clouds. The day of the Lord will come like a thief in the night, and they should not stop working now and become idle in waiting, because no one knows when this will happen.

He advised them to encourage one another, to admonish the idle, to encourage the weakhearted, to be patient with all, to refrain from repaying evil with evil, to hold fast to what is good, to abstain from all forms of evil, and to pray constantly.

SECOND THESSALONIANS

Time   A.D. 52.

Author   Paul. He was in Corinth when Timothy returned from delivering the first letter. He sent this second letter immediately thereafter, to clear up the issue of the second coming of Christ.

Theme   When Timothy returned after delivering Paul's first letter, he must have told of two things that Paul thought needed correction at once. The people were confused about the timing of the second coming of Christ; many were taking advantage of the idea of brotherly love and charity, and had stopped working. They were living on the charity of the others while waiting for the immediate coming of Christ. These ideas needed correction at once. A forged letter, supposedly written by Paul saying that the day of the Lord had come, had been circulated, and was confusing the members.

Paul praises the church for its growth, for the love of the members for one another, and for their steadfastness in the faith in spite of persecutions. They will be made worthy of salvation and will escape the affliction God will repay to those who persecute them. These persecutors will suffer the punishment of eternal destruction and exclusion from the presence of the Lord when He comes. He prays that the believers will be worthy, and that the name of Jesus Christ may be glorified in them.

Paul counsels them regarding the second coming of the Lord Jesus Christ.

They are not to understand, by any fraudulent letters or by anything that Paul has said, that the day of the Lord is here now. There must be a rebellion or apostasy (*see* definition), led by the activity of Satan, who will present great pretended signs, wonders, and wicked deception. Many will be followers of this rebellion because they refuse to believe the truth. But all of these will be condemned on the day in which the Lord returns in a flash.

Paul urges them to stand firm in their beliefs, as he has taught them. He prays for their comfort and progress in their faith. He urges them to pray for him, that he may be delivered from wicked and evil men.

Even though Paul is an advocate of charity, he is severe in his advice regarding those who have quit working and are being supported by the others in anticipation of the coming of Christ in the immediate future. He commands them not to tolerate this laziness. Any man able to work should earn his own living—if he doesn't, the members should cast him out. Paul sets an example for them by earning his own living while preaching to them, even though he should be entitled to payment for his work. He tells them to have nothing to do with any man who refuses to obey. Do not look upon him as an enemy, but warn him as a brother.

Paul prays that God will bless them in all they do.

FIRST TIMOTHY

Time   A.D. 65.
Author Paul. A letter from Macedonia to Timothy, who had always worked with Paul but was now being left alone in Ephesus. Paul had been released from his first imprisonment and was free for three or four years.
Theme Paul outlines general instructions about the organization, development, and administration of a church and the selection of officers and pastors, as well as conduct of the members. Timothy's mother was Jewish and his father Greek. He joined Paul on his second journey and worked very closely with him for about fifteen years. The territory was getting bigger, and there were more churches; Paul saw the need to put things in writing which formerly had been verbal, regarding the care of the Church. Second Timothy and Titus are similar books, covering the duties of officers, doctrine, and conduct.

Paul advises Timothy to be aware that, contrary to his instructions, there are false leaders trying to teach spiritual doctrines, which have been entrusted to Paul by God. The laws of the land are good, because they are made for the lawless and disobedient.

Paul says he thanks God for giving him the strength to do what he has done, and is doing, because he was God's worst sinner before God converted him and used him as an example for others. He urges Timothy to ". . . fight the good fight" for God (1 Timothy 1:18).

Firstly, Timothy should pray earnestly for all men and leaders. God desires all men to be saved through the knowledge that there is one God and one mediator between God and men; the Lord Jesus Christ, who gave Himself as a ransom for all. Men should pray and women should not adorn themselves with jewelry, but with good deeds. Women should learn in silence and should have no authority over men (Paul would not be very popular in today's women's liberation movement).

He outlines the qualifications for the offices of bishop and deacon. These people must be above reproach; should have one wife; should be temperate, sensible, dignified, hospitable; should be apt teachers; allow no drunkenness; be gentle, not quarrelsome; be no lover of money, be good managers of their own households; have proper children; be not recent converts, be not puffed with deceit; have a good reputation; be serious; should not be double-tongued; and must hold the mystery of the faith with a clear conscience and be tested first. The women likewise must be serious; there should be no slanderers, and they should be temperate and faithful in all things. They should hold the mystery of the faith with a clear conscience and let all men be tested, to prove themselves worthy of office.

The Spirit says that some will depart from the faith by listening to false teachers, who will forbid marriage and avoid certain foods that God created to be received with thanksgiving.

Timothy should be a good minister and follow these instructions. Have nothing to do with silly myths. All men should train themselves in godliness, because we have our hope set on the living God, who is the Saviour of all men, especially of those who believe.

Do not let your youth be a hindrance. Be an example by your speech and conduct; in love, in faith, and in purity. Attend to the public reading of the Scriptures, to preaching, and to teaching. Do not rebuke an older man, but exhort him as a father. Treat younger men as brothers, older women like mothers, younger women like sisters, in all purity. Honor widows, and help them in their adjustment.

Elders who rule well should be paid like anyone else. Never admit any charge against an elder unless there are two or three witnesses, but if any persist in sin, rebuke them in public. He tells Timothy to be courageous in carrying out his instructions. The sins of some men are conspicuous, pointing to judgment, but the sins of others appear later. Good deeds usually are conspicuous, but even if not, they cannot remain hidden.

Let slaves honor their masters. If anyone teaches contrary to the teachings of Jesus Christ, he is puffed with conceit and is just looking for disputes, which produce envy, dissension, slander, and wrangling among men, in the belief that godliness is a means of personal gain.

There is a great gain in godliness with contentment with just enough food and clothing. Those who desire to be rich fall into temptation and into many senseless and hurtful desires that plunge men into destruction. The love of money is the root of all evil and leads men away from the faith. Charge the rich men to do good deeds, to be liberal and generous, and to be rich in good deeds.

Paul concludes, "But flee from these things, you man of God; and pursue righteousness, godliness, faith, love, perseverance and gentleness" (1 Timothy 6:11). Fight the good fight, take hold of eternal life, and keep the commandments until the appearance of our Lord Jesus Christ.

SECOND TIMOTHY

Time   A.D. 67.
Author Paul. Written while he was in prison in Rome, awaiting execution.
Theme This was Paul's last letter. He asked Timothy to come and see him. He outlined the true course for a servant of Jesus Christ. The Christians were being arrested, persecuted, and killed by all kinds of vicious methods. Nero is said to have set fire to Rome so he could rebuild it. The Christians were blamed. Many Christians were fearful for their lives, and there was some backsliding.

Paul thanks God for Timothy, his loyal worker, whose grandmother, Lois, and mother, Eunice, are friends of his. He tells Timothy not to be ashamed of testifying for the Lord, nor for Paul, but if necessary to take his share of the suffering as a result of his teachings. Paul is proud of his own suffering, because he is a preacher, apostle, and teacher. He urges Timothy to follow the pattern of the sound words that he has heard from Paul in faith and love, which are in Christ Jesus.

He must be strong and take his share of the suffering as a good soldier of Christ Jesus. An athlete is not crowned unless he competes according to the rules. The Lord will grant him understanding. Paul says he endures his persecution for the sake of the members of the Church, that they may obtain salvation, which is in Christ Jesus.

Paul advises against getting into disputes and godless chatter, because it is like gangrene. Along with those who call upon the Lord from a pure heart, he should avoid youthful passions and aim at righteousness, faith, love, and peace. He must be kindly to everyone, be an apt teacher, and be gentle in correcting his opponents, in hopes that they may repent and come to know the truth.

He warns Timothy that in the last days there will come times of stress, for men will be egotistic, lovers of money, proud, arrogant, abusive, ungrateful, unholy, and slanderous, fierce haters of good and lovers of pleasure rather than lovers of God. He should avoid such people. They will not influence many men, and their folly will be plain to all.

Paul notes that Timothy has observed Paul's example in teaching, conduct, aim in life, faith, patience, love, and steadfastness and has seen the persecutions he has endured and how he has always been rescued by God. ". . . from childhood you have known the sacred writings which are able to give you the wisdom that leads to salvation through faith which is in Christ Jesus. All Scripture is inspired by God and profitable for teaching, for reproof, for correction, for training in righteousness; that the man of God may be adequate, equipped for every good work" (2 Timothy 3:15–17).

Paul charges Timothy, in the presence of God and Jesus Christ, to preach the Word: to be urgent all the time; to convince, rebuke, and exhort; but to be patient in teachings. People will be tempted and will drift off to myths.

Paul says that he is about to be sacrificed; that he has fought a good fight, finished the race, and kept the faith, and that he will be rewarded in heaven.

He urges Timothy to visit him soon and to bring a coat he left in Troas. (It was cold and damp in the prison in Rome where Paul was confined.) Paul gives all praise to God, forever and ever.

TITUS

Time A.D. 65.
Author Paul. Written to Titus, his trusted helper, who was a Greek. Titus was probably in Crete, where Paul had previously left him. He could have been in Dalmatia (Greece). Paul was in Macedonia.
Theme Paul was writing to Timothy and Titus from Macedonia at about the same time. He was principally concerned with the proper training of elders, instructions to the members, warning about backsliders and false prophets, and the constant need to preach and repeat the Gospel of God and salvation through Jesus Christ.

    Paul explains that he left Titus in Crete so that he might amend what was defective and appoint elders in every town. These men must be blameless, good husbands of one wife; their children must be believers and not insubordinate to their father. A bishop must be blameless; not arrogant, or quick-tempered, or drunken, or violent, or greedy for gain; but hospitable, a lover of goodness, upright, holy, and self-controlled. He must hold firm to the true teachings he has received, so that he will be able to give sound instruction in sound doctrine and also be able to overwhelm those who contradict it. There are many Jewish sects which are upsetting whole churches and teaching for personal gain.
    One of their own says, "Cretans are always liars, evil beasts, lazy gluttons" (Titus 1:12). Rebuke the members, so they will be sound in faith.
    Teach sound doctrine. Bid the older men to be temperate, serious, sensible, faithful, and steadfast in love. Teach the older women to be reverent, temperate in drink, and not slanderous. Teach what is good; train young women to love their husbands and children, to be sensible, chaste, domestic, and kind and submissive to their husbands, that the Word of God may not be discredited. Urge the young men to control themselves.
    Especially show yourself as a model of good deeds, and in your teaching show integrity, gravity, and sound speech that cannot be criticized, so that an opponent may be put to shame and left speechless. Bid slaves

to be submissive to their masters, obedient, and loyal, so they may be an example for their masters.

Remember always that the grace of God is here for the salvation of all men who will renounce ungodliness, worldly passions, and covetous lives to live godly lives in this world while awaiting our blessed hope—the appearing of the Saviour Jesus Christ—who gave His life for the forgiveness of our sins and redemption of our lives in heaven. Declare these things.

Remind the people to be submissive to the law of the rulers, to be ready for honest work, to speak no evil, to avoid quarreling, and to be gentle and courteous. We were once foolish in our conduct, but when the goodness and loving kindness of God our Saviour appeared, He saved us. Not because of deeds done by us in righteousness, but in virtue of His own mercy, by the washing away of our sins and renewal in the Holy Spirit through Jesus Christ, so that we might be justified by His grace and become heirs in hope of eternal life.

Insist on these things, and may the grace of God be with you.

PHILEMON

Time   A.D. 62.
Author Paul. Written from Rome, while in prison.
Theme Paul was in prison in Rome. Onesimus, a slave, had run away from his master Philemon, a wealthy Christian of Colossae, and had met Paul in Rome. He had also robbed his master. Paul's letter was delivered by Tychicus, who accompanied Onesimus back to his master. Paul very tactfully pleaded for forgiveness for Onesimus, who had accepted Christ as his Saviour.

Paul expresses his love for Philemon and his thankfulness for his efforts in the Church. It is possible that the church met in Philemon's home, because there were no church buildings until 200 years after Christ.

Paul relates that he is in prison and that Onesimus has come to him and has been as a son, and that he would like to keep him, but is sending him back to Philemon. Onesimus' help to Paul has been as though Philemon himself has helped him. He will return not only as a slave, but as a brother in the flesh and in the Lord.

Paul says that he himself will repay whatever Onesimus owes and reminds Philemon that he owes his own life of salvation to Paul. Paul thanks him in advance and knows he will do even more than Paul asks.

He hopes to visit Philemon soon and sends greetings from Epaphras, Mark, Aristarchus, Demas, and Luke.

HEBREWS

Time About A.D. 61–A.D. 65.
Author Attributed by many to Paul, but many other scholars say it could have been Apollos, Barnabas, Phillip, Priscilla, Timothy, Aquila, or Luke. Actually unknown. Written from Rome to all Jewish Christians.
Theme This book is addressed to the Hebrews at Jerusalem or in all of Palestine, and is similar to the book of Romans addressed to the Gentiles at Rome. James, who has been head of the church in Jerusalem, has been killed at about this time. The basic thought, from the reasoning standpoint of a Hebrew, is to establish Jesus Christ as the one and only High Priest of the Church. He was and is above the angels, Moses, and Joshua. He is the High Priest and the author of all salvation. The present Church does not need animal sacrifices, as Christ made the supreme sacrifice for all. All the people need to do is have faith and not backslide in their thinking to the old beliefs and rituals of the Old Testament.

In times past, God has spoken through the prophets, but now He has spoken by a Son who is superior to the angels and who will rule forever. This was foretold by the Lord and later by those who heard Him. We must not forget these things.

Those who did not obey Moses remained and died in their forty years of wanderings; those who now know of Jesus, the great High Priest, will be lost to salvation if they drift away from His teachings and the faith. Jesus learned obedience and gave His life for all who obeyed Him. ". . . by this time you ought to be teachers, you have need again for someone to teach you . . . ," said the author of Hebrews (Hebrews 5:12).

Therefore, it is impossible to bring to repentance those who have been disobedient and now harden their hearts. Land that receives rain and brings forth vegetation useful to those who cultivate it, receives the blessing of God. If it produces thorns and thistles, it is worthless and will be cursed and burned. We say these things so that you will not be sluggish, but will be imitators of those who, through faith and patience, inherit the promises.

In the time of Abraham there was Melchizedek, the king of Salem (Jerusalem 1400 B.C.), who was both king and priest of the most high God. After the exodus of the Hebrews from Egypt, there were Levitical priests. These mortals came and went. But now God has given a priest in

Jesus, "The Lord has sworn And will not change His mind, 'Thou art a priest forever'" (Hebrews 7:21). This makes Jesus the guarantee of a better promise.

". . . [Jesus] does not need daily, like those high priests, to offer up sacrifices, first for His own sins, and then for the sins of the people, because this He did once for all when He offered up Himself" (Hebrews 7:27). We now have a high priest seated at the right hand of the throne of the Majesty in heaven, which is set up, not by man, but by the Lord. The old covenant was written on stones, while the new covenant is written in men's hearts. In the days of the Tabernacle made by man, the priests made blood offerings once a year for the sins of the people. When Christ came as the high priest in heaven, in the presence of God, and offered Himself as a sacrifice for the sins of His people, He did this once and for all. Men will die once, and after that will face judgment. So Christ was offered once to bear the sins of many and will appear again to save those who are eagerly waiting for Him.

Therefore, let us hold fast the confession of our hope in Jesus without wavering. Help one another, meet regularly, and encourage one another. If we continually and willfully sin after receiving the knowledge of the truth, we face the judgment and a fury of fire. The Lord said, ". . . Vengeance is Mine, I will repay . . ." (Hebrews 10:30).

Faith is the assurance of things hoped for, the conviction of things not seen. For whoever would draw near to God must believe that He exists and that He rewards those who seek Him.

> By faith:
> Noah built the ark, when everyone said he was crazy.
> Abraham offered Isaac his son as a sacrifice.
> Moses kept the Passover.
> Joshua watched the walls of Jericho fall.
> Rahab, the harlot, cast her lot with Israel.
> Gideon won mightily in war.
> Daniel stopped the mouths of lions.
> Elijah raised the dead.
> And many, many others.

Do not regard lightly the discipline of the Lord, nor lose courage when you are punished by Him. The Lord disciplines him whom He loves, and chastises every son whom He receives. God is treating us as sons. We respect our earthly fathers who discipline us. Our heavenly Father disciplines us for our good, that we may share His holiness.

Let brotherly love continue, as well as hospitality to strangers. Remember those in prison. Hold marriage in honor, and avoid love of money, for, ". . . I will never desert you, nor will I ever forsake you" (Hebrews 13:5). Pray unceasingly.

JAMES

Time A.D. 45–A.D. 60.
Author James, the brother of Jesus. He was the leader, or moderator, of the church council in Jerusalem. He died a martyr's death by being stoned to death at the hands of his own people.
Theme This was one of the five general epistles (James, 1 Peter, 2 Peter, 1 John, Jude) and was addressed to all Christians, but primarily to Christian Jews. It was addressed to the twelve tribes scattered abroad, which could mean Jews scattered abroad or all the churches everywhere. In his book to the Romans, in his work largely with the Gentiles, Paul stressed justification in Christ by faith. James did not disagree with Paul, but spoke mostly to Jews and stressed the fact that faith without works is empty and that, "You see that a man is justified by works, and not by faith alone" (James 2:24). This book gave plain instructions as to those works.

Trials and hardships in life test our faith and produce steadfastness. God grants wisdom to those who ask and have faith. The rich should be humble, because their life is short, and their flower will fade in death like the poor. God does not tempt men; they tempt themselves with passion and material things. Blessed is he who can withstand temptation that gives birth to sin.

Every good gift is from God, who brought us forth as His first fruits. Be quick to hear, slow to speak, and slow to anger, for the anger of man does not work the righteousness of God. Be a doer of good works and not just a hearer of the Word of God. Religion that is pure and undefiled before God is to visit the widows and orphans in their afflictions.

Show no partiality to the rich rather than the poor. Is it not the rich who drag you into court and persecute you? Those who are poor on earth will be rich in heaven. Love your neighbor as yourself.

You must keep the whole law. You cannot sin in any part of the law, or you are guilty of sinning in all. Judgment is without mercy to those who give no mercy. Words without deeds are empty. Faith by itself, if it has no works, is dead.

Abraham justified his faith when he offered his son Isaac upon the altar. God blessed him. Rahab, the harlot, justified her faith by works when she received the messengers of Joshua and sent them out by another way. Faith without works is dead.

Use great care in the selection of teachers and preachers, for those who teach will be judged strictly. The tongue is very small and is only a small part of the body, but it is very powerful. The bridle in a horse's mouth guides the whole horse. The small rudder on a great ship guides the ship. A forest fire is set by a small flame. The tongue is a flame. All the reptiles and animals can be tamed, but the tongue in evil men cannot be tamed. Blessing and cursing cannot come from the same mouth. Fresh water and brackish water cannot come from the same spring. Fig trees will not yield olives.

Disorder will exist where there is jealousy and selfish ambition. Wisdom from above is pure, peaceable, gentle, open to reason, full of mercy, and without insincerity. Peace is reaped by those who sow peace.

Submit yourselves therefore to God. Resist the devil and he will flee from you. Draw near to God and He will draw near to you. Humble yourselves before the Lord and He will exalt you.

Do not speak evil against one another, or you put yourself in the position of a judge. There is only one lawgiver and judge who is able to save and destroy, and that is God.

Do not say what you shall do tomorrow, because you are as a mist that will vanish. Say, ". . . If the Lord wills, we shall live and also do this or that" (James 4:15).

The rich, who have taken from the poor, may live in luxury on earth, but their riches will eat their flesh like fire hereafter. Be patient until the coming of the Lord, as the farmer plants and waits. Do not swear by heaven or earth, but let your yes be *yes* and your no be *no*.

Let those who are happy sing praises, those who are sick ask for prayers, and the prayer of the faithful will heal. Elijah prayed that it would not rain for three and one-half years, and it did not rain. He then prayed for the rain, and it did rain.

Lead one another in righteousness as the way to salvation.

FIRST PETER

Time A.D. 65–A.D. 67.
Author Peter (Simon, Simon Peter, Cephas). The name means *rock*. Brother of Andrew, spokesman of the twelve apostles, leader of the group, and one of the three favorite disciples of Jesus. He and his brother Andrew were Galilean fishermen, partners with Zebedee and his sons James and John. According to tradition, Peter was married to Perpetua. He died a martyr in Rome, and tradition says his wife died the same way. Written from Babylon, generally interpreted as Rome.
Theme Peter addresses his letter to the Jews scattered, after Christ's resurrection, to Pontus, Bithynia (both in northern Asia Minor, bordering on the Black Sea), Cappadocia, and Asia (southern Turkey), all in Asia Minor. Paul probably founded most of these churches, and Peter had probably helped or visited them.

Peter reminds them that by God's mercy, men have been born anew through the sending of Jesus Christ as a man, His death for forgiveness of our sins, and His resurrection that we may be born again and have eternal life.

He counsels them as obedient children not to succumb to their former passions and lusts, but to follow Christ's example in their conduct. They were ransomed by Christ's blood, and not with gold and silver. They are born anew through the living and abiding Word of God. That Word is the Good News.

Peter urged them to look upon themselves as living stones, to be built into a great spiritual house, acceptable to God through Jesus Christ. ". . . you are a chosen race, a royal priesthood, a holy nation, a people for God's own possession, that you may proclaim the excellencies of Him who has called you out of darkness into His marvelous light" (1 Peter 2:9).

He suggested that they maintain good conduct among the Gentiles, so that they would see their good deeds and glorify God. They should submit to the law of the land, whether governed by emperor or governor. They should live as free men, without using their freedom as a pretext for evil, but live as servants of God.

The same thing is true of slaves and servants. They suffer in their servitude, but Christ also suffered as an example for them, and He committed no sin, and no guile was found on His lips. Christ bore our sins in His death that we might shed our sins and live to righteousness. By His wounds we have been healed.

Wives should be submissive to their husbands so that husbands can be won to the Lord, without a word, by the behavior of their wives when they see their reverent and chaste behavior. Believers should not adorn the body, but have the imperishable jewel of a gentle and quiet Spirit, which in God's sight is very precious. Husbands, likewise, honor your wife as the weaker sex, in order that your prayers may not be hindered.

All of you have unity of spirit, "For let him who means to love life and see good days Refrain his tongue from evil and his lips from speaking guile. And let him turn away from evil and do good; Let him seek peace and pursue it. For the eyes of the Lord are upon the righteous, and His ears attend to their prayer, But the face of the Lord is against those who do evil" (1 Peter 3:10–12).

Always be prepared to make a defense for your beliefs, but do it with gentleness and reverence. Remember that Christ suffered by men also. At all times love and help one another, practice hospitality, and use what gifts you have for one another, that God may be glorified through Jesus Christ.

Let none of you suffer as a murderer, thief, wrongdoer, or a mischief maker. But if you suffer as a Christian, do not be ashamed, for under that name you will glorify God. Elders, tend your flocks of God's children, not as a duty, but willingly, and lead by example. When the Chief Shepherd comes, you will receive the unfading crown of glory. Likewise, you who are younger, be humble, and trust God because He cares for you. Resist the devil and all his temptations, and God will establish and strengthen you.

Peace to all of you that are in Christ.

SECOND PETER

Time A.D. 67.
Author Peter. Written from Rome to same people as 1 Peter, to warn of present dangers. Peter's death was imminent.
Theme Nero, the Roman emperor, had been and was now persecuting the Christians unmercifully for being Christians. They were killed in the arenas by duels, tossed to the lions in sporting events, burned alive in public places, and generally persecuted unmercifully, in Rome especially. Nonbelievers were using this political climate to persecute the Christians throughout the Roman Empire. The effects were being felt. There was creeping into the brotherhood the acts of apostasy (desertion from the faith) and heresy (opinion opposed to accepted doctrine). Peter's letter is to warn of these dangers and strengthen the members to withstand these temptations to surrender. His first letter was to warn and guard from attack outside the Church. This letter warns of attack from inside the Church, especially from false teachers.

Peter tells the people to avoid corruption in the world by supplementing their faith with virtue, knowledge, self-control, steadfastness (patience), godliness, brotherly affection, and love. These things keep them from being ineffective or unfruitful in the knowledge of our Lord Jesus Christ. If they do this, they will never fail, and they will be provided an entrance into the eternal Kingdom of the Lord and Saviour Jesus Christ. Peter knows that his death is imminent, and he wants them to remember these things, even after he is gone.

He reminds them that his teachings are not myths. He was an eyewitness to the transfiguration of Jesus (Matthew 17:1–5) and heard God's voice say, ". . . This is My beloved Son with whom I am well-pleased" (2 Peter 1:17). He reminds them also that all Scripture is not by the impulse of man, but by men moved by the Holy Spirit spoken from God.

As there were false prophets in the past, there will be false teachers now and in the future. They will bring destruction to themselves and those who follow them. They are reminded that God cast disobedient angels into hell, destroyed all the world except Noah and seven other persons in the flood, destroyed the cities of Sodom and Gomorrah to ashes, but saved Lot from destruction because he was righteous. The Lord will punish the unrighteous and rescue the godly. Nevertheless, there will be among you those unrighteous revilers, preaching in their ignorance and reveling in their sinfulness, dissipation, and carousing. They entice unsteady souls with their hearts trained in greed.

They are like waterless springs, or mists driven by a storm; for them the gloom of darkness has been reserved. They promise freedom, but they are slaves of corruption. It would have been better for them never to have known the truth, than to know it and turn back from the holy commandments. ". . . 'A dog returns to its own vomit,' and 'A sow, after washing, returns to wallowing in the mire'" (2 Peter 2:22).

Remember the predictions of the holy prophets and commandments of the Lord Saviour through your apostles. Scoffers will come and ask, ". . . Where is the promise of His coming?" (2 Peter 3:4.) The heavens existed long ago, and the earth was formed by God to be stored up for fire, until His judgment shall destroy the ungodly.

Remember this fact: ". . . with the Lord one day is as a thousand years, and a thousand years as one day" (2 Peter 3:8). The day of judgment will come like a thief in the night, and the elements will be dissolved with fire, and the earth and the works that are upon it will be burned up.

We wait for a new heaven and a new earth, in which righteousness prevails. Therefore, be zealous to be found without blemish and at peace by Him. Paul wrote to you about these things. Do not be carried away by the errors of lawless men, but grow in grace and knowledge of our Lord and Saviour Jesus Christ. To Him be the glory, both now and forevermore.

FIRST JOHN

Time A.D. 80–A.D. 92.

Author John. Written from Ephesus, where he lived to an old age after Jerusalem was destroyed by the Romans in A.D. 70. He had taken care of Jesus' mother in Jerusalem until her death. John wrote the Gospels of John, epistles of John, and Revelation. He was the apostle "whom Jesus loved." He was a brother of James and son of Zebedee, a fisherman.

Theme This epistle was not addressed to anyone in particular, but it was probably intended as a circular letter for the churches in the area of Ephesus; however, it could easily apply to all the churches. He places the members in the position of a family. He was with Christ for about three years, and was, therefore, positive in his statements. There were other doctrines being preached. John's aim was to give assurances that the teachings of the Christians were right.

John reminds his readers that he has seen, heard, and touched Jesus—the Word of life. What he tells them is firsthand, so they can have his understanding of the real truth with the Father and the Son, Jesus Christ.

God is light, and if we walk in that light, the blood of Jesus, His Son, cleanses us of all sin. If we say we have no sin, we deceive ourselves. "If we confess our sins, He is faithful and righteous to forgive us our sins and to cleanse us from all unrighteousness. If we say that we have not sinned, we make Him a liar, and His word is not in us" (1 John 1:9, 10). We should not commit sins, and he who says he abides in Him, should walk the same way Jesus walked.

He who loves his brother, walks in the light. He who hates his brother is in the darkness still. John seems to classify his readers according to the depth of their belief as children, young men, and fathers.

Children, your sins are forgiven for His sake, and you know the Father. Young men, you have overcome the evil one; you are strong, and the Word of God abides in you. Fathers, you know Him from the beginning. Do not love the world and the things in the world, because they pass away, but he who does the will of God abides forever.

He warns them that there are many false teachers. They have been taught the truth, and they must hold to it. Those who deny the Christ lie.

No one who denies the Christ can have the Father. Abide in Jesus, so that when He appears, we may have confidence and not shrink from Him in shame at His coming.

He who does right is righteous, as God is righteous; He who commits sin is of the devil. The reason the Son of God appeared was to destroy the works of the devil. We should love one another and not be like Cain, who was of the evil one and murdered his brother, because his own deeds were evil and his brother's righteous. The world hates you because you are righteous. No murderer has eternal life abiding in him. By this we know love, that Jesus laid down His life for us, and we ought to lay down our lives for the brethren. Let us not love in word and speech, but in deeds and in truth. All who keep His commandments abide in Him, and He in them.

There is no fear in love, but perfect love casts out fear, for fear has to do with punishment, and he who fears is not perfected in love. He who believes that Jesus is the Christ is a child of God; everyone who loves the parent loves the child. For this is the love of God, that we keep His commandments, and His commandments are not burdensome. Believe in the name of the Son of God, that you may know that you have eternal life.

SECOND JOHN

Time   A.D. 90–A.D. 97.

Author   John. He was the last survivor of the twelve apostles and was at least ninety years of age, living in Ephesus.

Theme   Similar to 1 John. This letter appears to be to an individual lady, but could be interpreted as addressed to a church.

John calls himself The Elder. He rejoices to find her children following the truth, just as they have been commanded by the Father. He repeats what he has always taught—not a new commandment, but the same commandment as from the beginning—that we love one another.

He warns that there are many deceivers with new ideas, who will teach false doctrine and who will not acknowledge the coming of Jesus Christ in the flesh. Anyone who does not abide in the doctrine of Christ does not have God, but he who abides in the doctrine has both the Father and the Son. Do not receive into your home the deceivers and their wicked works.

THIRD JOHN

Time A.D. 90–A.D. 110.
Author John. He talked of visiting churches in his letters, but was probably too old to travel. He was bishop of the churches in his area.
Theme Paul had established many churches in and around Ephesus forty years earlier, but there were no seminaries in which to train new pastors, so the pastors were selected from the converts. There were bound to be mistakes, and this appears to be one of them: Diotrephes, a pastor of one of the churches, had taken a dictatorial attitude and would not allow John's emissaries in his church. John was writing to Gaius, a member of the church.

John calls himself The Elder and addresses this letter to Gaius, ". . . whom I love in truth" (3 John 1). He expresses his joy that some of the arriving brethren have said that Gaius follows the truth and that he has been helpful to the brethren and strangers.

John tells Gaius that Diotrephes refuses his letters, likes to put himself first, does not acknowledge John's authority, refuses to welcome the brethren, and stops the members from welcoming them.

Do not imitate evil, but imitate good. He who does good is of God; he who does evil has not seen God. Peace be to you.

JUDE

Time   A.D. 67. Possibly later.
Author   Jude. He is a half-brother of Jesus and brother of James, who wrote the epistle of James. Jude's writings are similar to those of Timothy and Peter, and he is probably writing to the same churches.
Theme   Jude, like other leaders, was concerned with the growing apostasy (desertion from one's faith) of some of the members, due to the efforts of false prophets. These false teachers generally offered bounty in their teachings, which permitted men to live in sin, immorality, and lust with no punishment involved, because God was too good to punish. This attracted some people. Jude used a vocabulary all his own in describing these leaders.

Jude had intended to write of the common salvation, but is concerned with those who would pervert the grace of God into licentiousness. He reminds them that the God who brought the people out of Egypt and then destroyed those who would not believe; who has kept the angels who left their proper dwelling in eternal chains; and who destroyed Sodom and Gomorrah by fire, is the same God who offers eternal life in heaven for those who will believe.

Yet these men defile the flesh, reject authority, and revile the glorious ones. They carouse together, like wild waves of the sea, casting up the foam of their own shame. It is these who set up divisions among the people, devoid of the Spirit of God.

You, beloved, build yourselves up on your holy faith, pray in the Holy Spirit, keep yourselves in the love of God, and wait for the mercy of our Lord Jesus Christ unto eternal life. Convince some who doubt and save some from the fire of God's fury.

The grace of God and the love of our Saviour, Jesus Christ, be with you now and forevermore.

REVELATION

Time   A.D. 96.

Author   John. (Some scholars say the author is unknown.) John, as the bishop of the churches at Ephesus, had been arrested and was living as a prisoner of Caesar or Domitian on the island of Patmos. This island is between Greece and Turkey off the coast of Ephesus, about sixty miles in the Aegean Sea. It is now one-half owned by the monastery of St. John. John was an old man, and probably didn't have to work in the rock quarries like the other prisoners. He probably had the visions for this book in A.D. 95, while on the island, but returned later to Ephesus, where it is felt he wrote the book in A.D. 96. He died in Ephesus, an old man.

Theme   This book is difficult to read and understand. The visions revealed and written by John are not comparable to anything with which we are familiar, which forces us to stretch our imaginations to try and find the meaning. The book is written to the seven churches in Asia Minor, which was the heart of world Christianity at that time.

There seems to be no single universal acceptance of interpretation among scholars and theologians. We must assume that if this book was not intended as a confirmation of the basic teachings of the rest of the Bible, it would not be a part of it. If it can be interpreted as conveying any other message, it makes a lie of the rest of the Bible. If the Bible is a lie, it would not exist as it has for all these centuries. Therefore, we must assume by its vagueness that the intention is to provide evidence in its testimony which can be interpreted by all men in a personal manner of reasoning, satisfactorily and clearly to each individual, to bring him and all others to the same conclusion.

All actions and decisions in law for settlement of disputes of presumed agreement are based on finding the true intent of the parties concerned. The same is true of this book. We assume beyond any question that the intent in its simplest form is to restate and confirm all the previous teachings in the Bible. They are, briefly and concisely, that God created the world and everything in it, including man. He gave man the freedom of choice between good and evil, and created the Bible for man's guidance by the writings of men inspired by God. He sent His only Son, Jesus Christ, into the world in the form of human flesh, that He might instruct men as to His Father's desire that all men should inherit eternal life in heaven. He sacrificed His life on the cross and was resurrected the third day for the redemption of men's sins. Anyone who had faith and belief in these things, repented of his sins, asked God's forgiveness, was baptized and received the Holy Spirit, and obeyed God's commandments, would inherit eternal life in God's heaven.

Those who choose to believe this will be accepted into eternal life in heaven. Those who reject it will burn in eternal hell. Man makes his own choice. There has been unending conflict between the believers and nonbelievers and between those who are good and those who are evil. This will continue until Christ comes again on the judgment day and claims the righteous into His Kingdom. It is never revealed when He will come, but He has said that it will be like a thief in the night.

John says that an angel of God instructed him to write this book, and blessed is he who reads and hears what he has written.

In the first three chapters, he addresses his writings to the seven churches of Asia around Ephesus. He tells them that while he was on Patmos he heard a loud voice and saw a vision. The vision was of seven lampstands, with a man in the midst, clothed in white robes, a golden breastplate, white head and hair, eyes like a flame of fire, feet like burnished bronze, seven stars in his right hand, a two-edged sword in his mouth, a face like the shining sun, and a voice like the sound of many waters. The voice (assumed to be the voice of Christ) said, ". . . Do not be afraid; I am the first and the last, and the living One; and I was dead, and behold, I am alive forevermore, and I have the keys of death and of Hades . . . the seven stars are the angels of the seven churches, and the seven lampstands are the seven churches" (Revelation 1:17–20). The messages were to the individual churches.

"To the angel of the church in Ephesus write: 'I know your deeds and your toil and perseverance, and that you cannot endure evil men, and you put to the test those who call themselves apostles, and they are not, and you found them to be false . . .' " (Revelation 2:1, 2). " '. . . repent and do the deeds you did at first' " (Revelation 2:5). " '. . . you hate the deeds of the Nicolaitians, [those who eat sacrificial offerings to idols and commit fornication] which I also hate . . . To him who overcomes, I will grant to eat of the tree of life . . .' " (Revelation 2:6, 7).

"And to the angel of the church in Smyrna write: . . . 'I know your tribulation and your poverty (but you are rich), and the blasphemy by those who say they are Jews and are not, but are a synagogue of Satan . . . you may be tested, and you will have tribulation ten days. Be faithful until death, and I will give you the crown of life' " (Revelation 2:8–10).

"And to the angel of the church in Pergamum write: . . . 'I know where you dwell, where Satan's throne is; and you hold fast My name, and did not deny My faith, even in the days of Antipas [a Christian martyr] . . . you have there some who hold the teaching of Balaam . . . Repent therefore . . . To him who overcomes, to him I will give some of the hidden manna, and I will give him a white stone . . .' " (Revelation 2:12–17).

"And to the angel of the church in Thyatira write: . . . 'your deeds of late are greater than at first . . . you tolerate the woman Jezebel, who calls herself a prophetess, and she teaches and leads My bond-servants astray, so that they commit acts of immorality and eat things sacrificed to idols . . . I will cast her upon a bed of sickness, and those who commit adultery with her . . . the rest . . . who do not hold this teaching . . . I place no other burden on you . . . and he who keeps My deeds until the end, to him I will give authority over the nations' " (Revelation 2:18–26).

"And to the angel of the church in Sardis write: . . . 'you have a name that you are alive, and you are dead . . . for I have not found your deeds completed in the sight of My God. Remember therefore what you have received and heard; and keep it, and repent. If therefore you will not wake up, I will come like a thief, and you will not know at what hour I will come upon you. But you have a few people in Sardis who have not soiled their garments . . . I will not erase his name from the book of life' " (Revelation 3:1–5).

"And to the angel of the church in Philadelphia write: . . . 'I know . . . you have a little power, and have kept My word, and have not denied My name. Behold, I will cause those of the synagogue of Satan . . . I will make them to come and bow down at your feet, and to know that I have loved you . . . I am coming quickly; hold fast what you have, in order that no one take your crown' " (Revelation 3:7–11).

"And to the angel of the church in Laodicea write: . . . 'So because you are lukewarm . . . I will spit you out of My mouth. Because you say, "I am rich, and have become wealthy, and have need of nothing" . . . I advise you to buy from Me gold refined by fire, that you may become rich, and white garments, that you may clothe yourself . . . Those whom I love, I reprove and discipline; be zealous therefore, and repent . . . He who overcomes, I will grant to him to sit down with Me on My throne . . .' " (Revelation 3:14–21).

The remaining eighteen chapters are highly visionary and portray future events. The figure seven is used fifty-nine times.

John is then shown the throne of God.

. . . a throne was standing in heaven, and One [God] sitting on the throne. And He who was sitting was like a jasper stone and a sardius [red] in appearance; and there was a rainbow around the throne, like an emerald in appearance. And around the throne were twenty-four thrones; and upon the thrones I saw twenty-four elders sitting, clothed in white garments, and golden crowns on their heads [possibly representing the twelve tribes of Israel and the twelve apostles]. And from the throne proceed flashes of lightning and sounds and peals of thunder. And there were seven lamps of fire burning before the throne, which are the seven Spirits of God; and before the throne there was, as it were, a sea of glass like crystal . . . and around the throne, four living creatures full of eyes in front and behind. And the first creature was like a lion, and the second creature like a calf, and the third creature had a face like that of a man, and the fourth creature was like a flying eagle. And the four living creatures, each one of them having six wings, are full of eyes around and within; and day and night they do not cease to say, 'Holy, holy, holy, is the Lord God, the Almighty, who was and who is and who is to come.' . . . And I saw in the right hand of Him who sat on the throne a book written inside and on the back, sealed up with seven seals. And I saw a strong angel proclaiming with a loud voice, 'Who is worthy to open the book and to break its seals?' And no one in heaven, or on the earth, or under the earth, was able to open the book, or to look into it . . . a Lamb standing, as if slain, having seven horns and seven eyes, which are the seven Spirits of God, sent out into all the earth. And He came, and He took it out of the right hand of Him who sat on the throne. And when He had taken the book, the four living creatures and the twenty-four elders fell down before the Lamb . . . And they sang a new song, saying, 'Worthy art Thou to take the book, and to break its seals; for Thou wast slain, and didst purchase for God with Thy blood . . .' I heard the voice of many angels . . . saying with a loud voice, 'Worthy is the Lamb [Christ] that was slain to receive power and riches and wisdom and might and honor and glory and blessing.'

Revelation 4:2–5:12.

When the Lamb opened the first seal, a white horse and rider came out to conquer. When He opened the second seal, a red horse and rider came out to make wars. When He opened the third seal, a black horse and rider, with a balance in his hand, came out, denoting famine. When He opened the fourth seal, a pale horse and its rider named death came out, to kill with famine and pestilence. When the fifth seal was opened, John saw under the altar the souls of all those who had been slain for witnessing to the Word of God. They were each given a white robe and told to wait until their number was complete. When He opened the sixth seal, there was a great earthquake, the sun became black, the moon like blood, stars fell from the sky, the sky vanished, mountains and islands disappeared, and the people of the earth hid from the wrath of the Lamb of God.

Four angels standing at the four corners of the world held back the four winds until the servants of God could be sealed on their foreheads. Those from Israel were one hundred and forty-four thousand, and from the rest of the nations on earth, so great a multitude that they could not be numbered, all clothed in white robes. ". . . These are the ones who come out of the great tribulation, and they have washed their robes and made them white in the blood of the Lamb . . . the Lamb . . . shall be their shepherd . . . and God shall wipe every tear from their eyes" (Revelation 7:14, 17).

The Lamb opened the seventh seal, and the seven angels who stand before God were given trumpets. The first angel blew his trumpet, and hail and fire mixed with blood fell on the earth and burned a third of it. The second angel blew his trumpet, and something like a great mountain burning with fire was thrown into the sea and became blood, and a third of all creatures and ships was destroyed. The third angel blew his trumpet, and a great star, called Wormwood, fell blazing from the heaven and made bitter a third of all the rivers and fountains, and many men died. The fourth angel blew his trumpet; a third of the sun, moon, and stars was darkened; and a third of the day and night was kept from shining. [Many scholars compare these exact events to the parallel events in the fall of the Roman Empire from A.D. 100 to A.D. 1450.]

The fifth angel blew his trumpet, a star fell from heaven, and he was given a key to a bottomless pit, from which came smoke that darkened the light. From the smoke came locusts, looking like horses arrayed for battle. On their heads were what looked like crowns of gold. They had faces like humans, hair like women's, teeth like lions, and scales like iron breastplates, and the noise of their wings was like chariots with horses rushing into battle. They were led by Abaddon-Apollyon [Satan]. They had tails like scorpions, and their sting hurt men for five months, so that men longed to die rather than to endure the pain. The locusts were told not to harm the grass, trees, or anything green, but only those of mankind who did not have the seal of God on their foreheads.

The sixth angel blew his trumpet, and a voice released the four angels who were bound at the Euphrates River. They released 200,000 troops of cavalry, whose riders wore breastplates the color of fire and sapphire and sulphur. The heads of the horses were like lions' heads, and fire and smoke and sulphur issued from their mouths. A third of mankind was killed by the fire, and smoke and sulphur came from their mouths. The rest of mankind still did not repent of its sins, nor did they give up their sinful ways.

Another angel came down from heaven with a little scroll in his hand and set his right foot on the sea and his left foot on the land. When he spoke, there were seven thunders. A voice from heaven said not to write what the seven thunders said, but a decree had been issued that when the seventh trumpet was blown, the mystery of God should be fulfilled. The voice said to eat the scroll, and it was sweet to the mouth, but bitter to the stomach. The voice said, ". . . You must prophesy again concerning many peoples and nations and tongues and kings" (Revelation 10:11).

In the vision, John was told to measure the temple and the altar, but not the court outside. The nations would trample over the Holy City for forty-two months, and two witnesses would have the power to prophesy for 1,260 days. These were the two olive trees and the two lampstands which stood before the Lord of the earth. They had the power to stop the rain, to turn the waters into blood, and to smite the earth with every plague. The beast from the bottomless pit would make war with them and they would lie dead in the streets for three and one-half days while the sinners rejoiced. Then God would breathe life into them, and they would rise into heaven in a cloud. There was great fear among the sinners as the earth quaked and 7,000 people were killed. The rest were terrified and gave glory to God in heaven.

Then the seventh angel blew his trumpet, and there were loud voices in heaven, saying, ". . . The kingdom of the world has become the kingdom of our Lord, and of His Christ; and He will reign forever and ever" (Revelation 11:15).

Then appeared the woman clothed with the sun, with the moon under her feet, and on her head a crown of twelve stars, and she was in pain with child. Also, there appeared a great red dragon with seven heads, ten horns, and seven diadems [crowns] upon his heads. His tail swept down a third of the stars in heaven to earth. The dragon stood ready to devour the newborn child at birth. The woman had a male child, who was to rule all nations, and he was caught up to God on His throne. She fled and hid in the wilderness, prepared by God to be nourished for 1,260 days.

A war arose in heaven between the angel Michael and his angels, who fought against the dragon and his angels, and the dragon was defeated and exiled from heaven. The dragon [the devil, or Satan], the deceiver of the whole world, was thrown down to the earth. A voice said, ". . . Now the salvation, and the power, and the kingdom of our God and the authority of His Christ have come, for the accuser [Satan] of our brethren has been thrown down . . . And they overcame him because of the blood of the Lamb . . . rejoice, O heavens . . . Woe to the earth . . . because the devil has come down to you, having great wrath, knowing that he has only a short time" (Revelation 12:10–12).

The dragon pursued the woman, but she was given the wings of the eagle and escaped. The dragon poured water like a river from his mouth, to drown the woman, but the earth opened its mouth and swallowed the water. The dragon then tried to make war on the rest of her offspring—those who keep the commandments of God and bear testimony to Jesus.

John saw a beast rising out of the sea, with ten horns and seven heads. It had ten diadems on its horns, and it was like a leopard with bears' feet and a lion's mouth. It received its power and authority from the dragon. One of its heads had a mortal wound, which had healed. Some men worshipped the beast, saying, ". . . Who is like the beast, and who is able to wage war with him?" (Revelation 13:4.) The beast was given authority for forty-two months, and it blasphemed God and those who dwell in heaven and made war on the saints. [It has been estimated that in the Middle Ages and during the Reformation Era, more than 50,000 Christians were killed.] Here is a call for the endurance and faith of the Christians.

Another beast rose out of the earth; it had two horns like a lamb and spoke like a dragon (pretending to be a lamb). It exercised the same authority as the first beast and made the people worship the first beast whose mortal wound was healed. It worked great signs, such as making fire come down from heaven. This deceived those on earth, causing them to make an image for the beast; it was allowed to give breath to the image, so that it could speak, and caused those who would not worship the image to be slain. Everyone was marked on the forehead or the right hand with a number, to enable them to buy or sell. Without the number, they could do neither. The number was six hundred sixty-six, the pretender lamb.

John then looked, and on Mount Zion stood the Lamb with the 144,000 people who had His name and His father's name on their foreheads. They were singing a song before the throne, which could only be sung by those who had been redeemed from earth, had not defiled themselves, and were the first fruits for God and the Lamb.

Another angel was flying in midheaven, saying, ". . . Fear God, and give Him glory, because the hour of His judgment has come; and worship Him who made the heaven and the earth and sea and springs of waters" (Revelation 14:7). A second angel followed, saying, ". . . Fallen, fallen is Babylon [generally considered to mean Rome] the great, she who has made all the nations drink of the wine of the passion of her immorality" (Revelation 14:8).

A third angel followed, saying, ". . . If any one worships the beast and his image, and receives a mark on his forehead or upon his hand, he also will drink of the wine of the wrath of God . . . and he will be tormented with fire and brimstone in the presence of the holy angels and in the presence of the Lamb" (Revelation 14:9, 10). His torment goes on forever.

Then came the call for the saints who keep the commandments of God and the faith of Jesus. The voice said, ". . . Write, 'Blessed are the dead who die in the Lord from now on!' . . . that they may rest from their labors, for their deeds follow with them" (Revelation 14:13). Then one like a son of man came out with a sharp sickle, and an angel said, ". . . Put in your sickle and reap, because the hour to reap has come, because the harvest of the earth is ripe" (Revelation 14:15). And the earth was reaped.

Another angel came out of the temple of heaven with a sharp sickle. An angel from the altar, who had power over fire, called to the angel with the sickle, ". . . Put in your sharp sickle, and gather the clusters from the vine of the earth, because her grapes are ripe" (Revelation 14:18). The vintage was cut and thrown into a great wine press of the wrath of God. The wine press was trodden outside the city, and blood flowed as high as a horse's bridle, for one thousand six hundred stadia (200 miles). The harvest by the first angel seems to be the saved, and the vintage of the second angel is the lost, or wicked.

The seven bowls of God's wrath were described. John saw those who had conquered the leopard-false-lamb beast, and they were singing with great joy and praising God. Then came seven angels, and one of the four living creatures gave the seven angels seven golden bowls, full of the wrath of God in the form of seven plagues, to be poured out on the earth, upon the unrighteous.

The first angel poured his bowl on the earth, and foul and evil sores came upon the men who bore the mark of the beast and worshipped its image. The second angel poured his bowl into the sea, and it became like the blood of a dead man; every living thing in the sea died. The third angel poured his bowl into the rivers and the fountains, and they became blood. The angel of water praised the Holy One because evil ones had shed the blood of saints and prophets, and now the evil ones had blood to drink. It was their due. A voice at the altar cried, ". . . Yes, O Lord God, the Almighty, true and righteous are Thy judgments" (Revelation 16:7).

The fourth angel poured his bowl over the sun, and it scorched men with fire and fierce heat. They cursed the name of God who had power over these plagues, and they did not repent and give glory. The fifth angel poured his bowl on the throne of the beast, and its kingdom was in darkness. Men cursed God, and did not repent of their deeds.

The sixth angel poured his bowl into the great river Euphrates, and its water was dried up. There issued from the mouths of the dragon, the beast, and the false prophet, three foul spirits like frogs. They were the demon spirits who were to go abroad to the kings of the whole world, to assemble them for battle on the great day of God the Almighty [God had said, "I am coming like a thief in the night."] They assembled at Har-Magedon (Armageddon).

The seventh angel poured his bowl into the air, and a voice from the temple said, "It is done." There was lightning, thunder, and an earthquake such as the world had never seen. Cities fell, including Babylon (Rome), the islands disappeared, and no mountains were to be found. There were hailstones as heavy as one hundred pounds. The sinful and unrighteous cursed God.

Then one of the seven angels with the bowls explained all of this to John (it is too detailed and complicated to explain here).

After these things I saw another angel coming down from heaven, having great authority, and the earth was illumined with his glory. And he cried out with a mighty voice, saying, "Fallen, fallen is Babylon [Rome] the great! And she has become a dwelling place of demons . . . the kings of the earth have committed acts of immorality with her, and the merchants of the earth have become rich by the wealth of her sensuality . . . in one day her plagues will come, pestilence and mourning and famine, and she will be burned up with fire; for the Lord God who judges her is strong."

Revelation 18:1–8

The kings of the earth who lay with her will weep and wail for her. The merchants who sold her their gold, silver, jewels, silks, ivory, and all costly articles will mourn for her. Alas, alas the great city, in one hour she has been laid waste for her sinfulness.

After this, John heard what seemed to be the mighty voice of a great multitude in heaven, crying, ". . . Hallelujah! Salvation and glory and power belong to our God; because His judgments are true and righteous; for He has judged the great harlot [Rome] who was corrupting the earth with her immorality, and He has avenged the blood of His bond-servants on her" (Revelation 19:1, 2). All those around the throne praised God. He then heard the voice of a great multitude, crying, ". . . Hallelujah! For the Lord our God, the Almighty, reigns . . . for the marriage of the Lamb [Christ] has come and His bride [the righteous saints] has made herself ready . . . to clothe herself in fine linen, bright and clean; for the fine linen is the righteous acts of the saints [believers]" (Revelation 19:6–8).

Then John saw heaven open and saw a man called Faithful and True sitting on a white horse. In righteousness He judges and makes war. He is clothed in a robe dipped in blood, and the name by which he is called is The Word of God. His armies are arrayed in white linen and mounted on white horses. On his robe he has inscribed the name King of Kings and Lord of Lords. An angel called all the birds that fly, to come and gather to eat the flesh of those to be slaughtered. The beast and the false prophet were captured and thrown alive into the lake of fire that burned with brimstone. The rest were slain, and all the birds were gorged with their flesh.

Then an angel came down from heaven holding the key to the bottomless pit. He seized the ancient serpent, the devil and Satan, bound him for one thousand years, and sealed him in the bottomless pit until the one thousand years were ended. After that, he would be loosed for awhile. Then those came to life who had not worshipped the beast, and they reigned with Christ for one thousand years. The rest of the dead did not come to life until the one thousand years were ended. This was the first resurrection.

When the one thousand years are ended, Satan will be loosed for awhile, to deceive the nations which are at the four corners of the earth and to gather his forces again. But fire will come down from heaven and consume them, and the devil who has deceived them will be thrown into the lake of fire and brimstone with the beast and the false prophet. They will be tormented day and night, forever and ever.

Then John saw a great white throne, and Him who sat upon it. All the dead stood before the throne, and the books were opened. The dead were judged by what was written in the books—by what they had done. The sea, death, and Hades gave up their dead to be judged. Death and Hades were thrown into the lake of fire. If anyone's name was not written in the Book of Life, he was thrown into the lake of fire.

Then John saw a new heaven and a new earth, for the first heaven and earth had passed away, and the sea was no more. New Jerusalem, the Holy City, came down out of heaven from God. A voice said that the dwelling of God would be with men, and He would be with them. And He would wipe away every tear, and death would be no more, for former things had passed away. He who sat upon the throne said, ". . . Behold, I am making all things new . . . It is done . . . He who overcomes shall inherit these things, and I will be his God and he will be My son. But for the cowardly . . . their part will be in the lake that burns with fire and brimstone . . ." (Revelation 21:5–8).

One of the seven angels who had the seven bowls said, ". . . Come here, I shall show you the bride, the wife of the Lamb" (Revelation 21:9). He took him to a high mountain and showed him the New Jerusalem in all its radiance and glory, with its new walls, new gates with the names of the twelve tribes of Israel, and the names of the twelve apostles of the Lamb. The city was four square and fifteen hundred miles around. The walls and gates were adorned with every kind of jewel and metal, and the streets were paved with gold.

There is no temple, for the temple is the Lord God the Almighty and the Lamb. There is no sun or moon, for the glory of God is its light, and its lamp is the Lamb. The gates will never be shut by day, and there is no night. Nothing unclean shall enter the city, nor shall anyone who practices abomination or falsehood, but only those who are written in the Lamb's Book of Life.

There is the river of the water of life, bright as crystal, flowing from the throne of God and of the Lamb [Christ] through the middle of the street of the city. On either side, the tree of life, with twelve kinds of fruit, yielding its fruit each month, and the leaves of the tree for the healing of the nations. There shall be the throne of God, and the Lamb shall be in it. They shall see His face, and His name shall be on their foreheads. The Lord will be their light, and they shall reign forever and ever.

The angel said to John, ". . . 'These words are faithful and true'; and the Lord, the God of the spirits of the prophets, sent His angel to show His bond-servants the things which must shortly take place. 'And behold, I am coming quickly. Blessed is he who heeds the words of the prophecy of this book' " (Revelation 22:6, 7).

When John heard these things, he fell down to worship at the feet of the angel, but the angel told him not to do this, because he was only a fellow servant. He said to worship God.

The angel said not to keep these words from the people, for the time is near. Let the evildoer still do evil, and the righteous still do right, and the holy still be holy.

"Behold, I am coming quickly, and My reward is with Me, to render to every man according to what he has done. I am the Alpha and the Omega, the first and the last, the beginning and the end."

Blessed are those who wash their robes, that they may have the right to the tree of life, and may enter by the gates into the city. Outside are the dogs and the sorcerers and the immoral persons and the murderers and the idolators, and everyone who loves and practices lying. "I, Jesus, have sent My angel to testify to you these things for the churches. I am the root and the offspring of David, the bright morning star." And the Spirit and the bride say, "Come." And let the one who hears say, "Come." And let the one who is thirsty come; let the one who wishes take the water of life without cost. I testify to everyone who hears the words of the prophecy of this book: if anyone adds to them, God shall add to him the plagues which are written in this book; and if anyone takes away from the words of the book of this prophecy, God shall take away his part from the tree of life and from the holy city, which are written in this book. He who testifies to these things says, "Yes, I am coming quickly." Amen. Come, Lord Jesus. The grace of the Lord Jesus be with all. Amen.

Revelation 22:12–21.

SUMMARY OF THE NEW TESTAMENT

The New Testament tells about the birth of Jesus Christ, which event had been prophesied throughout the Old Testament for hundreds of years. His early life and baptism at age thirty by His cousin John the Baptist, at the River Jordan are portrayed prior to His temptation by Satan.

Jesus Christ spent about three years in His ministry on earth, selecting His apostles and training them to help establish the Church of Christ. He was crucified by His own people, the Jews, rose from the grave three days later, talked to His apostles and many other people before ascending into heaven. He promised that He would return.

Saul, a Jew, a Roman citizen, and a Pharisee, was a persecutor of the Christians until he was converted by God to become a disciple. He then became the most dedicated believer and evangelist in the Bible. His name was changed to Paul.

The teachings of the New Testament all point in the same direction and toward one objective—to be saved and inherit eternal life, man must be born again.

To do this, man must, by voluntary action on his part, accept Christ as the Son of God and his Saviour, ask for the forgiveness of his sins, repent, be baptized, and receive the Holy Spirit for his comfort and guidance in his life here on earth. He will then inherit eternal life in heaven.

This digest of the Bible has been written to help you come to this conclusion. May God be with you in making your decision to seek eternal life through the reading, study, and understanding of the Holy Scriptures.

DEFINITIONS

Apocalypse   Any writing professing to reveal the future, especially in early Christian circles of the period 200 B.C. to A.D. 100. A revelation.

Apocrypha   Noncanonical literature, but specifically, in general terms, the books included in the Greek Septuagint and the Roman Catholic Bible, but not included in the Hebrew Bible or the Protestant Bible. All of the books of the Apocrypha were written by Jewish authors. There are fourteen books in the Apocrypha. There are a few similar books of Jewish origin, sometimes accepted in some oriental Christian churches, referred to as the Pseudepigrapha.

Apostasy   The abandonment, desertion, or departure from one's faith, holy orders, or religious state. Renunciation of a religious faith. Revolt or rebellion against the authority of God.

Asceticism   A disciplinary course of conduct in which certain actions, such as contemplation, fasting, or renunciation of the desires of the flesh and of worldly things, through self-torture or self-denial, are performed, not for their own sake, but for their moral or religious effect or in pursuit of a higher ideal, such as spiritual perfection.

Canon   A decree, decision, regulation, code, or constitution made by ecclesiastical authority. Hence, the Bible is a collection of Hebrew writings which are received as genuine and Holy Scriptures written by men inspired by God and called the sacred canon. The Protestant or Palestinian canon includes all of the Jewish canon. The Roman Catholic canon adds the books of the Apocrypha.

Coenaculum   Name of the traditional place of The Last Supper; possibly the home of Mary, the mother of Mark.

Essenes   A brotherhood among the Jews of Palestine, from 200 B.C. to A.D. 200. Organized on a pious, rigid, communistic basis, and practiced the strictest discipline of self-denial of desires of the flesh, pleasure of worldly things, contemplation, and fasting.

Gnosticism   A religious movement in early Christian times, which claimed that salvation came through knowledge (gnosis) of one's true self as explained in a myth revealed by a Saviour (Jesus Christ). It fused into one system some of the elements of Babylonian astral mythology, cabalistic Judaism, Persian dualism, and Greek philosophy.

God   The Supreme Being. The eternal and infinite Spirit, Creator, and Sovereign of the universe. God the Father, God the Son, and God the Holy Ghost, designate the first, second, and third persons of the Trinity, although the word *trinity* in this sense is not used in the Bible.

Holy Spirit (Ghost) God is three omnipotent, omnipresent beings, sometimes referred to as the Trinity; God the Father, God the Son, and God the Holy Spirit. The Holy Spirit is that person who is available to dwell spiritually in man as his Comforter, Paraclete, Advocate, and Intercessor with God the Father, through active faith in the Lord Jesus Christ. The Holy Spirit is available to man after having repented, after having been baptized, and having accepted Christ. Christ is the person who was made man in the flesh, lived among us on earth, was crucified, died, and was resurrected from death, that man might have remission of sin, enter into the Kingdom of God, and inherit eternal life in heaven. The Holy Spirit is available to all men who are willing to accept, through obedience, these spiritual truths into their lives, God as present and active in the spiritual experience of man.

Jesus Christ The son of Mary, the source of the Christian religion, and the Saviour in the Christian faith.

Justification That right of being eligible to eternal life with God through the grace of God, based on man's confession and repentance of his sins and faith in the belief that Jesus is the Christ, sent by God as a man, who died for the redemption of man, through the forgiveness of his sins, and who rose again to take His place with God.

Messiah The expected King and Deliverer of the Hebrews—the Christ. The divinely sent Saviour of the world.

Messianic Of or pertaining to the Messiah.

Mishnah A collection of oral Jewish laws, edited by Rabbi Judah ha-Nishi (A.D. 135–A.D. 220). Consists of sixty-three tractates (treatises or dissertations) dealing with prayer, marriage, festivals, agriculture, and so forth. Used as the basis of the Talmud.

Mysticism A doctrine or belief that direct knowledge of God or spiritual truth is attainable through immediate intuition, insight, or illumination in a way differing from ordinary sense perception, or without foundation.

Pentateuch The first five books of the Old Testament, collectively often called the law of Moses.

Pharisees A group of Jews, although not necessarily a political party, sect, or school of philosophy, noted for strict observance of the Pentateuch law, as modified by the oral and traditional interpretations of the elders. They differed from the Sadducees and believed in the traditional interpretations, the immortality of the soul, the resurrection of the body, future retribution, a coming Messiah, angels, spirits, divine providence, and freedom of the will. They were in existence from 200 B.C. to A.D. 200. The Pharisees were affected by the Greek influence. They determined who was worthy of admission to the synagogues. They usually had two scholarly leaders; one drawn from the aristocratic segment of society and one from the people. They were the majority party between the Pharisees and Sadducees. They were the successors of Ezra and cherished him next after Moses. Saul of Tarsus was a devout Pharisee. They were accused by Jesus of being hypocrites, although He did not hesitate to accept dinner invitations with them. Nicodemus, who sought an interview with Him, was a Pharisee and was the only voice in the Sanhedrin advocating fairness in Jesus' trial.

Sadducees Possibly named for Zadok, high priest in Solomon's age. In existence 100 B.C. to A.D. 100. They were the educated and wealthy element of the priestly aristocracy of Jewish society, few in number and aloof from the people. They were influential in the Sanhedrin and generally opposed to the Pharisees. They rejected the traditions of the elders and believed and observed only the written law of Moses. They denied the resurrection, personal immortality, retribution in a future life, fate, the existence of angels, spirits, and demons, and assumed the freedom of the will. They represented the vested interests in Jerusalem. Many were members of the Sanhedrin. They catered to the Roman government and were little heard about after the Romans destroyed the Temple. John the Baptist condemned the Sadducees and Pharisees jointly, and Jesus grouped them in His denunciation of their doctrines.

Sanctification That degree of justification reached when man can be perfect in the love he has for God and his fellow man.

Sanhedrin The chief judicial council or supreme court of the Jews, which had seventy-one members and had jurisdiction over religious matters and more important civil and criminal cases. It met daily, except the Sabbath and holidays. Organized by King Jehoshaphat of Judah in 875 B.C.–850 B.C., it lost its authority after destruction of the Temple by the Romans about A.D. 70. The Sanhedrin, working with the Roman procurator Pilate, was able to bring about the crucifixion of Jesus.

Septuagint The Greek version of the Old Testament still in use in the eastern church. So called from the legend preserved in the letters of Aristeas at the request of Ptolemy II (while Arsinae was queen, 278 B.C.– 270 B.C.). The church fathers made the number a round seventy and extended the tradition to the whole of the Greek Old Testament. Although the translation may have been begun under Ptolemy II, it was not completed until about the beginning of the Christian Era.

Talmud A compilation of Jewish tradition consisting of the Mishnah and the Gemara, a voluminous commentary on the Mishnah. The Palestinian Talmud was finished in A.D. 450, and the Babylonian Talmud, which is almost four times as large, was finished in A.D. 500.